1 SAMUEL

Indiana Studies in Biblical Literature

Herbert Marks and Robert Polzin,
General Editors

1 SAMUEL

A Literary Reading

**PETER D.
MISCALL**

INDIANA UNIVERSITY PRESS
BLOOMINGTON

To My Father and My Mother—

That my days may be long and that it may go
well with me in the land. (Deut. 5:16)

This book was brought to publication with the aid of a grant from the
Andrew W. Mellon Foundation.

Portions of chapters 4, 5, and 6 first appeared in *The Workings of Old Testament Narrative*.
Reprinted by permission of The Society of Biblical Literature.

Manufactured in the United States of America

Library of Congress Cataloging-in-Publication Data

Miscall, Peter D.
1 Samuel : a literary reading.

(Indiana studies in biblical literature)
Bibliography: p.
Includes index.
1. Bible. O.T. Samuel, 1st—Criticism,
interpretation, etc. I. Title. II. Title: First
Samuel. III. Series.
BS1325.2.M57 1986   222'.43066   85-42948
ISBN 0-253-34247-3
ISBN 0-253-20365-1 (pbk.)

1   2   3   4   5   90   89   88   87   86

CONTENTS

Introduction   vii

1. **1 Samuel 1–3**   1
2. **1 Samuel 4–7**   26
3. **1 Samuel 8–12**   41
4. **1 Samuel 13–15**   81
5. **1 Samuel 16–18**   115
6. **1 Samuel 19–23**   126
7. **1 Samuel 24–26**   144
8. **1 Samuel 27–31**   163

Postscript   184
Bibliography   186
Index   187

INTRODUCTION

The What

I claim much and I claim little for this work. I claim much, because the work is a decisive departure from and challenge to historical criticism and the biblical studies, whether historical, literary, or theological, based on it or associated with it. I accept few of historical criticism's presuppositions, modes of analysis, types of questions asked, or kinds of answers or meaning sought. At the same time, I claim little, because the work is only a beginning in new readings of Old Testament narrative and, indeed, is only a beginning in new readings of 1 Samuel. Fuller readings need to be done; individual themes, issues, characters, etc., traced and developed; implications of the reading further analyzed. At this stage, I can only point to some of these. Like the opening chapters of 1 Samuel, this book declares an older period at an end, heralds an as yet vague and indeterminate future, but cannot leave that past behind to approach the future with a clean slate.

A basic conviction—the Old Testament is different from Western literature, from classical to modern, but it is just as complex and sophisticated as any Western writing, whether narrative, poetry, philosophy, or theology. To be different is not to be less, is not to be simplistic and primitive. I read the Old Testament as on a par with, although different from, Homer, Tacitus, Plato, Augustine, Chaucer, Aquinas, Luther, Shakespeare, Hegel, Nietzsche, Yeats, and Robbe-Grillet. I depart from historical criticism and associated methods and disciplines, because they do regard and treat the Old Testament as simplistic and primitive. In this work I only hint at why I say this. I have said more in *The Workings of Old Testament Narrative,* but it remains for another work or works to delve more deeply into biblical studies of the last 200 years and to trace how they in fact treat Old Testament writing.

Genesis-Kings

My concern is OT narrative, not literature such as Isaiah and Psalms, and particularly the narrative corpus in Genesis through 2 Kings. Genesis-Kings is the book, *the work,* part of which I read and analyze. The corpus is an "entity" held together by plot—from creation to exile; by characters—the Lord and the people; and by themes—the word of the Lord, covenant, justice and mercy. The restriction to just Genesis-Kings derives in part from its size; 1 Samuel itself is more than I can deal with in one book. It also derives from a personal limit; I have not read the entirety of Genesis-Kings as closely as I have 1 Samuel, let alone the rest of the OT.

Practically, considering Genesis-Kings as a single work means that I treat all the material in the corpus on equal terms and do not divide it up or assign the divisions to different authors, places, and times. Because my focus is on 1 Samuel, at times it appears that I favor it over the rest of Genesis-Kings; this is a matter of focus and practical strategy, not necessarily favoritism. Because 1 Samuel comes after Joshua and Judges does not mean that it has superior, more complete, or later content—theological, historical, or whatever—than they do. In addition, I draw parallels to material in 1 Samuel from anywhere within the corpus, although I draw a limited number of parallels.

1 Samuel

Within the corpus, the main text I read is the Hebrew Masoretic text of 1 Samuel as it appears in the Hebrew canon. I am aware of the serious text-critical problems involved in any analysis of Samuel, due in large part to the divergent and often lengthy readings in the Septuagint and in the Qumran fragments of Samuel. (See McCarter 1980b, pp. 5–11, 32–34, for discussion and bibliography.) At times I note the problems, but I propose no corrections of the Masoretic text. (Occasionally I use a question mark in parentheses to indicate that the translation of a given word is uncertain.) I do not automatically consider the Masoretic text to be the best; I leave it as is, because text-critical study should be preceded by extended readings, wherever possible, of each version. Is it obvious that the Septuagint represents a better, or more correct, text? Perhaps the two, and others, can be read and compared and contrasted, but not necessarily used, to produce the correct and original text.

Unless otherwise noted, the translations of 1 Samuel texts are my own, although heavily influenced by the Revised Standard Version.

Many of the texts from other OT books are from the *RSV*, with a few changes to clarify specific points. The translations are literal, even if this produces a wooden or unusual English syntax; the translations clarify comments I make about the use of terms and phrases and about the structure of the passage. All italics in biblical texts are mine.

I include Hebrew transliterations at points to emphasize shared terminology and phraseology. The transliterations are for purposes of clarity and not for accurate transcription of the exact word or phrase. Frequently I give a simpler form than the actual Hebrew word, particularly if the latter would obscure the Hebrew root that is shared with other passages. Occasionally I use an asterisk to mark a root or form that does not occur in Hebrew.

1 Samuel is part of Genesis-Kings; it is analogous to a chapter in a book, except that our notions of "chapter" and "book" have limited application to the Bible. Focusing on 1 Samuel thus presents obvious problems, since considerable material both precedes and follows that is germane to a reading of 1 Samuel. Therefore I make some (at times lengthy) comments on other parts of the corpus that are in some way analogous to a given section in 1 Samuel. For me, a parallel exists where I can establish it in a feasible manner; the latter includes similar terminology, phraseology, themes, setting, characters, and plot. I do not treat parallels as based on some preexistent archetype, genre, or other foundational pattern. I note and develop parallels to assess their impact on a reading of the material in question and not to attempt to prove that they all share some "essence," structural or otherwise.

I restrict the number of parallels, or networks of parallels, that I develop because of the limits of this book and because the inclusion of additional parallels from Genesis-Kings, or from the rest of the OT and beyond, would not clear up the problems encountered in the reading of 1 Samuel. Ambiguity is not always a result of insufficient evidence or material; in many instances, it can be the result of too much evidence. In these cases, developing more parallels would only increase the ambiguity and complexity of the issues addressed. Focus on 1 Samuel does produce problems, but it does not determine the overall tenor of the reading. The ambiguity encountered would remain even if we were to attempt a similar reading of all Genesis-Kings.

Finally, I speak of Genesis-Kings as a work, an entity with unity and coherence, but the unity and coherence are its own and are not necessarily that of Western literature. The structure and style of Genesis-Kings are such that 1 Samuel can be isolated without the disruption and loss that would usually occur if one attempted a similar reading of a single chapter in a modern realistic novel.

Chronology

There are some issues that bear directly upon a reading of 1 Samuel that I do not treat extensively, since this would require analysis of large parts of Genesis-Kings. These are chronology, setting and locale, "poetry" and "poems," prophet and prophecy, and the appearance of God in the narrative coupled with the distinction between *yahweh*, the Lord, and *'elohim*, God. I discuss them in order. The discussion points to future analyses of the topics as they stand within the narrative and within the text, not as problems that have to be solved by some historical reconstruction outside the text.

A study of the chronology in Genesis-Kings would have to take into account at least the following points. First, is there a large-scale and explicit time frame? Genesis and 1-2 Kings have one; an overall time frame is given for the books, and most events within them are related to it. 1 Samuel does not have one; we are not told how much time elapses from the birth of Samuel to the death of Saul, and we are seldom told how much time elapses between individual events. Second, is the time frame consistent and coherent as in Genesis, or is it marked by breaks and gaps as in 2 Samuel -1 Kings 2? We are given forty years for David's reign in 2 Sam. 5:4, but we are not informed of the specific placement of events within his reign, e.g., Absalom's revolt. Further, is the time frame broken by inconsistencies that prevent the establishment of a consistent and continuous chronology? For example, in Judges, taking the terms of the judges as successive yields a period of time that does not accord with the rest of the chronology of Genesis-Kings, e.g., the note in 1 Kings 6:1 that Solomon began building the Temple 480 years after the Exodus. The judges' terms can be taken as simultaneous or as overlapping in various degrees, but this hinders the establishment of a strict and sure chronology.

Third, are individual episodes "timed," i.e., explicitly related to the time frame? Fourth, if not related explicitly, can a date be calculated? For example, we can calculate the length of Joseph's stay in Egypt until his brother's arrival, i.e., twenty years, from the notices of his age in Gen. 37:2 (seventeen years old), Gen. 41:46 (thirty years old), and the seven years of bounty. Finally, are explicit dates, when given, clear or ambiguous in themselves and in their relation to the context? For example, 2 Sam. 13:23 and 2 Sam. 13:38 allot five years for the period between the rape of Tamar and the return of Absalom to Jerusalem, but we cannot firmly attribute his return and revolt to a specific year within David's reign. The ark is at Kiriath-jearim for twenty years (1 Sam. 7:2). Does this mean that the events of 1 Sam. 7:3 ff. occur twenty years after the events of 1 Samuel 4-6 or during this twenty-year span? Does the twenty years refer ahead to the transfer of the ark to Jerusalem in 2 Samuel 6?

These comments are pointers to future study that should address the chronological issues and problems as they stand and not automatically assume different authorship or sources because a chronology is inconsistent. Such study should take chronological breaks and inconsistencies as deliberate and then assess what the "unity" and "coherence" are of a text that contains so many of them; the chronological problems, like all the problems I discuss, are not signs of a broken and incoherent text but do render problematic our notions of "unified" and "coherent."

Setting and Locale

Analysis of setting is similar to that of chronology in that attention is given to the presence or absence of a specific locale for an event, speech, or whatever. For example, the call of Samuel occurs at Shiloh, while Saul's first encounter with Samuel is at "this city" (1 Sam. 9:6, 11). The absence of such information is considered to be deliberate, i.e., it is not to be "filled in" by some historical or geographical surmise, and should be taken into account in a reading.

"Poetry" and "Poems"

Over and above small segments of verse, Genesis-Kings contain some lengthy "poems," e.g., the Blessing of Jacob in Genesis 49, the Hymn of Victory in Exodus 15, the Oracles of Balaam in Numbers 23–24, the Blessing of Moses in Deuteronomy 33, the Song of Deborah in Judges 5, the Song of Hannah in 1 Samuel 2, the Lament in 2 Samuel 1, David's Song in 2 Samuel 22, and Isaiah's Oracle in 2 Kings 19.

I put "poetry" and "poems" in quotes because of Kugel's impressive argument in *The Idea of Biblical Poetry* that they are words based on Western literature that have limited, and at times misleading, applicability to the OT. This is particularly so in the emphasis on meter and parallelism as distinguishing features of OT "poetry." Kugel demonstrates that there is no meter in OT "poetry" in the sense that there is meter in Greek, Latin, and English poetry; meter is a Western, not a biblical, phenomenon. There is parallelism in biblical "poetry," but it is also prevalent in biblical "prose." Kugel concludes that prose and poetry are not helpful or distinctive terms for the study of the OT. He does not equate Genesis and Isaiah but denies that the prose/po-

etry distinction accurately and adequately describes the difference between them.

However we term the above material, the "poems" are generally
dealt with as secondary insertions or additions to the text; they are
analyzed as independent works, and there are only a few comments
on how they relate to their context or how they affect a reading of
that context. Radday has made a beginning in analyzing the ones in
1-2 Samuel in their context but focuses almost solely on structural
rather than content or thematic issues. Polzin's discussion of Judges 5
briefly addresses thematic issues and the impact of the poem on a
reading of Judges (Polzin 1980, pp. 161–67).

The study I call for would regard the poems as integral parts of the
overall narrative and would study them as individuals and as a group,
both isolated from and in their immediate and general contexts. Some
problems that would have to be assessed are the association, or lack of
it, with the context. If there is an association, what constitutes it—
places, characters, structure, terminology, themes? What does the
poem add to or subtract from the context—specific information, different perspective, clarity? How do the poems relate to each other,
especially if they occur in the same "narrative block" as the Song of
Hannah, the Lament over Saul and Jonathan, and 2 Samuel 22? Do
they aid in reading Samuel, or do they muddy the waters?

Prophet and Prophecy

The issue of the identity and function of a prophet is central to
1 Samuel, especially the first sixteen chapters, where Samuel is a major
character. I deal with various aspects of the question in the analyses of
those chapters and include material from Deuteronomy, chiefly Deut.
18:15–22. However, I do not deal with the issue in an exhaustive
fashion, since this would entail discussing considerable segments of
2 Samuel (Nathan) and 1-2 Kings (e.g., Ahijah, Elijah, Elisha, and Isaiah). Indeed, 1 Samuel 1–16 forms, from one perspective, not an introduction just to 1 Samuel or 2 Samuel but also to Samuel-Kings.

Many issues, topics, and themes that are central to these chapters
are not dealt with again until 2 Samuel or even 1-2 Kings. Prophet
and prophecy are one example; king and kingship are another.
Chapters 8 and 12 give attention to these as general issues, particularly as they relate to the people and their standing before the Lord;
are kingship and the people's request for a king good or evil in the
Lord's eyes? However, 1 Samuel 13–31 deal with individuals, especially Saul, Jonathan, and David, and not with general and abstract

issues; the people and their standing before the Lord are not a significant theme. I stress that the ambiguity surrounding these issues in
1 Samuel 1–12 is not preliminary or temporary; it is such that it is not
definitively resolved in the rest of Samuel-Kings. I do not want to give
the impression at the outset that an extension of the study to all of
Samuel-Kings would result in a clear definition or evaluation of a
prophet and a king.

The Lord's Role

The Lord appears in the narrative in a variety of ways that differ in
significance, amount of information granted, and certainty about his
actual intervention in a story and his motives and purposes. (See Alter
1981, pp. 114–18, for background on characterization.) The Lord
may appear directly as an actor or speaker, e.g., 1 Samuel 3, 8, and
15; here we are granted a high degree of certitude about the Lord's
activity, intervention, and perhaps motives. His activity, presence, or
motivation is noted by the narrator, e.g., 1 Sam. 1:19, 2:25, 3:19, 5:6,
14:23, and 18:14; again there is a high degree of certitude. However,
in most of the examples with high certitude, limited information is
granted or the significance of the information is unclear; I discuss the
point at greater length in the analyses.

The Lord's appearance, especially his word, may be mediated, i.e.,
someone claims to be reporting a speech or action of the Lord, e.g.,
the man of God in 1 Sam. 2:27–36, Samuel in chapter 15, David's
men in 1 Sam. 24:5, and David in 1 Sam. 25:39. Inquiries of the Lord
are included in this category. We have to address the issue of the
reliability of the mediator when it is a person; questions of character,
setting, purpose for the statement, etc., must be raised. For example,
I see no reason to impeach the man of God but do find solid bases for
questioning the reliability of David's men and of David in chapters 24
and 25. I also discuss at length the issue of the literal accuracy of the
"prophetic speeches" of Samuel and the man of God; Samuel may
accurately report a "word of the Lord," but "accurate" does not mean
literal or word for word. Finally, with Samuel, the question of his
character and possible motives must be raised even if it means that his
"truthfulness" is impugned.

Inquiry of the Lord can grant sure information from the Lord, but
it is very limited. In the inquiries conducted in 1 Samuel, we are
informed of the Lord's action—or lack of it when he does not
answer—but are given no hint of his motivations; I detail this in
reference to chapter 23. Inquiry of the Lord needs examination as a

specific, yet limited, way of bringing God's word and action into the narrative; it should be approached as a narrative issue, not as an attempt to guess what type of formal procedure "actually happened." Attention has to be given to the Lord's precise answer, not to conjecture about how the answer was "really" obtained. For example, in 1 Sam. 23:10–12, the Lord responds to David's two lengthy questions with a one-word reply to only the second. David asks the first question again and receives another one-word reply. On the other hand, in 1 Sam. 30:8, David again asks two questions about pursuit and overtaking; the Lord answers both positively and adds information that David will certainly rescue. I discuss these and other individual instances of inquiry in 1 Samuel and some in Judges but do not attempt a comprehensive analysis of the topic.

The issue of the Lord's role is further complicated by the distinction between *the Lord* (*yahweh*), which is used only of Israel's God as a type of proper name, and *God* (*'elohim*), which can also mean god or gods and is not restricted to Israel's God. At times, *'elohim* refers to god(s) other than Israel's; at other times, it is interchangeable with *yahweh;* in another group of occurrences, it refers to uncertainty as to whether *yahweh* or some other unidentified deity is involved. Polzin discusses at length some examples of such equivocation drawn from the Gideon and Samson stories (Polzin 1980, pp. 168–76, 181–85). In my discussions, I do not stress a difference in the reference of the two terms, but I do pay attention to who uses which terms and when, i.e., as revealing something about the character. For example, the use of *yahweh* or *'elohim* by Saul is usually significant even if ironic; I comment on his use of *yahweh* in 1 Sam. 22:17 and of *'elohim* in 1 Sam. 28:15.

Retributive Justice and Mercy

Retributive justice involves reading both the OT and studies of the OT, particularly those with a theological bent. For my understanding and treatment of retributive justice, and of the holy war that is associated with it, I am indebted to Polzin's *Moses and the Deuteronomist*, although I take a different approach than he does. Retributive justice is a concept with a range of meaning. First, it is the doctrine that God necessarily and always both rewards good and righteous behavior and punishes sinful and wicked behavior. Mercy is related in the sense that sin might not be punished because God forgives it and has mercy on the sinner. God can also act graciously, i.e., give a reward to someone who has not acted righteously. Without specific reference to God, retributive justice can mean that good is always rewarded, always succeeds, and that evil is always punished, always fails. Even more generally, it can refer to a predictability of outcome based on observation of moral or religious behavior. The good should succeed, the wicked should fail.

It is generally assumed in biblical studies that most of OT narrative, especially the segment in Deuteronomy-Kings—the so-called Deuteronomistic history, is dominated by retributive justice, which is invoked to explain the destruction of Israel and then of Judah. Polzin has dealt the assumption a deadly blow. I agree with him that the biblical text (he treats Deuteronomy through Judges) questions and undermines, even though it does not reject, the doctrine of retributive justice by questioning and limiting its applicability and predictability. To a great extent, this work continues his attack, although the attack is only one aspect of my work and one whose full implications I do not trace.

When justice does not work, when it does not apply, God's mercy and graciousness, his compassion and love, can often be appealed to to explain the discrepancy. This is always possible and effective but not a thorough and completely complementary procedure. I do not talk as much of mercy and grace in the reading as I do of retributive justice, but most of my comments on the latter apply, in various ways, to mercy and grace. These are usually positive concepts, and much of Judges and 1 Samuel is not positive. The Lord's favor towards his chosen or elect (people or individual) results in disaster for others. Therefore, the dark side of grace and mercy is unpredictability, arbitrariness, and injustice.

Holy War

I also treat holy war as a textual issue and again acknowledge my debt to Polzin. I do not try to reconstruct an historical institution or practice of ancient Israel but deal with holy war as it is presented in the text, particularly in the Mosaic legislation in Deuteronomy 20 and in the conquest stories in Joshua 1–11. Polzin has shown how the legislation, the "word of the Lord," in Deuteronomy 20 is interpreted in Joshua by Joshua, Israel, and the Lord himself; the fact of interpretation undermines the notion that the legislation is a final or ideal statement of the ideology (Polzin 1980, pp. 73–91, 113–15, 117–23). The undermining continues in 1 Samuel and is dealt with in connection with chapters 11, 13, 15, 22, 27, and 30. Full treatment of the topic is beyond my scope, since it pervades large segments of Genesis-

Kings and is bound up with other issues, e.g., covenant, possession of
the land, the nations, and prophecy.

Mode of Reading

The reading is open and eclectic. There is no one method or approach employed here; there is no attempt to establish one consistent
interpretation of 1 Samuel. My mode of reading varies from section
to section. Some sections get more space and detailed analysis than
others, and I occasionally point out issues and problems to be dealt
with in future studies. My focus varies from comments on wordplay,
narrative style, and narrative techniques, to dominant themes, such as
retributive justice, the nations, and the word of the Lord.

I do not attempt to establish an essentialist interpretation—the true
meaning, the author's intention, what it really meant, what really happened, the purpose of the text, or any of the other diverse phrases or
categories employed to refer to an essential meaning. It is not my
purpose to overcome ambiguity or equivocation, either by ignoring or
explaining away details and repetitions or by filling in gaps and missing information. Gaps, details, repetitions, inconsistencies, and contradictions are considered to be deliberate, and their impact on the reading is assessed. This is a major departure from the majority of works
on OT narrative, regardless of orientation. Keil and Delitzsch's, Erdmann's, McCarter's and Ackroyd's commentaries all share the desire
to establish the true and essential meaning of 1 Samuel and frequently do not differ in their ways of establishing that meaning. I
have developed a few examples in *The Workings of Old Testament Narrative* and leave more thorough treatment for future study.

For example, Shiloh drops from the narrative after 1 Samuel 4.
Nothing is said to account for the disappearance. The text does not
even hint at the possibility that it was destroyed in the battle described
in 1 Samuel 4, as so many commentaries allege. Indeed, Eli receives
the news of the defeat at Shiloh; the battle was fought elsewhere.
Perhaps the death of Eli and his sons and the capture and subsequent
transfer of the ark from Shiloh can account for the lack of further
reference to it. Samuel is called by the Lord there but does not explicitly appear there again. These are possible explanations for Shiloh's
dropping from the narrative. My point is that they are *possible,* but not
one of them is *certain,* since the text says nothing—there is a gap—
about the fate of Shiloh.

The mode of reading is eclectic. I comment on some literary critical
influences in the second section of the introduction; here I wish to

acknowledge my debt to particular works on biblical narrative. Some I note in the body of the work and in the bibliography. Of greatest importance are Gunn's *The Fate of King Saul,* Alter's *The Art of Biblical Narrative,* and Polzin's *Moses and the Deuteronomist.* I comment on some points of agreement and disagreement in the discussion. It is not my intention to survey their content or approaches to note agreement or disagreement with them; I want only to indicate the general tenor of my relationship to them.

I am in agreement with many of Gunn's specific points and inter-pretations but go a quite different way in the overall reading of the last half of 1 Samuel. Alter's work is indispensable for a study of OT narrative. Much of my work has achieved its present form only after struggling with Alter's views, which are related, and sometimes op-posed, to mine. I share most of his views on the close reading of the biblical text but frequently depart from his interpretations. With Pol-zin, it is the opposite. I share many of his interpretations and thematic concerns, especially the word of the Lord and retributive justice, but I take little from his specific modes of reading, which are heavily influ-enced by Russian formalism.

The articles by Leach, Knierem, and Gros Louis have been influen-tial in the development of my reading of 1 Samuel. Leach, in his frustrating but inimitable style, provided me with a strong impetus for both accepting 1-2 Samuel as a single work and finding relevant par-allels to Samuel in unexpected places and with unexpected conse-quences for reading. Gros Louis's was the first convincing analysis I had read of 1 Samuel 16–17 as a literary unit; in addition, his distinc-tion between the public and the private David plays a role in my analysis of 1 Samuel, particularly in regard to succession and succes-sors. Knierem's thesis that a messianic concept was at the heart of a good deal of the material in 1 Samuel 9–31 bolstered my acceptance of the work as a whole. However, his insistence that this messianic concept explained Saul's rise and fall and David's subsequent rise led to my realization that although the text *seems* to fit with this interpre-tation, i.e., that in my terms it offers this resolution, it does not wholly or decisively fit with it. By trying to clarify and extend his thesis, I found that the text of 1 Samuel is in no way so clear and definite.

Other works have played an indirect role, mainly in my frequent strategy of deploying at least two opposed readings of a character, theme, or event. For example, McCarter argues that 1 Samuel 9 through 2 Samuel 5 defend David against charges that he assumed the kingship violently and illegitimately; the chapters are an Apology for David that clarify his legitimacy and propriety. Knierem makes a similar point, although he does not argue it to the same extent. This is one of the Davids about whom I read. On the other side, Humphreys argues in his articles for a tragic Saul, who, at least in part of 1 Samuel, is presented in sympathetic terms. This contributed to my development of a "good" Saul. For me, the strong implication is that there is a "bad" David and a "bad" Samuel.

Finally, some recent articles have appeared that are in agreement with some of the aspects of my work. Perdue develops a similar bifurcated reading of David in 2 Samuel, while Preston writes of Saul's heroism, which is compared, unfavorably, to David's despotism and luxury. Saul, the military hero, dies in battle with Israel's enemies; David, the despot, dies in bed demanding that Solomon kill his personal enemies. Preston emphasizes David's violence and cunning. One final article underscores my reliance on dual readings. Preston maintains that 1 Samuel closes with a harsh comment on David's attending to his own affairs in the south while Saul is dying in battle with the Philistines. Veijola claims just the opposite, since David trusts in God, evidenced through the inquiries, and Saul in military prowess.

I consider myself working alongside of these and other works on biblical narrative; there are many points of agreement and disagreement—some minor, some major. I find the image of parallel lines helpful; the lines are separate and not opposed, but they never meet. I do not think of my work as complementary or additive to that of other scholars; parallel lines never meet. Literary critical study of biblical narrative is not *the method* that can replace others and finally produce the true and total meaning of the Bible. That may be a dream of certain interpretive modes, but it produces only more readings, more texts, not the final reading.

The Why

The remainder of the introduction is an attempt to explain why I wrote this book, which departs so sharply from standard biblical studies. This is not a formal and consistent defense or description but instead an account of that part—some books, authors, and issues—of the contemporary critical scene that plays a role in the book. The role may be direct and explicit; I can cite books and pages that elucidate a point I make or use a mode of reading that I employ. The role may be indirect and implicit; I cite a book once and do not mention it again. However, several books play a most significant role in my work; *S/Z*, and most of Barthes's other work, is a prime example. Burke's *The Rhetoric of Religion* is another example. Sometimes works cited do not so much support a particular aspect of my work as relate to the general tenor of the reading—why I do not argue for an overall coherent interpretation of 1 Samuel or a section of it; why I do not try to fill in gaps or explain away details, repetitions, and contradictions; and why I speak of indeterminacy and ambiguity.

Contemporary literary criticism does not offer a single well-defined methodology or group of approaches that may differ in focus or type of meaning sought but is similar in presuppositions and goals. The contemporary critical scene is marked by division and debate as different schools, critics, and journals vie with one another for acceptance of their wares in the critical marketplace. The debate can be polemical and acrimonious, since what is at stake is not always a matter of varying focus or type of meaning but at times is the question of meaning and its possibility and determinacy.

However, the various approaches do share one technique—the close reading and painstaking observation of the text or texts being studied, the unswerving attention to the physical and literal text, the careful noting of what actually is and is not said. The dividing line comes when something more is made of the close and detailed reading, when the "So what?" is addressed. Are the details, the *ipsissima verba*, accorded prominence, or are they regarded as secondary, ornamental, only rhetorical? Does the actual text with all its details and lacunae support meaning, or does the text undermine meaning, render it problematic and indeterminate?

Critics can debate what the meaning of a given work is and may never agree on one meaning, but they do not challenge the assumption that the work does have a fixed and determinate meaning. It may be regarded as archetypal, connected with a "collective unconscious"; as authorial, in accord with the author's intention, conscious or unconscious; as historical and social, stemming from the social forms and issues of the time of writing (or the time of reading); or as textual and structural, based in the text itself, without necessary concern for historical setting or authorial intention. Regardless, there is one fixed and determinate meaning. David, after all, is good or bad, and either he or Elhanan killed Goliath.

Much critical debate questions this action of meaning. The questioning comes from different quarters; it would be a gross oversimplification to divide criticism into two competing schools. Hermeneutical, reader-oriented, structuralist, psychological, and deconstructive critics can challenge the notion of fixed and determinate meaning in their own distinctive ways and at the same time challenge each other. Iser and Fish can be put together as reader-oriented critics, but an exchange emphasizes the gap between them (Fish 1981, Iser 1981). There is no fixed and determinate way to challenge the concept of fixed and determinate meaning.

By way of a list, I acknowledge my debt, of varying type and extent, to other critics whom I otherwise do not mention—Todorov, Scholes, Frei, White, Johnson, Culler, and Felman; relevant works are in the bibliography. Deconstruction may form a frame for my work, but specific modes of reading, i.e., what I note in the text and what I expect in the text, are from structuralism and other critical approaches. This book is not a deconstructive reading of 1 Samuel, although deconstruction does account, at least in part, for my talk of indeterminacy and ambiguity and my refusal to argue for one interpretation of 1 Samuel.

Deconstruction

I lay out briefly my understanding of some aspects of deconstruction that are relevant to this book. As a mode of thought, as a way of reading and writing, deconstruction is not new. Its debt to structuralism is indicated by the fact that it is frequently called "poststructuralism." Some of the most often mentioned and studied forebears are Rousseau, Nietzsche, Freud, and Heidegger. Contemporary deconstruction, however, begins with Jacques Derrida and his studies of Husserl, Rousseau, Freud, Hegel, and others. It has many present adherents; some are disciples of Derrida, while others represent major alternatives to Derridean deconstruction.

One aim of deconstruction that is germane to my purposes is the questioning of metaphysical thought—the attempt to undermine it and its founding concepts, particularly the ubiquitous use of conceptual dyads (Gasché) or dichotomies that present themselves as hierarchies, i.e., one pole is granted privilege and primacy, while the other is considered secondary and irrelevant. The questioning, the undermining, is carried on from "within" metaphysics; deconstruction does not represent a new approach that is "outside" metaphysics and that can correct it or prove it wrong. "Inside/outside" is one of the prime dichotomies questioned in deconstruction.

Dichotomies, especially when presented as hierarchies, serve the drive to establish presence—the essential, the real, the true, the unified, the proper, that which is univocal and identical with itself. This is the privileged pole. Division and difference, in space and time, lead to the other pole, which can be excluded from whatever analysis or definition is being undertaken, since it is unessential, unreal, false, divided, and equivocal.

For example, a text always has essential meaning, whether it is called author's intention, deep structure, archetype, or historical function. The meaning is established and argued for on the basis of textual evidence; contrary textual evidence is excluded, because it is "ornamental," "mere rhetoric," or due to an editorial revision or addition. A deconstructive critic may then read the text and give prominence to just those features excluded by previous interpretations; I frequently do this in my analysis of 1 Samuel.

However, deconstruction is not concerned with denying all distinctions and dichotomies or the impressive results that can come from their establishment and use, e.g., the progress of structuralist linguistics based on the synchronic/diachronic distinction. Deconstructive critics are concerned with dichotomies or with that aspect of dichotomies that results in the exclusion of one pole and thereby permits the other pole to appear as the real and the true—from another viewpoint, that permits the overall method to appear as objective. Some forms of structural analysis can appear to be scientific, because they produce the deep structure, i.e., the essential and true meaning, but this is done only by relegating many textual elements to the surface structure as changing and unessential elements that can be safely ignored in establishing the deep structure.

Speech Act Theory

I develop this more fully, since it relates to my analysis of 1 Samuel; questioning of dichotomies is not denying them or their effective use but is an attempt to bare their ideological functioning and their ubiquity. Denial of a dichotomy can be followed by its reintroduction in another form. In "Signature Event Context" and "Limited Inc," Derrida discusses Austin and speech act theory. The articles are an excellent introduction to Derrida and deconstruction; they are discussed by Culler (1981a) and Spivak (1980).

Derrida questions the founding distinction between ordinary, everyday language, which is serious, and parasitical language, which is nonserious; examples of the latter are literature, especially novels and drama, and the citation of statements as illustrations in a grammar. The distinction is founding, for it authorizes the speech act theorist to establish a theory of speech acts solely on the basis of ordinary language and only then to apply the established theory to the various categories of "parasitical language" to account for them. The theory can be presented as objective and empirical, because it is based on "real and serious" speech acts. Derrida does not dispute that the distinction can be made or that speech act theory has yielded impressive results, but he does dispute its claim to scientific objectivity. How, he asks, can a speech act theory claim rigor and exhaustiveness when it begins, before any empirical analysis, by excluding a large set of speech acts as not really speech acts?

Derrida's deconstructive strategy proceeds in what can be called a two-step procedure. First is a reversal of the dichotomy, an upsetting of the hierarchy. Prominence and priority are granted to the excluded term, and this shows that the hierarchy is not based in some unchanging order of things; literature can be considered the starting point for speech act theory. However, such a move can leave the dyad unchallenged, since it entails the possibility that the reversed dichotomy will become a new hierarchy. Literature is now primary and serious, and everyday language is secondary and nonserious.

A second step, simultaneous with the first, is to move between the two terms of the dichotomy—to endeavor to subvert it from within or to account for it by using another term. In other words, the previously excluded term is "reinscribed" within the dichotomy. Such talk, aided by neologisms, italics, and quotes, signals that the deconstructive critic is alerting the reader that the writing both says and does not say what it says. The critic can only write within the tradition, being neither outside nor beyond it. The critic has only its concepts and language to use to undermine it and, therefore, while using them, must also indicate that they are to be read and understood in a mode different from a traditional mode.

Derrida frequently talks of strategy, of plural writing, of a plural style as an issue in deconstruction; he produces not just a different reading or commentary but also a different form or style of writing a critical text that contains a reading or commentary. The very form of Derrida's works deconstructs classical critical dichotomies—literature and criticism, creative and critical, criticism and philosophy, literature and philosophy.

Implications

Deconstruction struggles with dichotomies that are crucial to literary criticism and biblical studies; it does not attempt to deny them or their functioning, but it does undermine, subvert, their use to support an essentialist interpretation. Some of the classic dyads are text and reader, exegesis and eisegesis, author and text, "meant" and "means," explication and interpretation, finding meaning and making meaning, form and content, words and meaning, and theory and practice. For example, reader-oriented criticism can reverse the hierarchy of text and reader by focusing on the reader, the conventions employed in reading, and the types of meaning created from the text; New Criticism and structuralism focus on the text and its structure, imagery, and themes. Deconstruction does not want to stop there, for these critical approaches can end by granting privilege to the reader, the text, or the "conventions of reading," i.e., by establishing a new hierarchy.

I use multiple descriptions in this book. Although I seldom do so, I may speak of the author's intention to obfuscate issues deliberately, to block a definitive interpretation. Or I may focus on the text and speak of it, or the narrator, as blocking a definitive reading, withholding crucial information, or providing too much information. I may point to the very words and phrases of the text, "that which is really there," to support an analysis. Or I may talk in terms of myself as reader, of "us" as readers, or of an impersonal reader. There it is a matter of the conventions I use, the questions I ask of the text, the words and phrases that I isolate to support my analysis, the arguments I devise on behalf of my reading. Finally, I may resort to a dialectical description and speak of meaning arising from a dialogue or a confrontation between the reader and the text.

The distinctions are not collapsed by this strategy; I the reader and the biblical text do not merge; neither I nor the biblical text disappear. But the use of such distinctions to found a hierarchy that permits the emergence of the definitive and essential interpretation is rendered problematic. Meaning is not finally located in the text, in the reader, or in a dialectical process involving both. Hartman puts it well:

> Contemporary criticism aims at a hermeneutics of indeterminacy. It proposes a type of analysis that has renounced the ambition to master or demystify its subject (text, psyche) by technocratic, predictive, or authoritarian formulas. (Hartman 1980, p. 41)

The problem or danger is that such a drive for mastery can sneak in by the back door; deconstruction can become the new dogma.

Deconstruction also provides ways for me to think and to speak of the OT as other than and yet as complex and sophisticated as any Western text; however, this is at the limit of my work. I can speak of the OT as other, as different, but can only point to ways that this description might be developed. For example, my previous comments on character, setting, etc., pointed this way. I spoke of inconsistencies and contradictions within a text that is unified and coherent. I do not want to give up either set of words, even though I realize they are part of Western thought, and this forces me to think of them in "other" ways, to think of a deconstruction of a system that renders such a text an impossibility, a contradiction. The books of Samuel are a unified and coherent text that informs me that both David and Elhanan killed the same man, Goliath, and that Michal, the daughter of Saul, had no children to the day of her death and that she had five sons.

Despite this discussion of deconstruction, I reiterate that I will not be pursuing a deconstructive analysis in the sense of the close and painstaking readings of a Derrida, de Man, or Johnson. They seek to ferret out those places where the text undermines its own claims to some sort of closure or resolution; they seek to catch the ways in which the text breaks down and subverts the major dichotomies it is working with or proclaiming.

For me, the OT, here exemplified by 1 Samuel, is not attempting to establish and defend some clear, definitive meaning for either a character or a theme; it is not employing dichotomies so that it can claim one pole as the essential meaning. For example, the OT does not try to develop an understanding of the word of the Lord as a clear and distinct phenomenon that exists present and identical to itself in a state prior to any interpretation, because it is aware that the presentation of such an understanding will in some way undermine and subvert itself, i.e., it will deconstruct itself. This is one example of several that will be discussed in this book.

This to me is an important aspect of the Bible and deconstruction; the latter permits me to read the former on its own terms without having to force it into modes of meaning and interpretation that gloss over, harmonize, or remove its repetitions, contradictions, details, gaps, etc. This is not a deconstructive reading, since I see no need to deconstruct the Bible in the same sense that de Man or Derrida feels the need to deconstruct the texts he reads. It was put simply and effectively once to me by a colleague, Burton Feldman, "The OT is already deconstructed; now read it!" This book is such an attempt.

This idea of the OT as other is a limit, since much of my work has been fueled by the conviction that the OT shares much with the contemporary literature that is variously called modernist, postmodernist, or metafiction—the fiction of Joyce, Becket, Barth, Nabokov, Barthelme, and Robbe-Grillet. Structuralism and deconstruction, in one story, are critical responses to, and spurs to, this category of literature. For me, it is no coincidence that I have been influenced by them and employ them in sundry ways in my study of the OT. Dillard speaks of narrative collage in modernist fiction, and her words describe 1 Samuel and much of the OT:

> The point of view shifts; the prose style shifts and its tone; characters turn into things; sequences of events abruptly vanish. Images

clash; realms of discourse bang together . . . a world shattered, and perhaps senseless, and certainly strange. . . . We experience a world unhinged. Nothing temporal, spatial, perceptual, social, or moral is fixed. (Dillard 1982, p. 24)

For a final implication, I return to Derrida's discussion of speech act theory to isolate his term "iteration," which combines two terms—the Latin *iter,* "other," and the English "reiteration." "Iteration" combines senses of differing and deferring and represents another strategy in deconstruction—a strategy that turns to the definition of parasitic language as any use of language, or of a speech act, that can be considered some sort of citation or quoting of ordinary, everyday language. The ordinary speech act is separated from its context and grafted onto a new one; I do not present Derrida's discussion of the problematic status of context, since it is not germane to this reading of 1 Samuel. The distinction between primary and original and secondary and repeated is put into play; the privilege goes to the primary and original, since the citation is merely a copy and repetition of it.

"Iteration" moves between the poles and attempts to subvert the hierarchy. By repetition, "iteration," or iterability, marks the production, the effect, not only of difference and alteration but also of identity and sameness. Repetition alters (Spivak 1980, pp. 36–40). If it did not, we could never distinguish between an original and a repetition or citation. But if repetition alters, then alteration identifies. Without the repetition, the second, there can be no first, no original. Without repetition, alteration, why would we ever look for sameness or identity? This is akin to what Miller calls "the tradition of difference," as distinct from "the tradition of presence" (cited in Leitch 1983, p. 49). The tradition of presence is familiar—we notice difference, because there is a present and substantial identity, a shared essence. The tradition of difference holds that we notice, or establish, similarity and identity, because there is a difference; thus, difference founds sameness and resemblance, not vice versa. This has major implications for reading OT narrative, which is characterized by a wide variety of repetition; I pay close attention to prophetic speeches and historical retrospects like 1 Samuel 12. One very interesting repetition is:

David prevailed over the Philistine with a sling and with a stone; he struck the Philistine and he killed him; there was no sword in the hand of David.

David ran and stood over the Philistine. He took his sword and drew it out of its sheath, and he killed him and cut off his head with it.

· 1 ·

1 SAMUEL 1-3

1 Samuel 1

Related Texts

The birth story of Samuel introduces the main characters—Samuel, Eli, and Eli's sons, Hophni and Phinehas—and the two cities—Shiloh and Ramah. Saul (*sha'ul*) is introduced through wordplay on the Hebrew root *sha'al*, to ask, that underlies his name; the exact form is found in v. 28 (*sha'ul*, lent or asked).

The narrative presents some important individual themes and topics, e.g., the cultic order (sanctuary, priests, ark, etc.), asking or inquiring of the Lord, the word of the Lord, and retributive justice. The themes and other aspects of the story call into play a number of preceding texts. For example, Elkanah has two wives, Hannah and Peninnah, and Hannah is without children. Barrenness is an appropriate beginning for a birth story ⁞ OT narrative. Specifically, the fact of two wives, one barren and one fertile, is reminiscent of and analogous to Sarah and Hagar, Rachel and Leah. The latter are here inserted into the text, and it will not be surprising to encounter other and more extendable parallels to them, especially Rachel.

A second example is the category *birth story*, which leads to several analogous texts in Genesis, to that of Moses in Exod. 2:1–10, and to that of Samson in Judges 13. I do not develop the Genesis parallels, since this would entail a lengthy analysis of them and their context. Moses' birth occurs in a situation that is threatening to him and the people; he eventually saves himself and the people. Samson's birth is set during a period of Philistine rule, and he is to "begin to deliver Israel from the hand of the Philistines" (Judg. 13:5). The comparisons between the birth stories of Samuel, Moses, and Samson raise questions about Samuel as a savior and about the threatening situation from which he could save the people. Will he be like Moses or Samson, or will he be a new type of savior? Or, not to prejudge the issue,

1

will he be a savior at all? But, first, what type of savior are Moses and Samson?

The angel of the Lord announces to Manoah's wife that Samson is to "begin to deliver Israel from the hand of the Philistines"; if he does so, it is a meager beginning. Samson and those around him, Israelite and Philistine, are ignorant of what is happening, particularly about the Lord's role or lack of role (Judg. 16:20) in the events (Polzin 1980, pp. 181–95). Whether or not Samuel is to be similar to Samson, the parallel between their birth stories has indicated some important themes for the reading of 1 Samuel—Philistines, savior and salvation, ignorance and knowledge.

Moses is a far more complex character than Samson. Unlike Samson, his work is not just a beginning. He saves the people from the hand of the Egyptians. He brings them forth from Egypt to Sinai and then to the border of Canaan. More importantly, Moses is a legislator and mediator; he is the one who receives and then both reports and interprets the word of the Lord to Israel. He is a "wonder-worker" who has a privileged relation with the Lord (Deut. 34:10–12). Unlike Samson, Moses has a successor, Joshua, who is appointed by the Lord himself (Num. 27:12–23; Deut. 34:9).

On the other hand, akin to Samson, Moses' work is only a beginning, since he does not complete the task of bringing the people into the promised land. The generation he brings out of Egypt dies with him in the wilderness on the way to the land. It is Joshua who brings the people, the next generation, into the land, but his work is also just a beginning, since "the Lord said to [Joshua] . . . 'There remains yet very much land to be possessed' " (Josh. 13:1). The land and the peoples who remain are listed in Josh. 13:2–6; a similar list is in Judg. 3:1–3, after the death of Joshua. The latter, however, is a list of the nations left by the Lord, the nations that he will never drive out from Israel; the "there yet remains . . ." of Josh. 13:1 is no longer a beginning but a final state of affairs. "The people of Israel dwelt among the Canaanites, the Hittites, the Amorites, the Perizzites, the Hivites, and the Jebusites" (Judg. 3:5). In both lists, one of the groups left is the "five rulers of the Philistines: of Gaza, Ashdod, Ashkelon, Gath, and Ekron" (Josh. 13:3; cf. Judg. 3:3).

I turn now to a comparison of Moses and Samuel with the above in mind. It may well be that

> there has not arisen a prophet since in Israel like Moses, whom the
> Lord knew face to face, none like him for all the signs and wonders
> which the Lord sent him to do in the land of Egypt, to Pharaoh and
> to all his servants and to all his land, and for all the mighty power

and all the great and terrible deeds which Moses wrought in the
eyes of all Israel (Deut. 34:10–12)

Moses was a privileged prophet and wonder-worker. He himself told
the people, "The Lord your God will raise up for you a prophet like
me from among you . . . 'and I [the Lord] will put my words in his
mouth, and he will speak to them all that I command him' " (Deut.
18:15–19). Is Samuel to be a "prophet like Moses" who will speak the
word of the Lord to Israel?

It is striking that in the beginning of 1 Samuel there is no threat
either to Samuel or to Israel. Moses' situation of oppression in a
foreign land does not apply here directly, and I leave aside any indirect applications. Samson's situation is relevant, since it is nearer in
time and space, geographical and textual, but its application is not
immediately obvious.

Samson appears when the Lord has given Israel "into the hand of
the Philistines for forty years" (Judg. 13:1); it is not stated whether
Samson comes during or at the end of the forty-year period. Reference is made twice to the Philistine rule over Israel (Judg. 14:4,
15:11), but there is no explicit mention of oppression. The first occurrence of the Philistines in Judges is in Judg. 10:6–8; because of their
worship of other gods, including Philistine gods, the Lord sells Israel
"into the hand of the Philistines and into the hand of the Ammonites,
and they crushed and oppressed the Israelites that year." Jephthah
defeats the Ammonites, but there is no mention of the Philistines
after "that year." Samson may be saving Israel from Philistine oppression or from Philistine rule that is not oppressive.

In any case, the Philistines, so central to the narrative in Judges 13–
16, disappear from it after Judges 16 and do not reappear until the
battle of Ebenezer in 1 Samuel 4. By "disappear from the narrative," I
mean that a person, group, place, or theme no longer appears in the
text and that the text gives no reason for the disappearance. For
example, Moses dies; he does not disappear from the story. On the
other hand, no reason is given for the lack of any mention of the
Philistines in Judges 17–21 and 1 Samuel 1–3. Based only on Samuel's birth story, it cannot be confidently stated that Samuel will, or
will not, have something to do with salvation from the hand of the
Philistines.

Judges 17–21, nevertheless, present another class of threats to Israel—internal threats, particularly the violence perpetrated by Israelite upon Israelite. In Judges 19–21, the tribe of Benjamin is almost
annihilated, and the survivors face possible extinction because of the
other tribes' oath never to give their daughters as wives for the Ben-

jaminites. All this transpires in a time when "there was no king in Israel; every man did what was right in his own eyes" (Judg. 17:6, 21:25). Before turning to these chapters, however, a discussion is in order of some relevant issues from 1 Samuel that will bring us back to the end of Judges.

Cultic Order

This appears in the opening chapters of 1 Samuel in the persons of the house of Eli and in the sanctuary at Shiloh. By "cultic order," I intend all that pertains to the cult, e.g., priests, sanctuaries, and the sacrificial system; I do not intend a sharp break with other orders. In Exodus-Deuteronomy, the cultic order is given a central, authoritative status by the sheer amount of space devoted to its description and regulation. (I do not suggest that the description is consistent.) The authority extends beyond what we would consider priestly or religious duties into matters of war and justice, e.g., in Deut. 17:8–13, 19:15–21, and 20:1–8.

In Joshua and Judges, there is a significant change in the importance of the cultic order. The priests and the ark lead the people across the Jordan and play a crucial role in the ritual destruction of Jericho. However, it is Joshua who comes "before the ark of the Lord" to inquire about the debacle at Ai (Josh. 7:6); there is no mention of priests in Joshua 7. The conquest of Ai (Josh. 8:1–29) is accomplished without the aid of priest or ark, in contrast to the taking of Jericho and to a "holy war" text such as Deut. 20:1–8. The assembly between Mts. Ebal and Gerizim, following the conquest of Ai, is conducted by Joshua (Josh. 8:30–35); "the Levitical priests who carried the ark of the covenant of the Lord" are there but play no active role.

Eleazar and his son Phinehas play parts in the division of the land, but the roles are less than those of ark and priests in Joshua 3–6. Phinehas, indeed, is mainly a messenger to the Transjordanian tribes (Josh. 22:13, 30–32). The shift in importance is evident in the few verses allotted to noting the presence of Eleazar and Phinehas, e.g., Eleazar in Josh. 14:1, 17:4, 19:51, and 21:1.

Sanctuaries, or at least central and important sites, appear in Joshua. The base camp at Gilgal is the first mentioned. The conquest is launched from here and the division of the land begun here (Josh. 14:6). The site between Mts. Ebal and Gerizim, which is Shechem, is the second place and is noteworthy because of the absence of the name Shechem in Josh. 8:30–35.

"The entire congregation of the people of Israel assembled at Shiloh; they erected the tent of meeting there" (Josh. 18:1). The final seven inheritances are apportioned at Shiloh (Josh. 18:8–10). The distribution is accomplished by lot "before the Lord at the door of the tent of meeting" (Josh. 19:51). Except for the enigmatic reference in Gen. 49:10, Josh. 18:1 is the first mention of Shiloh in the OT. No background on Shiloh is provided; no reason is given for the establishment there of a central base. After the transfer to Shiloh, Gilgal is not mentioned again in Joshua. Finally, although Shiloh is the site for the allotment of much of the land, it itself is not allotted to any tribe.

Shiloh remains the base until the assembly at Shechem in Joshua 24. However, the latter may not involve a change of the central camp to Shechem, because after the ceremony "Joshua sent the people away, everyone to his inheritance" (Josh. 24:28). The status of Shiloh and Shechem is left open at the end of Joshua. Indeed, the question of any central site or sanctuary in Israel is open. "After the death of Joshua, the people of Israel inquired of the Lord" (Judg. 1:1), but no location is indicated. There is no base of operations, no central camp, in Judges, at least in chapters 1–16, since each judge operates from his own place. There can be no central place, because there is no central authority or leader for all the people of Israel. Joshua has no successor as sole leader.

Priests and sanctuaries appear in Judges 17–21. In Judges 17–18, Micah has a "house of God" with an ephod and teraphim in it and eventually a Levite as priest, but the Danites take both the objects and the priest. Micah's "house of God" disappears from the narrative. The priest turns out to be a certain Jonathan, and he "and his sons were priests to the tribe of the Danites until the day of the captivity of the land" (Judg. 18:30). The Danites set up the graven image of Micah but only for "as long as the house of God was at Shiloh" (Judg. 18:31).

Gibeah of Benjamin

The Danite episode is followed in Judges 19–21 by the horrendous events involving Gibeah and Benjamin. In response to the Levite's gory challenge to the tribes, "the congregation assembled as one man to the Lord at Mizpah" (Judg. 20:1). They march on Gibeah and end in war with Benjamin. Confronted by the Benjaminite army, the people do not remain at Mizpah; they go up to Bethel to inquire (*sha'al*) of the Lord not once but three times (Judg. 20:18–28).

Bethel is a site with an honored history stretching back to the days of Abraham and Jacob. We are informed, in the account of the third inquiry, that "the ark of the covenant of God was there in those days, and Phinehas the son of Eleazar, son of Aaron, ministered before it in those days" (Judg. 20:27–28). Does this provide a motivation for making inquiry at Bethel; if so, why was it not furnished with the report of the first inquiry in Judg. 20:18? Or is this an incidental fact for our information, a fact that has little or nothing to do with seeking the Lord and perhaps has more to do with demonstrating the narrator's detailed knowledge of the period? To put the question in other terms, are the ark and the priest associated or not with inquiring of the Lord? The issue is undecidable, because both responses—associated and not associated—are possible.

We are informed, in retrospect, of an oath sworn at Mizpah—"No one will give his daughter in marriage to Benjamin" (Judg. 21:1). Enforcement of the oath threatens the Benjaminite survivors with extinction. "The people came to Bethel and sat there until evening before God; they lifted up their voices and wept bitterly" (Judg. 20:2). The action is similar to that in Judg. 20:23 and 26. "They said [they do not *inquire* as in Judg. 20:18, 23, 27], 'O Lord, God of Israel, why has this come to be in Israel that there is today one tribe lacking in Israel?' " (Judg. 21:3). The people either get no answer from God, do not wait for one, or perhaps do not even expect one. "On the morrow the people rose early and built an altar there; they offered burnt offerings and peace offerings." This bears comparison with Judg. 20:26: "They sat there before the Lord and fasted that day until evening; they offered burnt offerings and peace offerings before the Lord." The later precedes the act of inquiry and may have been intended to affect the favorable response from the Lord: "Go up for tomorrow I will give them [Benjamin] into your hand" (Judg. 20:28).

The ritual at Bethel in Judg. 21:4 may or may not have anything to do with the question asked the previous evening; analogously, the rituals at Bethel in chapter 20, regardless of the Israelites' intentions, may or may not have anything to do with the response received. The relationship between ritual acts and inquiry of the Lord is clouded in the two episodes. The ambiguity is present in an earlier incident. The Danites asked Micah's priest to inquire of God " 'so that we may know whether the journey on which we are setting out will succeed.' The priest said to them, 'Go in peace. The journey on which you go is under the eye of the Lord' " (Judg. 18:5–6). Apparently the priest does not actually inquire of God but gives the Danites the answer they want to hear. The Danites depart and "succeed in their journey."

> The people of Israel said, "Which of all the tribes of Israel did not come up to the assembly of the Lord?" For they had taken a serious oath concerning him who did not come up to the Lord at Mizpah: "He must be put to death." The people of Israel had compassion for Benjamin their brother and said, "Today one tribe is cut off from Israel. What can we do for wives for those who are left since we swore by the Lord that we will not give them any of our daughters for wives?" (Judg. 21:5–7)

The ludicrousness of the situation needs little comment. "The people of Israel dwelt among the Canaanites, the Hittites, the Amorites . . . and they took their daughters to themselves for wives, and their own daughters they gave to their sons; and they served their gods" (Judg. 3:5–6). The people of Israel may not keep the covenant of the Lord, alluded to in Judg. 20:27, but they will keep an oath they have made regardless of its disastrous consequences.

The slaughter of the inhabitants of Jabesh-gilead and the rape of its virgins and the rape of the virgins of Shiloh during "the yearly feast of the Lord" underscore the grotesqueness of the solution and the horrible consequences of the oath. Yet, surprisingly, it works; Benjamin is saved.

> The Benjaminites did so. They took wives according to their number, from the dancers whom they carried off. They went and returned to their inheritance and rebuilt the towns and dwelt in them. The people of Israel left there at that time . . . each man to his inheritance. (Judg. 21:23–24)

The surprise can extend to the entire book of Judges. No matter what Israel does—"The Israelites continued doing what was evil in the eyes of the Lord"—she is not destroyed. She may be subject to periods of foreign rule and oppression, but she also enjoys lengthy periods of peace—eighty years (Judg. 3:30), forty years (Judg. 5:31), and forty years (Judg. 8:28). Despite the questionable origins of the family, the Danites do get their new territory and are able to set up a priestly house that lasts until the day of the land's captivity. In chapters 19–21, an Israelite city acts like Sodom. There is civil war and the near extinction of a tribe, but the people and the tribe survive.

Conclusion

"In those days there was no king in Israel; every man did what was right in his own eyes" is a formulaic statement that occurs in Judg. 17:6 and Judg. 21:25 (the final verse in the book of Judges). (A shorter form is in Judg. 18:1 and Judg. 19:1.) At this juncture, I focus attention on the latter half of the verse, since it has a parallel in the narrator's frequent intonation of the fact that the Israelites "did what was evil in the eyes of the Lord." The fact serves to explain why Israel is so often sold into the hands of her enemies.

The phrase "do what was evil in the eyes of the Lord" occurs for the last time in Judg. 13:1 in the introduction to the story of Samson. He and those around him are generally ignorant of the Lord's role in events. The narrator, however, does not share their obtuseness and realizes that the source or beginning of Israel's problems is her continuing to do what is evil in the Lord's eyes. But what is not provided is an explanation of why Israel survives. She is sold into the hands of her enemies, but she cries to the Lord, who sends a savior, a judge, to rescue her even while she continues to do evil. The doctrine of retributive justice apparently is not in force in the book of Judges. The problem of Israel's survival is emphasized by the clarity of the evil that she continues to do. Despite the ambiguity and obfuscation in Judges, there is little doubt that worship of the Baals and the Ashtaroth, the gods of Syria, the gods of Sidon, etc., and the events of chapters 17–21 are evil in the Lord's eyes. The absence of a king may account for the lawlessness in the land, but it does not address the issue of why the lawlessness can achieve its goals.

The initial discussion of the cultic order has led into Judges 17–21 and far afield from priest, sanctuary, and 1 Samuel 1, yet not too far. They have not been forgotten. Cultic concerns remain in Judges 17–21 in the theme of inquiry of the Lord and its relation to ritual acts; many of the other points raised in the preceding analysis of Joshua and Judges will play a part in the reading of 1 Samuel. An ongoing concern of the reading will be the issue of retributive justice and what, if any, sense it makes.

Before returning to the reading of 1 Samuel, we must evaluate the space between Judg. 21:25 and 1 Sam. 1:1. There is no indication of the amount of time elapsed between the two incidents at Shiloh, the rape of the virgins and the birth of Samuel. Is this the space between two adjacent verses so that we continue reading without pause or break, assuming that little time has elapsed? Or is it the space between two books so that we mark a major pause before continuing the reading and then expect new material, the beginning of a new period? It may be another type of space, e.g., the pause that comes before a return to and a repetition of previous material. In other words, does 1 Samuel continue the narrative of Judges; does it begin something new; does it repeat Judges, or some part of Judges, in some way? The question is crucial, for it bears upon the way in which we will read 1 Samuel and how we will treat any parallels between Judges and 1 Samuel.

The question cannot be definitively decided in favor of just one alternative. All three, and probably more, hold. 1 Samuel continues the narrative of Judges; it marks a break, since something new is to happen; it repeats Judges, particularly from chapter 13 on, since Samuel's birth story "repeats" Samson's. Practically, this results in my employing analogous material in a variety of ways at different times or at the same time; it also means that the above themes, e.g., the cultic order and retributive justice, will continue to be significant in the narrative; they will continue and yet be changed.

A Reading

Shiloh

We turn to the reading of 1 Samuel with initial focus on Shiloh and the house of Eli. Shiloh is an important site because of its past and present status. A major priestly family is there, and they may be descendants of Aaron. The temple of the Lord is there (1 Sam. 1:9, 3:3) along with the ark and the tent of meeting (1 Sam. 2:22, 3:3). Earlier we were apprised of the fact that at the time of the outrage of Gibeah, the ark of the covenant of God was at Bethel; "Phinehas the son of Eleazar, son of Aaron, ministered before it in those days" (Judg. 20:27–28). In these days, the ark of the covenant of God is at Shiloh (1 Sam. 4:3–4), where Hophni and Phinehas, sons of Eli, minister before it. The ark has been transferred from Bethel to Shiloh; has the house of Aaron also been transferred?

The reoccurrence of the name Phinehas argues in favor of the supposition that the house of Aaron has been transferred, as does the congruence between the man of God's pronouncement to Eli in 1 Sam. 2:28–30 and the Lord's pronouncement to Phinehas, son of Eleazar, in Num. 25:10–13. Both speak of eternal (`olam) priesthood. However, the correspondence is not conclusive evidence, since the Lord's promise was made to Eli's ancestors "when they were in Egypt subject to the house of Pharaoh" (1 Sam. 2:27). The promise to Phinehas in Numbers 25 was made in Moab forty years later. On the other hand, it could be argued that the choice mentioned in 1 Sam. 2:27–28 is earlier than the promise referred to in 1 Sam. 2:30 and that the latter, therefore, is the promise made to Phinehas in Moab, so that Eli is a descendant of Phinehas, son of Eleazar, perhaps his son.

This is a fine example of a *lure*. Enough evidence is offered to suggest a particular interpretation, e.g., that the house of Eli is the house of Aaron, but not enough evidence is provided to clinch the argument. Specific evidence is lacking, e.g., the statement "Eli, son of Phinehas, son of Eleazar," or the evidence is presented in a way that is open to two or more interpretations, e.g., the assertions in 1 Sam. 2:27–30. On the other hand, the evidence is sufficient in amount and clarity to prevent its disproof and rejection. We can ask of the house of Eli what another will ask of the band of prophets, "Who is their father?" (1 Sam. 10:12). The question is unanswerable. The lack of a clinching genealogy for Eli is emphasized by the presence of one for Elkanah.

Shiloh's importance is clouded. The priestly family there may or may not be of Aaronite ancestry, but it, the house of Eli, is to stand under divine judgment. The fact that the "temple of the Lord" is there (1 Sam. 1:9, 3:3) is rendered moot, since Shiloh disappears from

the narrative after 1 Samuel 4. In Joshua, the inheritances of many of
the tribes were distributed at Shiloh "at the door of the tent of meeting" (Josh. 19:51). Eli "heard all that his sons were doing to all Israel
and how they lay with the women who served at the door of the tent
of meeting" (1 Sam. 2:22)—an ironic comment that marks the sad
state of affairs at Shiloh.

The presence of the ark at Shiloh says little about the significance of
Shiloh, but it does point to two issues introduced above—inquiry of
the Lord and the "word of the Lord." The ark has a revelatory function. It contains the tablets given to Moses by the Lord (Exod. 25:10–
16, 40:16–21; Deut. 10:1–8). The cover of the ark has two cherubim
on it, where the Lord will meet and speak with Moses (Exod. 25:22;
Num. 7:89). Moses' "book of the law" is placed "by the side of the ark
of the covenant of the Lord" (Deut. 31:26). The motif, the ark, will be
picked up again in the reading of 1 Samuel 4.

Shiloh's status is ambiguous. It was the site for the distribution of
the land to separate tribes, including Benjamin, but it was also the site
for the "preservation" of Benjamin in Judges 21. Benjamin seized
virgins from there during "the yearly feast of the Lord" (Judg. 21:19;
1 Sam. 1:3). Shiloh has both a glorious and an ignominious past. In
1 Samuel, it has more of the latter than the former, but its precise
status is left open, since it disappears from the text. It is replaced not
by one other site but by several—Bethel, Gilgal, Mizpah, and Ramah
(1 Sam. 7:16–17); the latter is a new entry in the list of important
cities. Shiloh goes as suddenly as it first appeared in Josh. 18:1. Shiloh
appears again in 1 Kings 11–14 as the home of Ahijah, the prophet
who is instrumental in the division of the kingdom; the analogy with
Samuel requires a separate study.

Hannah
The narrative in 1 Samuel 1 moves at a leisurely pace. Background is
provided for the scene between Eli and Hannah and the subsequent
presentation of Samuel at Shiloh; there is a follow-up on Hannah's
later years, including the notice that she has five other children. We
are given, in 1 Sam. 1:1–2:26, the full story. However, the birth story
concerns itself more with Hannah's distress and request of the Lord
than with Samuel (see Alter 1981, pp. 81–86).

Hannah's distress is augmented by Peninnah, who irritates her; Elkanah is concerned because of Hannah's sadness. In her distress,
Hannah

> prayed to the Lord and wept bitterly. She made a vow, "O Lord of
> hosts, if you will look on the misery of your maidservant, and re-

> member and not forget your maidservant, but will give to your
> maidservant a son, then I will give him to the Lord all the days of
> his life." (1 Sam. 1:10–11)

This is a reflex of the bitterness of the Israelites because of the oppression of the Egyptians. They cry to God; he hears their cry and
remembers his covenant. Moses is sent to bring them out of the house
of slavery. The Lord remembers Hannah, and Samuel comes to relieve her misery, to blunt her rival's provocations. The reflex calls
attention to the lack of a threatening situation from which Samuel can
rescue the people. The moving and human portrait of Hannah, told
with detail and completeness, brings into relief the questions of who
Samuel is and what he is to accomplish. Unlike Joshua and Judges,
1 Samuel does not begin with a specific problem or crisis that is to be
addressed and corrected; there is no overview like Joshua 1 and
Judges 2 that tells us in advance what the book is to be "about."

The birth story is marked by the theme of eating and drinking,
food and drink; this is a ubiquitous theme in 1 Samuel and in most of
OT narrative. Hannah "wept and would not eat." Elkanah asks why
she does not eat, and Eli and Hannah speak of drink, drunkenness,
and not drinking. After her conversation with Eli, Hannah "went her
way and ate." Samuel is returned to Shiloh with a bull, flour, and
wine; the bull is slain, "and they brought the child to Eli."

Two readings can be followed here, the "everyday" and the "ritual."
"Hannah wept and did not eat," or "Hannah lamented and fasted."
She eats and drinks because she is famished and weak, or she performs a ritual eating and drinking and then goes to pray to the Lord.
The food sent with Samuel is a gift of appreciation for Eli, a demonstration of proper etiquette akin to Jesse's gifts to Saul and the army
commander (1 Sam. 16:20, 17:17–18). Or it is a mandatory offering
to be presented in such a situation.

The possibility that the acts may be either everyday acts or mandatory ritual raises the question of the relation between inquiry or
prayer and ritual. Are the two related? If so, how? I cite two passages
from Judges.

> All the people of Israel, the entire army, went up and came to
> Bethel and wept/lamented; they sat there before the Lord and
> fasted that day until evening. They offered burnt offerings and
> peace offerings before the Lord. The people of Israel inquired of
> the Lord . . . "Should we again go out to battle with the Benjami-
> nites our brothers, or should we cease?" The Lord said, "Go up for
> tomorrow I will give them into your hand." (Judg. 20:26–28)

> The people came to Bethel and sat there until evening before God.
> They lifted their voices and wept/lamented bitterly. They said, "O
> Lord, God of Israel, why has this come about in Israel that there is
> today one tribe missing from Israel?" On the morrow the people
> rose early and built an altar there and offered burnt offerings and
> peace offerings. (Judg. 21:2–4)

I have already highlighted the lack of an explicit relation between
ritual and inquiry in the passages (see pages 6–7). The two texts
together may be asserting that Judges 20 represents the "proper
order" of things and that Judges 21, by representing a distorted
order, is stressing the "distorted order" of Judges, in which evil frequently leads to success and even prosperity. This reading accords
with the statement that in the midst of its obfuscations, Judges is
definitive about "what is evil in the eyes of the Lord."

On the other hand, the two texts may be asserting that there is no
one determined relation between ritual and inquiry or prayer, i.e.,
both texts represent a "proper order" or both represent a "distorted
order." This neither affirms nor denies the necessity of ritual or its
opposite, the rejection of all ritual. The narrative places us in a zone
somewhere "between" the either/or of accepting or rejecting the necessity of ritual. I maintain that the ambiguity, the indeterminateness,
surrounding questions such as the status of Shiloh, the identity of the
house of Eli, inquiry of God, etc., is related to the undecidability of
the status and function of ritual, indeed of the entire cultic order.

I am aware that the ambiguity and the lack of clear distinctions
apply to the idea of a cultic order. There is no separate cultic order in
the sense of a group of people, places, and actions that are unified in
themselves and that exclude all others. There are no sharp demarca-
tions between the cultic order and other orders, e.g., prophecy and
monarchy. I speak of sanctuaries, priesthood, and sacrifice but do not
mean that, for example, only priests can sacrifice. Samuel and Saul
build altars and offer sacrifices without thereby becoming priests and
without usurping priestly prerogatives.

> O Lord of hosts, if you . . . will give to your maidservant a son, then
> I will give him to the Lord all the days of his life, and a razor will
> not touch his head. (1 Sam. 1:11)

The closing phrase is a Nazirite theme: "All the days of his Nazirite
vow a razor will not come upon his head" (Num. 6:5). The first
requirement for a Nazirite is to "separate himself from wine and
strong drink; he shall drink no vinegar made from wine or strong
drink and shall not drink any juice or grapes or eat grapes fresh or

dried" (Num. 6:3). The latter appears in 1 Samuel 1 not as a Nazirite provision but as a one-time event:

> Eli said to her, "How long will you be drunken? Put away your wine from you." Hannah answered, "No, my lord, I am a deeply troubled woman; I have drunk neither wine nor strong drink." (1 Sam. 1:14–15)

In Samson's birth story, the angel tells Manoah's wife, "Drink no wine or strong drink and eat nothing unclean, for look, you will conceive and bear a son. A razor must not touch his head for the boy will be a Nazirite to God from birth" (Judg. 13:4–5). In Judges 13, but not in 1 Samuel 1, the Nazirite association is explicitly noted; in 1 Samuel it is difficult to speak of Samuel as a Nazirite. ("Nazirite" does occur in a Qumran fragment [McCarter 1980b, pp. 55–56] of 1 Sam. 1:22, but do we regard this as an original, variant, or secondary reading?)

This is *metonymic dispersion*, already encountered in the reflex of Moses' birth story in 1 Samuel 1. A text is repeated and altered. Many of the themes and words of the "first text" reoccur, but they are in a different order with a different context, emphasis, and significance; new material is added, e.g., "eat nothing unclean" in Judg. 13:4. There is no need to trace the *dispersion* within Numbers 6, Judges 13–16, and 1 Samuel 1, but I do draw attention to it, since other cogent examples follow.

> As she continued praying before the Lord, Eli watched her mouth. Hannah was speaking in her heart; only her lips moved and her voice was not heard; therefore, Eli took her to be a drunken woman. (1 Sam. 1:12–13)

Eli is mistaken. His mistake stems from partial observation; he sees, but he does not hear. It is significant that it is hearing that would correct the error, and I pay close attention to the theme of hearing.

In this instance, we as readers are privileged, since we both see and hear; we are presented with the "true" situation and know what we are seeing and how to judge it. However, 1 Samuel does not always allow us such privilege, since it usually presents only part of the situation. We are then in Eli's position and have to accept the possibility that we can misjudge what we are seeing, but, unlike Eli, we are not then provided with the means to decide whether we have judged correctly or incorrectly. We are akin to Eli in his later condition—blind, unable to see—in the sense that we are unable to decide exactly what we are seeing. 1 Samuel 1, with its detail and completeness, is a misleading introduction to 1 Samuel, which will frequently share the detail but not the completeness.

> She called his name Samuel for "I have asked him (*she'iltiv*) of the
> Lord." (1 Sam. 1:20)

The Hebrew root *sha'al,* to ask, to dedicate, and to inquire, occurs
nine times in the story—1 Sam. 1:17, 18, 20, 27–28, and 1 Sam. 2:20;
each refers to Samuel as the one asked for or dedicated. It takes
ingenuity to explain the play on *sha'al* as offering a legitimate etymology for the name Samuel (*shemu'el*). The association of *sha'al* with
Saul, *sha'ul,* is patent (see page 1).

Wordplay is metonymic play as the proffered etymology shifts from
one character to another. With it, the focus of the narrative shifts and
blurs. Is this Samuel's birth story or, as many have suggested, a reflex
of Saul's? If there is a savior, who is it—Samuel or Saul? The play on
sha'al also involves the meaning "to inquire" and leads us not just
forward but back to Judges 17–21 and instances of inquiry of the
Lord. Yet the play leads forward again, since inquiry of the Lord, and
asking something of the Lord, are significant acts in the coming narrative and involve Samuel and Saul.

Inquiry is one mode of seeking the word of the Lord.

> Elkanah her husband said to her, "Do what is good in your eyes;
> wait until you have weaned him; only may the Lord establish *his
> word.*" (1 Sam. 1:23)

What is the word (*dabar*) that he is to establish, to raise up (*yaqem*)?
What could Elkanah have in mind? What can we as readers make of
the wish over and above Elkanah's intention? Is his wish to be taken as
intending an implicit promise made by the Lord through the birth of
Samuel? If so, what is the promise? Taken as referring to the immediate context, we are left in the dark as to the reference of "his word."
But "establish" (*qum*) and "the word of the Lord," separate or together, play significant roles in 1 Samuel and are put into play by
Elkanah's enigmatic wish.

In the judgment speech against the house of Eli, the man of God
quotes the Lord, "I will raise up (**qum*) for myself a faithful priest"
(1 Sam. 2:35). The Lord tells Samuel, "On that day I will raise up
(**qum*) against the house of Eli all that I have spoken (*dibber*) against
his house" (1 Sam. 3:12). In chapter 15, the Lord repents having
made Saul king, "for he has turned back from following me and *has
not raised up my words.*" Saul claims that "I *have raised up the word* of the
Lord" (1 Sam. 15:11–13).

A converse of Elkanah's wish concerns Samuel and similarly has no
explicit referent: "Samuel grew and the Lord was with him and *let
none of his words fall to the ground*" (1 Sam. 3:19). This text raises the

possibility that in 1 Sam. 1:23 Elkanah refers to Samuel's, not the Lord's, word, and this possibility in 1 Sam. 1:23 connects the word of Samuel with the word of the Lord (cf. 1 Sam. 3:21–4:1). Although the referent of Elkanah's wish is not determinable, the wish does set in motion a consideration for words, particularly the Lord's, and their establishment or lack of establishment. Elkanah's wish is pregnant, since its range of meaning and effect extends far beyond its context.

1 Samuel 2

The Song of Hannah (1 Sam. 2:1–10)

In the introduction, I discussed the limitations of my treatment of the Song. The following reading traces the general movement of the Song and illustrates what it "sets in motion." Although it is a lengthy, pregnant expression, there are no obvious or extended parallels between the song and the narrative. The hymn is not a theological statement that is verified and exemplified in dramatic and narrative form. There are hints and lures that point in the direction of a theological manifesto, but they are not developed. The specific lures are simultaneously frustrating and fascinating. I note a few in this section and indicate others at relevant points in the reading of 1 Samuel.

Hannah praises the Lord, but the praise is general and universal and does not include his specific action on her behalf. Her praise moves the narrative from the confines of Shiloh and Israel to the panorama of heaven and earth. But Israel is not lost sight of, for this is "our God," who will "judge the ends of the earth" and who will "give strength to his king and exalt the power of his anointed." Unlike so many who precede her in Judges, Hannah is a knowledgeable woman who confesses that "the Lord is a God of knowledge." She knows to whom to pray in her distress—Yahweh, not just Elohim. She also knows of a king who is considered the Lord's anointed.

Yet many of Hannah's statements in the Song have the flavor of platitudes with no predictable relevance to the context. There is no proportion, direct or inverse. For example, "The bows of the mighty are shattered, while the feeble [literally, stumbled] are girded with armor." The mighty are defeated in 1 Samuel, but they include the Israelites, the Philistines, the Ammonites, and even Saul and Jonathan; the relation is not specific. On the other hand, some rise from lowly positions, but it is impossible to speak of Samuel, Saul, David, or Jonathan as feeble and stumbled. The verse, nevertheless, does introduce the ubiquitous theme of war and the military.

"The full have hired out for food (*lechem*), while the hungry have ceased to hunger." Any associations are of questionable importance, although the theme of eating and drinking pervades 1 Samuel. In one reading of 1 Samuel 1, Hannah does not eat and becomes weak; she then eats and drinks. There are two parallels at the other end of the book. Saul is weak "because he had eaten nothing all day and all night"; the "witch of Endor" prepares a fine meal for him, which he eats. The Egyptian found by David in the wilderness is given food and water. "He ate and his spirit revived for he had not eaten food or drunk water for three days and three nights" (1 Sam. 30:12). There is a reflex in the speech against the house of Eli: "Any who is left in your house will come to implore him for a piece of silver or a loaf of bread (*lechem*) and will say, 'Please attach me to a priestly position to eat a morsel of bread (*lechem*)!' " (1 Sam. 2:36).

"The childless has borne seven, while she with many sons is bereaved." Hannah has Samuel and five more children, for a total of six (1 Sam. 2:21). Also given in 1 Samuel is reference to the eight sons of David's father, not mother (1 Sam. 17:12). The numbers six and eight emphasize that the Song has no simple, mechanical relation to the narrative. Neither bereavement nor birth is a major theme in 1 Samuel. Finally, in 1 Samuel, generational conflict involves fathers and sons, not mothers and sons. Saul's mother is named only in passing (1 Sam. 14:50), and David's mother is only mentioned, not named (1 Sam. 22:3).

"He guards the way of his faithful, while the wicked perish in darkness." If this is so, it will mark a change from the stories in Judges, where the wicked seldom perish and where it is difficult to speak of any as faithful. Will this statement of retributive justice hold, or will the perverse justice, the mercy, of Judges prevail?

The grandiose panorama of the Song of Hannah and its uncertain and tenuous relation to 1 Samuel draw attention once more to the absence of an overview or introduction that would have a substantial relation to the context. The Song as a whole is a lure; it offers much but produces little.

Sons: Samuel and Hophni and Phinehas

"Elkanah went home to Ramah and the boy was ministering to the Lord in the presence of Eli the priest" (1 Sam. 2:11). The focus shifts from parents to children—from Hannah and Elkanah to Samuel, from Eli to Hophni and Phinehas. It also shifts from priest and sanctuary to Samuel and the Lord. There is no mention in the verse of

Shiloh, temple of the Lord, tent of meeting, or ark. What is significant is that "the boy was ministering to the Lord," not where or how. Samuel's ministering associates him with "priest," since this is a priestly function (Exod. 28:35, 39:1; Num. 1:50; Deut. 10:8, 21:5). It also marks him as a leader like Joshua, who is the "minister of Moses" (Exod. 24:13, 33:11; Josh. 1:1). Samuel ministers "in the presence of Eli the priest," who moves to the side and does not mediate the relation between Samuel and the Lord.

1 Sam. 2:11–36 begins to chart, in alternating sections, the rise of Samuel and the fall of the house of Eli. "The sons of Eli were worthless men; they did not know the Lord." "Worthless men" (*bene beliyya`al*) places the sons of Eli in the company of the men of Gibeah of Benjamin, who are "worthless men" (Judg. 19:22, 20:13), and dissociates them from Hannah and thereby from Samuel. Hannah is not a "base woman" (*bath beliyya`al,* 1 Sam. 1:16). Ignorance is characterized as not knowing and as disregarding the Lord and his word.

"The custom [*mishpat*] of the priests" is described in 1 Sam. 2:13–16. The details of the description parody previous statements about sacrifice. In particular, I note the legislation in Deut. 18:1–8, especially v. 3: "This will be *the custom* [*mishpat*] *of the priests* with the people who are sacrificing a sacrifice. . . ."

1 Sam. 2:12–17 ends, as it began, with an evaluative comment. "The sin of the young men was great *before the Lord* for the men treated the offering of the Lord with contempt." The young men contrast with Samuel, who is ministering *before the Lord.* The evaluative statements in vv. 12 and 17 clarify the status of Hophni and Phinehas; they are doing that which is evil in the eyes of the Lord. Matters in 1 Samuel have so far progressed according to the "proper order" to the extent that the good, Hannah and Elkanah, are rewarded; we can therefore expect that the wicked will perish in darkness.

"Samuel was ministering before the Lord, a boy girded with a linen ephod and a little robe his mother would make for him and take to him each year" (1 Sam. 2:18–19). Ephod and robe (*me`il*) are associated elsewhere with priestly garments (Exod. 25:7, 28:1–43, 39:1–29; Lev. 8:7). The ephod is linked with divination, since "the breastpiece of judgment" is attached to the ephod and "in the breastpiece of judgment you will put the Urim and the Thummim" (Exod. 28:30). Samuel's link with priesthood is strengthened and a divinatory function is intimated, but there are serious qualifications.

The linen ephod is apparently part of his official garb at Shiloh; the little robe is an annual gift from his mother and not necessarily any type of cultic attire. Additionally, "robe" (*me`il*) does not appear elsewhere in 1 Samuel in an exclusively ritual setting. In Judges, the ephod is a cultic object, but it is associated with apostasy, not proper worship. The people give Gideon all the gold earrings taken from the Midianites, "and Gideon made an ephod of it and put it in his city, in Ophrah; all Israel played the harlot after it there" (Judg. 8:27). Five times Micah's images are spoken of as an ephod—Judg. 17:5 and Judg. 18:14, 17, 18, 20. Elsewhere in 1 Samuel, e.g., 1 Sam. 23:6–12, the ephod connotes priestly and divinatory functions; through the ephod, the word of the Lord is given thematic prominence.

> The boy Samuel grew in the presence of the Lord. Eli was very old.
> He heard all that his sons were doing to all Israel and how they lay
> with the women who served at the entrance of the tent of meeting.

The antithesis between Samuel and the house of Eli is stressed. There is no mention of the "presence of the Lord" in regard to Eli and his sons, who are priests of the Lord. In this instance Eli hears and hears correctly; he does not need to see anything.

> I hear [*shome`a*] of your evil doings [*debarim*] . . . it is no good report
> [*shemu`ah*] I hear [*shome`a*] the people of the Lord spreading abroad.

Eli hears, but Hophni and Phinehas "would not listen [*lo'yishme`u*] to the voice of their father." "To hear" expands to "to listen to" and "to obey"; in Hebrew, all are the same word—*shama`*. (Dis)obedience is introduced.

Hophni and Phinehas do not listen to their father, "because it delighted the Lord to kill them" (1 Sam. 2:25). The wicked are indeed to perish in darkness. The Lord has brought life through Hannah, and now he will kill through the house of Eli. Eli's voice can be merged with those of Samuel and the Lord: "Has the Lord as great delight in burnt offerings and sacrifices as in *obeying the voice* of the Lord?" (1 Sam. 15:22). The texts, in chapters 2 and 15, present a striking configuration of sacrifice, obedience/hearing, disobedience/sin, life, and death. The themes are dispersed through the text, and tracing them is part of the task facing the present reading of 1 Samuel.

Eli concludes his rebuke of his sons,

> If a man sins against a man God will mediate [*pillo*] for him, but if a
> man sins against the Lord, who can intercede [*yithpallel*] for him?

What can Eli understand this to mean? And beyond that, what can it signify for us the readers? What are we to make of such a weighty theological pronouncement? First, is this a rhetorical or a literal question? Is Eli sincerely asking who can intercede for the man who has sinned against the Lord, or is he emphatically denying the possibility of such intercession? I leave aside the problematic issue of what a "sin against the Lord" is. In the first case, several answers suggest themselves, e.g., the priest through sacrifice and offering or the prophet, as Samuel, through prayer and intercession (1 Sam. 7:5–11). That a priest could intercede in such a situation is implied by the Lord himself, "Therefore I swear to the house of Eli that the iniquity of Eli's sons *will never be expiated by sacrifice and offering*" (1 Sam. 3:14). With this interpretation, Eli is offering his sons an opportunity for repentance and atonement, which accords with the Lord's subsequent charge that Eli did not restrain his sons in an emphatic way (1 Sam. 3:13).

On the other hand, if Eli is denying the possibility of intercession, he is thereby accusing his sons of a sin for which they must inevitably be punished. This is a harsh denunciation and requires us to read the Lord's later charge as perhaps meaning that Eli did not restrain his sons with force. The issue is further complicated by the third possibility—that this is a mild rebuke, if it can be called a rebuke at all, and that Eli's "question" is a platitude that fails, since the sons pay no attention to their father. The rest of the OT does not witness such a sharp distinction between sins against humans and sins against the Lord, particularly if the distinction means that the latter cannot be atoned for in ways similar to the former.

However, Eli's question does relate the important themes of sin and intercession with the latter regarded, or denied, as a means of expiation for sin. Hannah's intercession (*tithpallel*, 1 Sam. 1:10, 12) succeeds, but it is related to distress, not sin.

"The boy Samuel continued to grow both in stature and favor with the Lord and with men." "With the Lord and with men"—have Hophni and Phinehas sinned against both the Lord and men? Samuel is an enigma at this point. What is he to be and to do? Why him? Hannah's fortunes stem from her piety, Hophni's and Phinehas's from their sin. But there is no balancing "cause" for Samuel's growth in favor. Even when retributive justice seems to be working, there are limits to its applicability and predictability. "The Lord kills and brings to life" does not have to correlate with his treatment of the faithful and wicked. We are in the realm of what theologically is called mercy or grace; the Lord can act without a "just" cause.

Judgment

The alternating descriptions of Samuel's rise and the house of Eli's decline lengthen into the speech of the man of God against the house of Eli (1 Sam. 2:27–36) and the call of Samuel (1 Sam. 3:1–4:1a). The speech of the man of God is complex, and in a partial reading I dwell on those parts that are germane to my reading of 1 Samuel.

The speech is a quote of another speech: "Thus says the Lord. . . ." First is a pronouncment of the Lord's past benefactions for the house of Eli:

> Did I plainly reveal myself to the house of your father when they were in Egypt subject to the house of Pharaoh? And I chose him from all the tribes of Israel to be my priest, to go up on my altar, to burn incense, to wear an ephod before me; I gave to the house of your father all my offerings by fire from the people of Israel.

The statement brings together themes of revelation, choice, and priesthood and sacrifice.

The accusation, in v. 29, is addressed mainly to Eli but concerns both Eli and his sons. It is followed by the formula, "Therefore the Lord the God of Israel declares. . . ," which should introduce an announcement of judgment, but the latter is followed by another review of the past: "I promised that your house and the house of your father would go in and out before me forever." There is a theme of perpetuity, "forever" (`ad `olam; cf. 1 Sam. 1:11, 22). "*But now [we`atah]* the Lord declares. . . ." A divine promise for perpetuity is to be taken back, denied, because of sin. Retributive justice takes priority and cancels a divine election and promise; justice prevails over grace.

"But now the Lord declares: 'Far be it from me! Those who honor me I will honor, and those who despise me will be lightly esteemed.' " This is another theological principle which is confirmed in the preceding verse and in the Song of Hannah but which is contravened in the book of Judges. It may be another platitude that has occasional, but not predictable, relevance. For future reference, I note the Hebrew roots *kabed,* to honor and be heavy, and *qalal,* to be light and treat lightly.

The pronouncement of the specific judgment to befall Eli's house in vv. 31–36 includes the promise of a future replacement, a faithful priest, in v. 35. The judgment is not annihilation but the curse "that there will not be an old man in your house" and the reduction to beggars of Eli's descendants. The speech, including the promise in v. 35, provides a masterful example of the displacement and dissemination of an OT text. The judgment does befall Eli's house but with modifications. Eli and his sons die at the time of the battle of Ebenezer. On the same day, Ichabod is born to Phinehas's wife and immediately disappears from the narrative. Eli's line is carried on by Ichabod's nephew, "Ahijah the son of Ahitub, Ichabod's brother, son of Phinehas, son of Eli, the priest of the Lord in Shiloh" (1 Sam. 14:3);

the detail leaves no doubt as to the identification. Ahijah is with Saul in Gibeah, but, like his uncle, he disappears from the text after 1 Samuel 14. The effect of the judgment on Ichabod, Ahijah, and their families is not stated, but we can assume that their insignificance for the continuing story is a sign that the judgment has befallen them; the judgment perhaps has expanded to the complete disappearance of the family.

Another branch of the line of the house of Eli may be represented by Ahimelech, the son of Ahitub, who is at Nob; he and his family are almost annihilated by Saul and Doeg (1 Sam. 21:2–8, 22:6–19). Abiathar, son of Ahimelech, son of Ahitub, flees to David for asylum (1 Sam. 22:20) and becomes one of his main priests. If this is the same Ahitub who is the father of Ahijah in 1 Sam. 14:3, then this is the line of the house of Eli. On the other hand, it may be another Ahitub, and then there is no line of the house of Eli at Nob. Or, third, he may not be the same as the father of Ahijah, but Ahitub, father of Ahimelech, could still be a descendant of Eli. The question of this Ahitub's identity is raised by the lack of the genealogical specificity granted in 1 Sam. 14:3.

A later text apparently confirms that the priests at Nob are representatives of Eli's house. Solomon banishes Abiathar to Anathoth because of his support for Adonijah in the succession conflict. "Solomon expelled Abiathar from being priest to the Lord, thus fulfilling the word of the Lord he had spoken against the house of Eli in Shiloh" (1 Kings 2:27). The family is not annihilated, only removed from power, and we can imagine Abiathar and his descendants begging for their sustenance. The word of the Lord against Eli is not mentioned again after 1 Kings 2.

However, if Abiathar is a member of the line of the house of Eli through Ahitub, what of "Zadok son of Ahitub," who is David's other priest with Abiathar (2 Sam. 8:17)? This is a lure in the same vein as the possibility that the house of Eli is the house of Aaron. Abiathar is banished, but Zadok remains as Solomon's priest. Yet Zadok disappears from the narrative in 1 Kings. Indeed, priestly houses disappear. There are priests in Kings, but no houses, of Eli or otherwise, which supports the supposition that Eli's house is the house of Aaron. The disintegration of Eli's house means the end of the one legitimate priestly line or house. But, as with the fate of Shiloh, a definitive resolution is blocked, because the narrative simply drops the matter.

Fulfillment/Dissemination
The judgment upon the house of Eli is not "fulfilled" if we understand the term to mean a neat, literal, point-by-point effectuation, i.e.,

"literal" in the accepted sense of conforming to or upholding the explicit or primary meaning of the words of a text. (*American Heritage Dictionary*). To put the question of fulfillment or nonfulfillment in these terms is not in accord with the text. Judgments, prophecies, etc., are not fulfilled in an exact, proportional manner, i.e., literally. Yet they are fulfilled "literally," taking "literal" as meaning "letters," "words," and "written." The very words of the speech are significant, even when their supposed "explicit and primary" meaning is not. The terminology and phraseology of the speech set much in motion; the terms of the speech are disseminated into the text to attach themselves, in various ways, to others beyond the house of Eli.

For example, "The days are coming when I will cut off your seed and the seed of your father's house so that there will not be an old man in your house" applies to Eli's house, and it also applies to the house of Saul. Violent, and generally early, death is the fate of Saul and his sons at Mt. Gilboa, of Ishbaal, of other children and grandchildren of Saul (2 Sam. 21:1–9), and of Shimei, "a man of the family of the house of Saul" (2 Sam. 16:5). Mephibosheth is spared, but he is dependent on David for his livelihood, a reflex of 1 Sam. 2:36, the curse of being beggars.

Even David's descendants are contaminated by the judgment speech, since many of his sons die young. Although David, Solomon, and other Davidic kings live to old age, the other aspect of the judgment, being beggars, echoes in the closing verses of 2 Kings:

> Evil-merodach king of Babylon . . . freed Jehoiachin king of Judah from prison; he spoke to him kindly and gave him a seat above the seats of the kings who were with him in Babylon. Jehoiachin changed his prison garments. He ate food regularly at the king's table for the rest of his life; his allowance, a regular allowance, was given him by the king, every day a portion for the rest of his life. (2 Kings 25:27–30)

David's house, like Saul's, ends up eating at another king's table.
What of the promise?

> I will raise up for myself a faithful (*ne'eman*) priest who will do according to what is in my heart and in my mind; I will build him a sure (*ne'eman*) house; he will go in and out before my anointed forever.

There is play on the verb *'amen*, which means to be sure, faithful, established, and to believe, trust. There is no later comment on the fulfillment of the promise analogous to the note on the end of the house of Eli in 1 Kings 2:27. In 1 Sam. 3:11–14, the Lord speaks to

Samuel only of what he has said against Eli's house, not about any replacement. The narrative in Samuel and Kings speaks of no "faithful priest" who has a "sure house" and who goes "in and out before my anointed forever."

However, Samuel is recognized by all Israel as "established (*ne'eman*) as a prophet of the Lord" (1 Sam. 3:20), and he can be said to "do according to what is in my heart and in my mind." Yet Samuel does not have a "sure house," and he certainly does not "go in and out" before either Saul or David.

Although Saul is not an established or faithful king with a sure house, David is spoken of as a "faithful (*ne'eman*) servant" of Saul (1 Sam. 22:14). Surprisingly, Abigail knows that "the Lord will certainly make my lord a sure (*ne'eman*) house" (1 Sam. 25:28); the assertion is confirmed by the Lord. "Your house and your kingdom will be made sure (*ne'eman*) forever before me; your throne will be established (*nakon*) forever" (2 Sam. 7:16). The motif of perpetuity recurs. The Philistine Achish trusts (*ya'amen*) David and considers him a "perpetual servant" (`*ebed* `*olam*, 1 Sam. 27:12). David is the Lord's anointed, although for a brief period he can be said to go in and out before Saul (1 Sam. 18:5–16). Most problematic and a central concern of the reading is whether David does or does not act according to what is in the Lord's heart and mind.

The judgment speech against Eli's house is significant not because it points ahead to its own systematic realization but because it marks its own dispersion into the narrative. The mark of an authentic "prophetic" speech is its literal effectuation—"literal" in the sense that the very words, phrases, and themes of the speech are loosed into the narrative to appear, then disappear, reappear, then disappear again. The "other direction," e.g., the effective and accurate historical survey or the notice of a fulfillment, will be discussed in relation to 1 Sam. 12:6–15; 1 Kings 2:27 will be noted in the discussion.

To summarize, the judgment speech again reminds us of the lack of an overview for 1 Samuel, yet by now we can detect a type of overview in chapters 1 and 2. Many issues and themes have been brought into play. I have isolated some of them. There is an interest in "words," especially speeches. A specific role is given to the word of the Lord. I use the phrase "the word of the Lord" in an expanded sense to include actual quotes from the Lord and the search for the who, the how, and the why. To have "the word of the Lord" is to have an explanation and understanding of what is happening. A corollary of the interest in the word of the Lord is the theme of inquiry, asking, and seeking.

In the concern for "words," at one stage I treat them as material entities on the page with little or no regard for their primary and explicit meanings. There is wordplay, dissemination, dispersal of the words. The text is not to be reduced finally to a set of meanings. However, I do not remain always at that stage of reading but also talk of themes and meanings. The text is not to be reduced finally to just the words on the page. The two approaches, "words" and "meanings," undermine each other and prevent each other from producing the true reading or interpretation of the text.

Finally, I focus on the issue of retributive justice, which ties together a disparate group of themes—(dis)obedience, hearing, sin, evil in the eyes of the Lord, intercession, ritual, etc. The latter themes are not clearly distinguished from one another. The relationships between them are various. For example, if sin should inevitably lead to punishment, what of the role of intercession, whether prayer or sacrifice? If intercession, in whatever form, works as expiation for sin, then the issue of justice is complicated, since the intercession is rewarded but the sin is not punished. In other words, do prayer and intercession fit in a system of mercy or in a system of justice? I will return to the question at a relevant point.

1 Samuel 3

The Call of Samuel

"The word of the Lord was rare in those days; no vision broke through." The second situation will not be remedied, since visions will not become frequent. But the word of the Lord will no longer be rare after the call of Samuel.

> Samuel grew, and the Lord was with him and let none of his words fall to the ground. All Israel from Dan to Beersheba knew that Samuel was established as a prophet of the Lord. The Lord continued to appear at Shiloh for the Lord revealed himself to Samuel at Shiloh by the word of the Lord, and the word of Samuel came to all Israel. (1 Sam. 3:19–4:1a)

The Lord reveals himself, i.e., "makes himself appear or be seen"; the emphasis, however, is on the word(s), not on a visionary experience.

"The word" is underscored by Eli's blindness ("he could not see") and by the narrative of the Lord's call. The Lord calls (*qara'*); "he came and stood and called as before." He does not appear in a dream even though the call occurs at night. Eli, dependent only on sight, mistook Hannah for a drunken woman. Here, even though blind, Eli can comprehend that it is the Lord who is calling the boy. Samuel does not, because he "did not yet know the Lord, and the word of the Lord had not yet been revealed to him." Ignorance, however, does not prevail in this instance.

The Lord's pronouncement gives prominence to words, speech, and hearing.

> I am about to do a thing (*dabar*) in Israel at which the *two ears* of everyone that *hears* it will tingle. On that day I will establish against Eli all that I have *spoken* against his house from beginning to end. I *tell* him that I am about to punish his house forever because of the iniquity which he knew, because his sons were blaspheming, and he did not restrain them. Therefore, I *swear* to the house of Eli that the iniquity of Eli's house will never be expiated by sacrifice or offering. (1 Sam. 3:11–14)

It is noteworthy that the Lord tells this to Samuel but does not instruct him to report it to Eli. Samuel has a message but no commission.

1 Sam. 3:19–4:1a, quoted above, give Samuel a prominent position in Israel. Yet the generality of the statement raises questions about Samuel's precise status and authority, since we are informed only about "his words" and "the word of the Lord." We are not informed what the content of the words is; we do not know what they are about or how far-reaching, in time and space, they are. Do the words concern great issues like the condemnation of a priestly house, the defeat of Israel, or the establishment of a king? Do they concern more mundane issues like the location of lost asses? The statement does not provide enough information to answer the question.

·2·

1 SAMUEL 4-7

The Ark's Last Hurrah

1 Sam. 4:1b–7:2 is generally called the Ark Narrative and treated as a separate and independent work embedded in 1 Samuel. I deal with it as an integral part of the context. Samuel's exalted position in 1 Sam. 3:19–4:1a is qualified by the narrative, since Samuel is absent from it, even though the word of the Lord is a major issue. Both the Israelites and the Philistines are concerned with why, who, and how; the Israelites send to Shiloh for the ark but not for Samuel. The qualifying of Samuel's position and authority extends to the availability of the word of the Lord. It may be that it is no longer rare, but that does not mean that it is always available or that there is a word of the Lord for every situation. One of the main interests of the following reading is "the word of the Lord" and its relation to inquiry, to seeking certitude on the who, the why, the how.

Even though most of the narrative is composed of questions and answers, certitude is not achieved; definitive resolutions are not arrived at. The text is rife with unanswered, and unanswerable, questions. Samuel's absence is significant, since he is the one, in chapters 3 and 7, who brings the word of the Lord to Israel.

Ebenezer

Chapter 4, the battle of Ebenezer and its aftermath, is narrated matter-of-factly with little comment. Israel is defeated.

> When the army came to the camp, the elders of Israel said, "Why has the Lord put us to rout today before the Philistines? Let us bring the ark of the covenant of the Lord here from Shiloh so that he/it may come into our midst and save us from the power of our enemies." (1 Sam. 4:3)

26

The elders speak, not Samuel or the priests of Shiloh, even though the ark is brought from Shiloh. "Why has the Lord put us to rout?" They apparently want a word from the Lord but do not act accordingly. They do not consult Samuel or the priests, and they bring "the ark of the covenant of the Lord of hosts, who is enthroned on the cherubim" (1 Sam. 4:4). The title highlights the revelatory function, yet the elders want the ark as a guarantee of victory—that he/it may come into their midst and save them—and not as an oracular implement.

The elders repeat a previous pattern, e.g., in Judg. 18:5–6 and 21:1–7; a question is asked and an answer provided without formal inquiry of the Lord, if there is any inquiry of the Lord. The question itself is put into question. Are the elders asking a sincere question of the Lord, truly seeking his word—a why—or are they making a statement, presuming they already know the word of the Lord—because the ark was not with them—or perhaps not even caring to know it?

"Why has the Lord put us to rout today before the Philistines?" This is a pregnant question for the reader regardless of the elders' intention. It assumes that the Lord has, in fact, put Israel to rout, but the assumption is not confirmed in the text. The construction is passive in vv. 2 and 10: "Israel was put to rout before the Philistines." Even if we accept the elders' assumption, we are still left with their question—why? They propose an answer, the absence of the ark; we are presented with no other explanation of why the Lord defeated Israel, if he did.

The ark is brought from Shiloh, "and the two sons of Eli, Hophni and Phinehas, were with the ark of the covenant of God." They are not referred to as "priests of the Lord," as in 1 Sam. 1:3; it is the ark of the covenant "of God," not "of the Lord." The Israelite army responds to the ark's arrival with "a mighty shout and the earth resounded"; the response continues the Judges pattern, since it reflects the certitude of Micah in a "cultic solution." "Now I know that the Lord will do well by me because I have a Levite as priest" (Judg. 17:13). As a counterpoint, the Philistines respond with fear and a question of their own. "Woe to us! Who can deliver us from the hand of these mighty gods? These are the gods who smote the Egyptians with every sort of plague in the wilderness." The Israelites speak of the ark of the covenant of the Lord, but it is the Philistines who speak of the mighty acts of the Lord that found the covenant. They demonstrate an awe, not so much of the ark, but of the "gods" that it represents; the Israelites manifest no such awe or respect.

The Philistines have an answer to their question, "Strengthen yourselves and act like men, O Philistines!"

> The Philistines fought, and Israel was put to rout and they fled,
> every man to his tent; there was a very great slaughter for there fell
> of Israel thirty thousand foot soldiers." (1 Sam. 4:10)

The pattern of Judges is and is not completed, depending on one's
viewpoint. Israel's "solution" does not work; the Philistines' does. The
ark has not produced the expected deliverance; courageous fighting
has. One explanation for the turn of events is that preparation for a
battle is more effective than reliance on a magical implement. Even
though both the Israelites and the Philistines refer to the activity of
God, there is no hint from the narrative that God plays any role in the
defeat of Israel and the victory of the Philistines. Yet this does not
definitively deny God a part in the battle of Ebenezer.

The inversion, marked by the shift to the Philistine point of view, is
striking. Israel plays the role of the loser, the defeated, played in
Judges 17–21 by Micah, Laish, Jabesh-gilead, and Shiloh. 1 Sam.
4:1—10 presents a balanced account of the battle; we see both sides
and can sympathize with both the victors and the vanquished. The
analogy requires a rereading of Judges to which I only point here.
More consideration would have to be given to the vanquished, since,
from their vantage point, the outcome is not so clear even if unexpected. Destruction (punishment?) has befallen them in a time of
continued evil, yet in Judges, they, particularly Laish and Jabesh-
gilead, seem innocent and undeserving of the devastation visited
upon them.

The House of Eli
1 Samuel 4 closes with the effect of the battle on the vanquished.
"The ark of God was captured, and the two sons of Eli, Hophni and
Phinehas, *died*." The matter-of-factness of the report is striking given
the evaluation of Hophni and Phinehas in 1 Sam. 2:12–17, the assertion that "it delighted the Lord to *kill* them" (1 Sam. 2:25), and the
prediction that "this which will befall your two sons, Hophni and
Phinehas, will be the sign to you: both of them will *die* on the same
day" (1 Sam. 2:34). The Hebrew root *muth* is employed in all three
texts. The delight of the Lord has been realized and the sign fulfilled.
Judgment is befalling the house of Eli, and its effects spread to all
Israel and even to the ark of God. Again it is the ark of God, not of
the Lord, that is associated with the two men. However, the narrative
is not explicitly claiming that the defeat of Israel and the capture of
the ark are signs of judgment, that they are the delight of the Lord.

News of the defeat, the death of his sons, and the capture of the ark
is brought to Eli in Shiloh. At the mention of the ark, "Eli fell over

backward from his seat by the side of the gate; his neck was broken and he died for he was an old man and heavy." Hearing can have a deadly effect. Eli's death is ascribed to his old age and weight; it is a chance occurrence. Or does the note on his age indicate fulfillment of the curse "that there will not be an old man in your house"? "Heavy" (*kabed*) would then be a play upon his "honoring" (*kibbed*) his sons above the Lord (1 Sam. 2:29).

Not everyone in the house of Eli dies. Eli's death is framed by stories about his children—two sons and a daughter-in-law die, but a grandson, Ichabod, is born. Ichabod brings ambiguity with him, or, better, he adds to the ambiguity attached to the messenger from the battle lines, who is a man of Benjamin. Benjamin's birth is akin to Ichabod's, since his mother Rachel dies giving him birth (Gen. 35:16–20). In Benjamin's case, there is an equivocation on his name and an attempted clarification. "As her life was departing (for she died), she called his name Ben-oni; but his father called his name Benjamin" (Gen. 35:18). Ben-oni may mean "son of misfortune" or "son of vigor."

A similar uncertainty pervades the end of 1 Samuel 4. The *RSV* reads: "And about the time of her death the women attending her said to her, 'Fear not for you have borne a son.' But she did not answer or give heed" (1 Sam. 4:20). This is generally taken to mean that she was crushed by misfortune and grief. In a footnote, McCarter offers another translation, "And she was downcast and paid no heed (to her affliction)." The interpretation "assumes that the words of comfort have had some effect or, more probably, that the woman is bearing her misfortune stoically. Faced with the loss of the ark she can have no thought of herself." He acknowledges the undecidability of the text: "There is no compelling reason to choose between these alternatives" (McCarter 1980b, p. 115), i.e., misfortune or strength.

Jacob attempts to resolve the ambiguity of Ben-oni by changing the name to Benjamin, "son of the right (side, hand, or the like)" (Speiser 1964, p. 274), which is a positive name referring to the child's good fortune or his support for his father. Nevertheless, Rachel's name, Ben-oni, remains in the text to disturb Jacob's attempt. The unsettling manifests itself in Judges 19–21, where the tribe of Benjamin is both vigorous and cursed.

There is a reflex of Jacob's naming in 1 Samuel 4 when Ichabod's mother attempts to clarify the narrator or perhaps herself. "She named the child Ichabod, 'Glory has departed from Israel!' because the ark of God had been captured and because of her father-in-law and her husband." The latter explanation could be the narrator's comment or the woman's motive expressed indirectly. The mother repeats the etymology and limits the explanation to one event. "She said, 'Glory has departed from Israel because the ark of God has been captured.' "

Judgment has come to pass for Eli's house. Has it also fallen upon Israel, Shiloh, and the ark? Has the Lord put Israel to rout, and, if so, why? Has he delivered the Philistines? Or have the Philistines delivered themselves with valiant fighting? Whose perspective should we take? "Glory has departed from Israel." Does this intend just the capture of the ark (v. 22), or is something more inclusive meant (v. 21)? Is 1 Samuel 4 a tale of death and misfortune or of life and vigor? Or is it of both at the same time? Has anyone delivered the Philistines "from the power of these mighty gods"? To put it more simply, does the Lord have anything to do with Ebenezer and its aftermath?

The Ark in Philistia (1 Sam. 5:1–7:1)
The text operates with the limitations of v. 22, since the next two chapters narrate the fate of the ark and do not mention Eli or Ichabod. Nothing is said of Shiloh; indeed, more interest is shown in the house of Dagon in Ashdod, where the tale of the ark among the Philistines opens. First let us turn to the only other mention of Dagon in Genesis-Kings. (The only other reference to Dagon is in 1 Chron. 10:10.)

> The Philistine lords gathered to offer a great sacrifice to Dagon their god and to rejoice. They said, "*Our god* has given Samson *our enemy* into *our hand*." When the people saw him, they praised *their god;* they said, "*Our god* has given *our enemy* into *our hand*, the ravager of *our country*, who has slain many of *us*." (Judg. 16:23–24)

This is not the work of Dagon; their certainty, their concern with "us" and "our" is mistaken. It is a symptom of their ignorance (Polzin 1980, p. 194). Samson ravages them again and kills more when he brings the house down "upon the lords and all the people that were in it" (Judg. 16:30).

In 1 Samuel, the Philistines are not so obtuse.

> When the men of Ashdod saw how things were, they said, "The ark of the God of Israel must not remain with us because his hand is heavy upon us and upon Dagon our god." (1 Sam. 5:7)

Exemplified in the detail of 1 Sam. 6:2–11, the Philistines demonstrate a "proper attitude" toward the ark and toward the Lord, the same attitude they had when they knew of the ark's presence in the Hebrew camp—an attitude Israel does not have.

The narrative in 1 Samuel 5–6 is marked by detail and clarity but also by an obscurity stemming from truncation of the story. Individual episodes are not finished; they merely stop and do not conclude. Dagon falls over in the presence of the ark at least twice. He is set back up the first time. The next morning, he is again lying on his face before the ark, "and the head of Dagon and both his hands were lying cut off upon the threshold." (This presages the frequent "cutting off's," particularly beheadings, that occur in Samuel.) However, the narrative of the second morning stops, and the narrator comments, "This is why the priests of Dagon and all who enter the house of Dagon do not tread on the threshold of Dagon in Ashdod to this day." "To this day"—unlike Shiloh, we are immediately informed of the future of the house of Dagon, even though we are told no more of Dagon himself. The house continues to exist, and thus the succeeding story is not about a final conquest and destruction of Ashdod or of the Philistines. Finally, we have a knowledgeable narrator who knows of specific practices among the Philistines.

The next episode, the movement of the ark from Ashdod to Gath and then to Ekron, begins with a statement of the "who": "The hand of the Lord was heavy upon the people of Ashdod, and he terrified them and afflicted them with tumors." (The play upon *kabed,* to honor and to be heavy, continues.) The ark may be a magical instrument, an automatic guarantee of salvation or of judgment, as the Israelites thought at the time of the battle of Ebenezer. The Ashdodites associate the ark and the hand of God—"The ark of the God of Israel must not remain with us because his hand is heavy upon us"—but the narrator does not. We know who is afflicting the Philistines but not why. The presence of the ark *may be* the reason, but it certainly does not operate as the automatically effective implement of the previous story.

The Philistines ask and answer a question. " 'What should we do with the ark of the God of Israel?' They answered, 'Let the ark of the God of Israel be brought around to Gath.' " But the solution does not work, since Gath is afflicted like Ashdod. The Philistines in Ekron, not afflicted by ignorance, want the ark sent back "to its own place" (1 Sam. 5:11); they propose a definitive answer to the question of what to do with the ark. Before the how of returning the ark is addressed, there is another narrational comment.

> For there was a deathly panic throughout the whole city. The hand of God was heavy there; the men who did not die were stricken with tumors, and the cry of the city went up to heaven. (1 Sam. 5:11–12)

Two texts echo in the background. The cry of Sodom and Gomorrah has come to the Lord, and it ushers in their total destruction (Gen.

18:20–21). Second, God hears the cry of his people in Egypt (Exod. 2:23–24), and he brings them out of Egypt into Canaan. The latter holds for the Philistines in 1 Samuel 5–6. They and their cities are not destroyed; the ark goes up from them "into Canaan." But does this mean that the Philistines are "saved"? "The cry of the city went up to heaven" may be saying that the cry went to God and he responded to it, or it may mean that the cry was loud because of the deathly panic in the city. The text provides no answer, only the enigmatic comment: "The ark of the Lord was in the country of the Philistines seven months" (1 Sam. 6:1). The comment refuses to resolve the tale; as 1 Sam. 5:5 does, it truncates the story; we hear no more of Dagon or of the "cry of the city."

The people turn to "the priests and the diviners" and repeat their concern for the ark and their decision to return it "to its own place." "What should we do with the ark of the Lord? Tell us with what we should send it to its place" (1 Sam. 6:2). They now know that it is "the ark of the Lord," not just of "the God of Israel." The priests and diviners tell them that the ark is to be returned with an appropriate guilt offering; "then you will be healed, and it will be known to you why his hand does not turn away from you." A familiar pattern—a cultic solution that will have clear results, healing and knowledge. This is the proposal and conviction of the priests and diviners. However, the knowledge concerns why the Lord's hand has not turned away, not why his hand was heavy in the first place. The narrative does not provide an explanation, explicit or implicit, for why his hand does not turn away or why it afflicted them.

Israelites speak of the departure of glory (*kabod*); Philistine priests and diviners speak of giving "glory to the God of Israel" (1 Sam. 6:5). The play on *kabed* is continued and augmented by *qalal*, to lighten and treat lightly (see page 20). If they give glory,

> perhaps he will lighten (*qalal*) his hand from off you and your gods and your land. Why should you harden (*kibbed*) your hearts as the Egyptians and Pharaoh hardened (*kibbed*) their hearts? After he had made sport of them, did they not let the people go, and they departed?

The Philistines again draw a lesson from the events of the Exodus, the necessity of respecting the Lord and his power; it is a lesson that Israel is reluctant or unable to draw. Moreover, as the plagues in Egypt are spoken of as "sport" (*hith`allel*, Exod. 10:2; 1 Sam. 6:6), as the display of the Lord's power and might, so can the ravaging of the Philistines show the heaviness of the Lord's hand.

The Ark Returns

The departure of the ark is a model of a narrative that is detailed yet obscure at many points in its meaning. After the priests and diviners give details on the cart that is to carry the ark and the guilt offering, they propose a test, a sign.

> And watch! If it goes up on the road to its own land, to Beth-shem-esh, then it is he who has done us this great harm; but if not, then we will know that it is not his hand that struck us, it happened to us by chance. (1 Sam. 6:9)

They will definitely know the who, but they mention no why. However, this knowledge is superfluous, since they have already expressed their conviction that "it is he who has done us this great harm." What has become of their original offer of knowing "why his hand does not turn away"? The narrative continues with precision as though a final answer, a definitive word of the Lord, were to be provided.

> The men did so. They took two milch cows and yoked them to the cart and shut up their calves at home. They put the ark of the Lord on the cart and the box and the golden mice and the images of their tumors. The cows went straight to Beth-shemesh along one high-way, lowing as they went; they turned neither to the right nor to the left, and the lords of the Philistines went after them as far as the border of Beth-shemesh. (1 Sam. 6:10–12)

Their earlier conviction is confirmed.

The return of the ark and its reception by the Israelites are told with similar detail; there is emphasis on the joy and the sacrificial rites. There is one final comment on the Philistines who had come to the border of Beth-shemesh. "The five lords of the Philistines saw it, and they returned that day to Ekron" (1 Sam. 6:16). Instead of a scene in Ekron and confirmation of the healing and the knowledge gained, we are given in vv. 16–18 a section akin to 1 Sam. 5:5 and 6:1 in its refusal of resolution, in its truncation of the text.

We hear no more of the affliction of the Philistines, particularly whether or not it was lifted because of the return of the ark or why it befell them in the first place. This may be expecting too much, since the Philistines had apparently given up the desire to ascertain the why and had returned to confirmation of the who. In lieu of any information on the why or the who, we are presented a list of what the golden tumors and mice stood for and are informed that the great stone upon which they set the ark is still there "to this day in the field of Joshua of Beth-shemesh." This is a very knowledgeable narrator, who does not truncate his story because of lack of knowledge. The obscurity of the text is deliberate. "Deliberate"—we should question it further and not write it off as Hebrew style or simply assume that there is a clarity, an answer, here.

Summary

The Philistine encounter with the ark and the hand of the Lord ends with knowledge of the who but not the why. They and we know that "the hand of the Lord was heavy" upon them; at least they seem convinced of this. They and we look first to the ark for an explanation of the disaster. They may determine "why his hand does not turn away," but we do not, and we do not even know whether they discover it. However, to support the assumption that the affliction has something to do with the ark, we can note the disastrous consequences for Israel when her people look into the ark of the Lord—50,070 men die (1 Sam. 6:19). (I do not emend the text.) Ritual infractions can entail deadly effects. On the other hand, the slaughter of the Israelites makes it improbable that the Philistines have been afflicted, because they are foreigners, the uncircumcised. The narrative leaves open the question of why the Philistines were afflicted.

The obscurity, the openness, is deliberate. Search for the word of the Lord—the who, the why, the how—is an explicit theme in the Ark Narrative in the form of questions and assertions. But the absence of the word of the Lord, of sure answers, is also an explicit theme. Presence and absence support and undermine each other.

In contrast to the Philistines, the Israelites have no certain knowledge about the defeat at Ebenezer. They do not know who or why. They may have been struck by the hand of the Lord; they may have been defeated by a valiant Philistine army; it may have happened to them by chance. The pattern of Judges does not prevail in the Ark Narrative, since proffered "solutions" do not work; the "clarity" of Judges is also gone. In Judges, Israel did what was evil in the eyes of the Lord, even though she survived and at times prospered. Why the Israelites survive may be undecidable, but their sin is manifest. Not so in 1 Samuel. What have the people done that can be considered good or evil in the Lord's sight, that can be grounds for regarding their defeat as expected or as a surprise? The house of Eli has sinned and stands under condemnation, but why should this affect all Israel?

The Ark Narrative closes, as it opened, with questions and answers.

> The men of Beth-shemesh said, "Who is able to stand before the Lord, this holy God? To whom can he/it go up away from us?" They sent messengers to the inhabitants of Kiriath-jearim, "The

Philistines have returned the ark of the Lord. Come down and take
it up to you." (1 Sam. 6:20–21)

The status of the first question is open. It can either be an assertion
that no one is able to stand before the Lord or a sincere question
about who, in fact, is able to stand before the Lord. The men answer
immediately. The ark goes to Kiriath-jearim. Once there, Abinadab
consecrates his son to watch over the ark, not to be a priest, as Micah
once consecrated his son.

Digression: The Land and the Nations
The discussion of "land and nations" is not exhaustive; it requires a
separate study, including extensive material beyond 1 Samuel. Kiriath-jearim is one of the four cities ascribed to the Gibeonites (Josh.
9:17). They are Hivites or Amorites (Josh. 9:7; 2 Sam. 21:2) who trick
Joshua and Israel into a covenant; they are not destroyed but instead
become part of the community. The mention of Kiriath-jearim raises
the topic of the peoples "in the land" and Israel's relationship(s) to
them.

In geographical descriptions of the promised land in the Penta-
teuch and in Joshua 1, the Philistines are implicitly included in the
land to be conquered. "I will set your bounds from the Red Sea *to the
sea of the Philistines* and from the wilderness to the Euphrates" (Exod.
23:31). However, they are never included by name in the lists of the
peoples who are to be dispossessed, e.g., Gen. 15:19–21; Exod. 23:23,
33:2; Num. 13:29; Deut. 7:1, 20:17; Josh. 3:10, 9:1. The first time the
Philistines are "listed" is in Joshua 13 and again in Judges 3, where
they are among the groups and territories that are left and that are
not to be conquered. The Philistines are subdued, but not conquered
or destroyed, by Samuel and David (1 Sam. 7:13; 2 Sam. 8:1). Solomon's kingdom extends "from the Euphrates *to the land of the Philistines* and to the border of Egypt" (1 Kings 5:1); contrast with Exod.
23:31.

Thorough treatment of the issue of the peoples of the land would
require analysis of Genesis, where the people who are not dispossessed by Israel are introduced; almost all are blood relatives of the
patriarchs. It is no coincidence that Saul's first victory is over the
Ammonites, the sons of Lot; the Lord will not give Israel Ammonite
land (Deut. 2:16–23). The Philistines may be "grandchildren" of the
Egyptians (Gen. 10:13–14), and they stand in close association with
Israel because of their treatment of the patriarchs, Abraham and
Isaac, and their wives, Sarah and Rebekah. Both Abraham and Isaac
make a treaty with Abimelech of Gerar, king of the Philistines, not to

deal falsely with him, but to treat him honestly, as he treated them
(Gen. 21:22–34, 26:26–33). The treaty is not mentioned again in the
OT.

The theme of "the peoples of the land" in 1 Samuel at this point
emphasizes, in obverse fashion, its overall absence from the book.
Conquest of the rest of the land and continued possession, or loss of
the land, are not explicit concerns in 1 Samuel. There are neither
promises nor threats about the land and its inhabitants. Samuel and
the people speak of being delivered from the hand of the Philistines,
e.g., in 1 Sam. 7:3–8, but not of driving them out or dispossessing
them. Samuel threatens the people, "If you still do wickedly, you will
be swept away, both you and your king" (1 Sam. 12:25), but does not
mention loss of the land. The lack of concern for conquest of the land
is underscored in 1 Sam. 7:14: "The cities which the Philistines had
taken from Israel were restored to Israel, from Ekron to Gath; Israel
rescued their territory from the hand of the Philistines." Territory
changes hands, but there is no conquest of all Philistia. Indeed, "there
was peace between Israel and the Amorites," the opposite of conquest
and dispossession.

Another "classic sin" is absent from 1 Samuel:

> Samuel said to all the house of Israel, "If with all your heart you are
> returning to the Lord, then put away the foreign gods and the
> Ashtaroth from among you and direct your heart to the Lord and
> serve him only so that he will deliver you from the hand of the
> Philistines." Israel put away the Baals and the Ashtaroth, and they
> served the Lord only. (1 Sam. 7:3–4)

Worship of other gods will not be a problem again until the reign of
Solomon; Baal will not be worshipped again until the days of Ahab
and Jezebel.

1 Samuel 7

Repetition and Counterpoint

1 Samuel 7 is ambiguous, because the narrative is laconic and truncated; I read it as a parallel and counterpoint to the Ark Narrative.
"From the days that the ark lodged at Kiriath-jearim, a long time
passed, some twenty years, and all the house of Israel lamented (?)
after the Lord." A specific time period is noted, but its relation to the
subsequent verse—Samuel's demand to serve the Lord alone—is not
clear; the demand could be during or at the end of the twenty-year

period. Nor is it evident that Samuel's demand and Israel's response in v. 4 are a particular manifestation of their lamenting after the Lord.

Locale is not specified in vv. 3–4 or for Samuel's call for all Israel to gather at Mizpah. "Gather all Israel at Mizpah, and I will pray (*'ethpallel*) to the Lord for you." No reason is given for prayer or intercession, and there is no specification in the Israelites' confession, "We have sinned against the Lord." The absence of an account of how they have sinned is underlined by the parallel confessions in Judg. 10:10 and 1 Sam. 12:10. In the latter ("We have sinned because we have forsaken the Lord and have served the Baals and the Ashtaroth"), Samuel is apparently alluding to the Judges passage—"The people of Israel cried to the Lord, 'We have sinned against you because we have forsaken our God and served the Baals.'"

In 1 Samuel 7, the action which precedes Israel's confession is a clear example of unclarity due to the brevity of the description. "They gathered at Mizpah. They drew water and poured it out before the Lord. They fasted on that day and said there, 'We have sinned against the Lord.'" Is this a standard ritual or a one-time event? "Samuel judged the people of Israel at Mizpah." What does "to judge" mean in this instance? I discuss possibilities for the term in the analysis of 1 Sam. 7:15–8:3.

1 Sam. 7:7–11 "repeats" the battle at Ebenezer. As in 1 Samuel 4, the Philistines hear, but now it is the Israelites who hear and fear (cf. 1 Sam. 4:7 and 7:7). Their demand to Samuel is analogous to their previous expectation of the ark. "The people of Israel said to Samuel, 'Do not cease to cry to the Lord our God for us so that he may save us from the hand of the Philistines.'" The "magic" has been transferred from ark to prophet. This time it works. The Philistines are routed before Israel (cf. 1 Sam. 4:4, 10). Yet, from one perspective, the outcome is the same as after the battle of Ebenezer, since "*the hand of the Lord* was against the Philistines all the days of Samuel" (1 Sam. 7:13; see 1 Sam. 5:6, 9, 11).

We encounter some of the same themes in the Ark Narrative and in the Mizpah episode—defeat, the Lord's role in it (who), his motivation (why), and cultic and ritual actions. Yet in neither story are the relations between the themes spelled out in a definitive fashion, if they are stated at all. It is in the area of possible correlations that ambiguity and equivocation reign supreme.

> (9) Samuel took a suckling lamb and offered it as a whole burnt offering to the Lord. Samuel cried to the Lord for Israel, and the Lord answered him. (10) While Samuel was offering up the burnt

offering, the Philistines drew near to attack Israel. The Lord
thundered with a mighty voice that day against the Philistines, and
he threw them into confusion, and they were routed before Israel.
(1 Sam. 7:9–10)

The episode can be read according to the canons of retributive justice.
Israel has returned to the Lord to serve him alone; gone are the Baals
and the Ashtaroth. Samuel has interceded, cried to the Lord, and
offered sacrifice. The Lord is moved and responds by thundering
against and defeating the Philistines. Proper ritual behavior has been
rewarded.

This is a possible, but not necessary, interpretation. First, the sacrifices may or may not be related to the "crying" to the Lord, i.e., v. 9
may be describing separate and coincidental actions. V. 10, then,
simply notes that the Philistines attacked while Samuel was sacrificing, and it is not connecting as cause and effect Samuel's sacrificial
act and the Lord's thundering. In fact, it may not even be connecting the Lord's answering with his thundering. The latter can be a
second, independent act of the Lord. Second, "Samuel cried to the
Lord for Israel," but why is not stated, although v. 8 does lead us to
believe that it was for salvation from the Philistines. Thus Samuel's
sacrificing can be related to his appeal to the Lord as a necessary or
as a coincidental action. And the defeat of the Philistines may or
may not be the Lord's answer to Samuel's appeal. The text is ambiguous on the point. The Lord throws the Philistines into confusion,
but they are routed—passive construction—before Israel.

Even if we accept this reading of the Mizpah episode, the Ark
Narrative, as a counterpoint, requires us to look at the "other side"—
that of the Philistines—which gives us an opportunity to bring together some of the preceding discussion of the ambiguity and obfuscation of the narrative in 1 Samuel. 1 Sam. 7:5–11 is a fine example
of the ambiguity.

Is Retributive Justice Just?
It may be in accord with the ideals of retributive justice that the Lord
responds to Israel's prayers and sacrifices, that he rewards her for
proper ritual, but what then of the Philistines? Can it be considered
just that they are put to rout so that the Lord may reward Israel?
What is a reward for Israel's proper ritual or behavior is a curse for
the Philistines, a perversion of justice. Any attempt to sidestep the
conclusion by asserting that Israel's actions vis-à-vis God and his actions vis-à-vis Israel are solely their own concern is subverted by the
Ark Narrative, which presents the Philistine point of view. The
Judges stories are also subversive of the attempt. Just because retribu-

tive justice does not hold for "all Israel," just because "all Israel" is not punished for her continued evil, does not mean that others, e.g., Laish and Jabesh-gilead, are not punished.

Perhaps it would help if we dropped the canons of retributive justice and read the episode from the perspective of God's mercy. God is not rewarding prayer or sacrifice; he is responding to an appeal to act on Israel's behalf when she does not deserve it. He is acting graciously. (I note and do not develop the question of whether God's action can be gracious, unmotivated, if Israel, even if undeserving, has to appeal for mercy.) But the Philistines are then, if anything, treated even more unjustly and unmercifully. God's compassion and love for his people can have a harsh and capricious look to others.

Full discussion of the cultic order is beyond my present scope, but the material in 1 Samuel and in Judges allows us a glimpse of why ritual action is so frequently presented in an ambiguous and indeterminate manner. At times it may be unclear whether a given action is to be considered ritual or not, e.g., Hannah's weeping/lamenting and not eating/fasting in 1 Sam. 1:7. What is even more frequently left in doubt is the relation between the ritual act and a request of the Lord and the Lord's response and subsequent action or lack of action. Ritual has an undecidable status "between" justice and mercy. It is both proper action and behavior that should be rewarded, and it is an appeal for divine help and forgiveness that is undeserved. Its necessity is both affirmed and denied, neither affirmed nor denied. Focus on the cultic order leads into a deconstruction of the dichotomies that found it—justice and mercy, reward and punishment, deserved and undeserved, ritual and social, proper and improper; the OT text does not maintain them as rigorous dyads whose poles must exclude one another. I emphasize my contention that OT narrative is not so much deconstructing the dichotomies as it is presenting the matter in a deconstructed fashion, in an undecidable mode.

The ambiguities of the Mizpah episode are underscored in the narrative by the stone (*'eben*) set up by Samuel. He "called its name Ebenezer; he said, 'Up to here the Lord has helped (*'azar*) us' " (1 Sam. 7:12). Is this the same Ebenezer as in chapter 4? If so, how is God's help associated with the defeat at Ebenezer? If not, what can be made of the identity of the name, since it inevitably links this episode with chapter 4? "Up to here"—does this intend time, space, or both? God has helped Israel in the event at Mizpah, but not in those before it, whether the battle of Ebenezer or the slaughter of 50,070 men at Beth-shemesh. 1 Sam. 7:12 can be read as a refusal of meaning; we want to hear more of the gathering at Mizpah and are informed instead of the stone, analogous to 1 Sam. 6:14–18.

Summary

Despite the ambiguity and undecidability surrounding this and preceding chapters, some points can be listed as a summary and as an
introduction to much of the rest of 1 Samuel. Retributive justice is a
theme, even though it has been undermined as an effective, explanatory principle. It is not a simple issue. Things do not always accord
with it. Even when they seem to, this can be the result of a narrow
focus rather than the full application of the principle of retributive
justice. Hophni and Phinehas are punished for their sin, but why is
Israel defeated at the same time? God may answer his people's prayer,
but the Philistines experience such mercy or justice as an unjust and
arbitrary disaster.

Eli's death is a capstone on the displacement of the priests from the
central positions and functions they occupied and performed in Exodus through Deuteronomy. I trace the displacement from Joshua into
1 Samuel. Noteworthy, for our purposes, is the loss of the judicial
function allotted them, for example, in Deuteronomy 16–17. Many of
these functions and much of their authority pass to others, e.g.,
Joshua and the judges.

Samuel has inherited some of this. He performs priestly functions
and is noted as prophet and judge. I use the terms "priest," "prophet," and "judge" because they appear in the text, but I do not
intend them as referring to three separate and identifiable functions
or offices. Samuel is Samuel and does things that, in the OT, are
usually done by those called priest, prophet, and judge. It is the
burden of the following chapter on 1 Samuel 8–12 to examine what
the terms "prophet" and "judge" and the new term "king" may mean
and how they can be distinguished from one another. Attention will
be given to issues of governance and types of leaders. (I do not include the priest, since he plays no important role in these chapters.)
As the reader probably suspects, 1 Samuel 8–12 will not be very
helpful if one is expecting clear distinctions and definitions.

· 3 ·

1 SAMUEL 8-12

Judges and Judging

1 Samuel 8–12 are discussed together because of kingship, which is explicitly treated in chapters 8 and 12. They, from one viewpoint, frame chapters 9–11—the introduction of Saul, who will be the first king. However, there is no developed, unified presentation of "king" here or elsewhere in 1 Samuel; some aspects of the issue will be dropped after 1 Samuel 12 and not raised again until 2 Samuel or 1 Kings.

In the midst of chapters 8 and 12, chapters 9–11 appear to talk of anything but the king. Therefore, the treatment of these three chapters will emphasize the absence of "king" or "kingship," which is present in chapters 8 and 12 and at points in chapters 9–11, and at the same time will demonstrate how much of chapters 9–11 talk around the king, i.e., they are not irrelevant but are lures and teases. The analysis of chapters 8–12 will be more broken and digressive than much of the preceding and will frequently attempt a delicate balancing act between characters, themes, and the literal text.

The previous material closed with a comment on 1 Sam. 7:12, the stone set up by Samuel "between Mizpah and Shen." The remainder of the chapter, vv. 13–17, can be read in various ways, e.g., as a continuation of chapter 7, as a summary, or as a summary and a transition. The variety is indicative of the subsequent chapters.

"The Philistines were broken and did not again enter the territory of Israel, and the hand of the Lord was against the Philistines all the days of Samuel." V. 14 speaks of cities being returned to Israel and of peace between Israel and the Amorites; there is no mention of Samuel. This could be the continuation and result of the Lord's and Israel's rout of the Philistines in 1 Sam. 7:10–11; "all the days of Samuel" would mark a time period and not relate the events to his

41

activity. This is the work of the Lord, not Samuel. Vv. 15–17 would then shift to Samuel and would be a continuation and clarification of the comment in 1 Sam. 7:6 that Samuel judged Israel at Mizpah; it would also serve as a transition to chapter 8. Or vv. 13–17 could be a summary of the rest of Samuel's life between the Mizpah episode and his old age; vv. 15–17 would still serve as transition to chapter 8. They mark Samuel's elevated status and his successes. However they are read, the verses do contain two themes that will be important for the continuing reading—military victory and governance. The latter is marked by the term "to judge" (*shapat*) and the question of its meaning and extent.

The importance of "judge" is marked by the occurrence of the root *shapat* nine times in 1 Sam. 7:15–8:20, in three different forms and with a wide range of meaning—one verb (to judge) and two nouns (justice and judge). We are told three times that Samuel judged (*shapat*) Israel—"all the days of his life"; at Bethel, Gilgal, and Mizpah; and finally at Ramah. His sons are judges (*shopetim*) at Beersheba, where they pervert justice (*mishpat*). The people want a king to govern or judge (*shapat*) them like all the nations. Samuel, at the Lord's behest, describes to the people the justice or custom (*mishpat*) of the king.

In this section, 1 Sam. 7:15–8:20, the root's meaning extends from judging in a judicial sense to ruling or governing in general. The latter includes, or is at least associated with, a military function—"he [the king] will fight our battles" (1 Sam. 8:20). This accords with the function of the judges in the book of Judges—they govern and lead the army. They save and deliver Israel from her enemies. So does Samuel in 1 Sam. 7:6–9: "Samuel judged the Israelites at Mizpah . . . Samuel cried to the Lord on Israel's behalf and the Lord answered him." The Philistines are routed.

Samuel and his sons are portrayed in the judicial roles presented in Deut. 16:18–20 and Deut. 17:8–13. The first speaks of "judges and officers in all your towns." The second describes a system akin to a "superior" or "supreme" court that can be appealed to in "any case within your towns which is too difficult for you" (Deut. 17:8). Samuel's movement between Bethel, Gilgal, Mizpah, and Ramah makes him similar to a circuit-riding judge hearing the difficult cases at four cities.

According to the Mosaic legislation in Deuteronomy, the decision given by such a judge is a weighty matter; priests are absent from this position in 1 Samuel, and I omit them from the discussion.

> You will consult them [the priests and the judge], and they will declare [*higgid*] to you the decision [*mishpat*]. You must do according

to what they declare to you . . . you must be careful to do according to all that they teach [*yarah*] you; according to the instruction [*torah*] which they give you and according to the decision [*mishpat*] which they tell you, you must do. You must not turn from the verdict [*dabar*] which they declare to you. . . . The man who acts presumptuously, by not obeying the priest . . . or the judge, that man must die; you must purge the evil from Israel. The people must hear and fear and not act presumptuously again. (Deut. 17:8–13)

The judge is to declare (*higgid*) and teach (*yarah*) an instruction (*torah*; same root as *yarah*), a decision (*mishpat*), and a verdict (*dabar*). This makes the judge, in his limited sphere, akin to Moses in the larger sphere, since Moses declares and teaches instruction, decisions, and verdicts or words. With both judge and Moses, the emphasis is on the necessity of the people's hearing and obeying; disobedience leads to severe punishment, including death. Thus to say that Samuel *judged* is a serious pronouncement and makes Samuel akin to Moses. I read 1 Sam. 8:1–3 before returning to this phrase.

1 Samuel 8

Samuel's Sons

When Samuel became old, he appointed his sons judges over Israel . . . they were judges in Beersheba. His sons did not walk in his ways. They went after profit, took bribes, and perverted justice. (1 Sam. 8:1–3)

Samuel's sons are judges in the judicial sense; they do not seem to have political or military status. They, like Eli's sons, have violated particular prescriptions of the Mosaic law, especially that in Deut. 16:18–20. I quote the final two verses.

You must not pervert justice; you must not show partiality; you must not take a bribe for a bribe blinds the eyes of the wise and subverts the cause of the righteous. Justice, and only justice, you must follow, that you may live and inherit the land which the Lord your God gives you.

The absence of the final statement from 1 Samuel accords with the fact that possession of the land is not at issue in 1 Samuel. 1 Sam. 8:3, in view of this passage, stresses Samuel's prestige and authority, since "his sons did not walk in *his ways*," not Moses' or the Lord's ways.

Samuel's sons are named and listed in order of birth, but we hear no more of them except for Samuel's general remark to the people, "My sons are with you" (1 Sam. 12:2). They may or may not have continued as judges in Beersheba. Treatment of them is in contrast with treatment of Eli's house, where we do learn something of the fate of Eli's descendants, in particular his sons. But the text veers away from Samuel's family and does not return to them. The focus is now on Samuel and the king.

The sons are judges in Beersheba, which is mentioned one other time in 1 Samuel: "All Israel from Dan to Beersheba knew that Samuel was established as a prophet of the Lord" (1 Sam. 3:20). Samuel is akin to Moses as a judge. Is he also a "prophet like Moses"? I digress to discuss "prophet" and "prophet like Moses" and begin with the relevant passages from Deuteronomy.

Prophet like Moses
Deut. 34:10–12 were discussed above in relation to a comparison between the birth stories of Moses and Samuel. The question was asked whether Samuel was to be the "prophet like Moses" spoken of by Moses and the Lord in Deut. 18:15–22. I cite this entire passage and set off the Lord's statement, since such quotes are rare in the law code in Deuteronomy 12–26. The italics indicate the importance of speech, words, and hearing/obeying.

> The Lord your God will raise up a *prophet like me* from among you, from your brothers—you *must listen to* him—just as you *asked* of the Lord your God at Horeb. . . . "Let me not *hear* again the *voice* of the Lord my God or see this great fire any more, lest I die." The Lord *said* to me,
>
>> "It is good what they have *spoken*. I will raise up a *prophet like you* from among their brothers; I will put my *words* in his *mouth*, and he will *speak* to them all that I *command* him. Whoever will *not listen to my words* which he will *speak* in my name, I myself will require it of him. But the prophet who presumes to *speak a word* in my name which I have *not commanded* him to *speak*, or who *speaks* in the name of other gods, that same prophet must die."
>
> If you *say* in your heart, "How may we know the *word* which the Lord has *not spoken*?" When a prophet *speaks* in the name of Lord, if the *word* does not come to pass or come true, then that is a *word* which the Lord has *not spoken*; the prophet has *spoken* it presumptuously, and you need not be afraid of him.

The prophet is a potentially disruptive figure, since he will speak words other than those already spoken by the Lord and by Moses.

The prophet can be distinguished from the judge in several ways, most importantly through the fact that the prophet will speak, in the name of the Lord, *a word* which the Lord has spoken to him. The prophet is similar to a spokesman or messenger for the Lord. There is no hint in Deuteronomy that the judge speaks a word from the Lord, even though the judge's decision is to be treated as seriously as the prophet's.

The prophet's very words receive far more attention in Deuteronomy 18 than do the judge's in Deuteronomy 17; in accord with this, there is concern for how the people are to know whether a prophet, speaking in the name of the Lord, is speaking truthfully or presumptuously. The question of true or false prophecy is raised. This is a grave matter, since the Lord has stipulated the death penalty for false prophecy, but he gives no criterion for how to decide. Moses does, but the guide introduces the category of time and is stated negatively; the people will have to wait to ascertain whether they should fear a given prophet. It is strongly implied, but not explicitly stated, that if what the prophet says occurs, then he is a true prophet.

We can now begin to work our way back to 1 Samuel 8 via 1 Samuel 3, which establishes Samuel's credentials as a prophet, but the credentials have some interesting qualifications and omissions. In 1 Sam. 3:1–14, Samuel is called and given a message but no commission; he is not told to do something. For contrast, note the commissioning of Moses in Exodus 3 and Deut. 5:22–31, especially v. 31; he is respectively to bring forth and to teach the people. Thus the "call" of Samuel raises the question of whether Samuel has been commissioned for some future task beyond the end of the house of Eli.

Apparently he has been. There is a hint in 1 Sam. 3:7—"Samuel did not yet know the Lord, and the word of the Lord had not yet been revealed to him"—and a confirmation of sorts in 1 Sam. 3:19–4:1a:

> Samuel grew, and the Lord was with him and let none of his words fall to the ground. All Israel from Dan to Beersheba knew that Samuel was established as a prophet of the Lord. The Lord continued to appear at Shiloh for the Lord revealed himself to Samuel at Shiloh by the word of the Lord, and the word of Samuel came to all Israel.

I cited the above passage earlier and noted the lack of specification of content for "the word of the Lord" and "the word of Samuel." Here I focus on other phrases and issues.

The Lord "let none of his words fall to the ground." Apparently Samuel's words *come true, come to pass;* he is a prophet like Moses. "All Israel . . . knew that Samuel was established as a prophet of the Lord."

This is the only place in Samuel that Samuel is called a *prophet* (*nabi´*). We are told specifically of *Israel's knowledge*; we are not provided the certain fact that Samuel is a prophet, a *nabi´*. The next verse, however, adds further evidence that he is a prophet, as it connects Samuel's and the Lord's word, and this is very close to the identification of the prophet in Deut. 18:15–22—he will bring the word of the Lord to Israel. Yet the 1 Samuel passage lacks the corresponding stress on the people's hearing and obeying; all Israel knows, but there is no mention of the people's fearing and obeying.

We come to 1 Samuel 8 with at least three possible pictures of Samuel—the prophet, the judge, and a combination of the two. (I remind the reader that I am restricting "judge" to its judicial sense.) Both involve declaring a word that must be listened to and obeyed; the prophet's word is explicitly from the Lord and spoken in the Lord's name. However, the texts analyzed, in both Deuteronomy and 1 Samuel, and my analysis do not permit a clear demarcation of two different leaders or offices that can be separately defined. There can be prophets, there can be judges, and there can be characters who act as both prophet and judge (and perhaps as other officials). Moses and Samuel are two excellent examples. Again, Samuel is like Moses. Both are legendary figures of authority who play many roles; prophet and judge are the two presently focused on.

"Give Us a King!"
Samuel's authority is recognized by the narrator in 1 Sam. 8:3 and by the elders of Israel in 1 Sam. 8:5; all condemn Samuel's sons for not walking in their father's ways, not the Lord's ways or Moses' ways. The elders, however, recognize Samuel's authority by noting that it has reached its limit—he is old and his sons are not worthy successors—and by asking him to appoint another leader, i.e., to replace himself.

> All the elders of Israel gathered and came to Samuel at Ramah and they said to him, "Look, you are old and your sons do not walk in your ways. Now set up [*śim*] for us a king [*melek*] to govern [*shapat*] us like all the nations." And the matter [*dabar*] was evil in Samuel's eyes when they said, "Give [*natan*] us a king to govern us." And Samuel prayed to the Lord. (1 Sam. 8:4–6)

The people's request introduces another leader into the text. The king is a leader who is to govern or judge; the king has been anticipated in the Song of Hannah in 1 Sam. 2:10 and in the closing verse of Judges: "In those days there was no king in Israel." The establishment of a king was foreseen by the Lord and Moses; the description has some significant restrictions.

(14) When you come to the land which the Lord your God gives you, and you possess it and dwell in it and say, "I will set [*śim*] a king over me, like all the nations that are round about me"; (15) you may indeed *set* as king over you him whom the Lord your God will choose. One from among your brethren you will *set* as king over you; you must not put [*natan*] a foreigner over you, who is not your brother. (16) Only he must not multiply horses for himself or cause the people to return to Egypt in order to multiply horses since the Lord has said to you, "You must never go back there." (17) He must not multiply wives for himself lest his heart turn away; he must not greatly multiply silver and gold for himself. (18) When he sits on the throne of his kingdom, he will write for himself in a book a copy of this law from that which is in charge of the Levitical priests; (19) it will be with him, and he will read from it all the days of his life that he may learn to fear the Lord his God by keeping all the words of this law and these statutes by doing them. (20) So that his heart may not be lifted up above his brethren and that he may not turn aside from the commandment either to the right or to the left and that he may continue long in his kingdom, he and his children, in Israel. (Deut. 17:12–20)

Given the centrality of the king and monarchical issues from Samuel through Kings, the passage is striking in its brevity. It is one section among several and regards the establishment of a king as a near certainty and as an acceptable action for Israel. The king's establishment is not here associated with crisis.

Unlike with a prophet and a judge, there is no command here that the people must fear and obey the king; he also is to fear and obey the Lord and the law. Indeed, the stress is on what the king cannot and should not do, not on what he should do. In contrast to the prophet like Moses, the king as described here is not potentially disruptive. He is presented as one leader among many, with no apparent power to introduce significant change.

The people's demand for a king in 1 Sam. 8:4–6 is in accord with the Deuteronomic legislation, including Israel's desire to be "like all the nations." There is no explicit concern that the king be chosen by the Lord, but this does not necessarily signal the absence of any concern, since the demand is addressed to Samuel and can follow from all Israel's recognition that Samuel is a prophet of the Lord. Why then is the request "evil in Samuel's eyes"? I raise one possibility here that I will trace through relevant portions of 1 Samuel 8–12. The elders say, "Now set up [*śim*] for us a king to govern us"; what explicitly distresses Samuel is their statement, "Give [*natan*] us a king to govern us." Both verbs appear in Deut. 17:14–15, but here they are imperatives; this is a demand to establish a king. Samuel deeply resents the people's demand that he exercise his authority to demote or even remove himself by appointing another leader, a king, especially one who will govern or judge (*shapat*) the people as he has been doing.

Rejection

Samuel prays to the Lord, and Lord's response is susceptible of several interpretations.

> The Lord said to Samuel, "*Listen to/obey the voice* of the people *in all that they say* to you. For it is not you they have rejected, but it is me they have rejected from ruling [*malak*] over them. According to all the deeds which they have done from the day I brought them up out of Egypt even to this day—they have abandoned me and served other gods—thus they are doing to you. Now then, obey their voice; only, you must indeed warn them; you must tell them the justice/ custom of the king [*mishpat hammelek*] who will rule [*malak*] over them." (1 Sam. 8:7–9)

If Samuel's prayer was for the Lord to reject the people's request or punish the people, he is surprised, for the Lord turns the tables on him. It is he, prophet and judge, who is to obey all that the people say to him. The reversal is confirmed at the end of the episode. "The people refused to listen to the voice of Samuel . . . and the Lord said to Samuel, 'Listen to their voice and make them a king'" (1 Sam. 8:19–22). Samuel has an explicit command to obey the people and to make them a king, even though the act is evil in his eyes.

Samuel's surprise cannot be lessened by the Lord's express reason for his command—"They have rejected me." This would seem to be strong reason to reject the people and their request. But, first, how have the people rejected the Lord from being king over them? Is it by the request, by the establishment of an actual king, or by something else? Is there an implication that the Lord is Israel's only king? The latter is assumed by most commentaries on 1 Samuel and developed into an interpretation that the establishment of a human king is a rejection of the divine king. I follow a different tack, since the implication is weak at best.

The major thrust of the Lord's response is the reversal—the command that Samuel obey the people—and the Lord consoles Samuel by noting that the people are not so much rejecting him as they are rejecting their own God. However, the latter rejection does not refer specifically to the people's demand for a king but rather to their consistent abandonment of him to serve other gods, as they have done from the time of the Exodus. The Lord is presenting Samuel with an analogy, not a particular accusation against the people. As the people have abandoned him to serve other gods, so they are abandoning Samuel to serve another leader; as the Lord still continues with the people, so should Samuel. The Lord employs the root *malak,* to rule or be king, not because he is Israel's true king but to relate the anal-

ogy better to the context. The Lord gives no evaluation of the request
or of a king; he is directing and supporting Samuel, his judge and
prophet.

The Lord's response to Samuel then veers away from concern for
him. Samuel is to warn (`ed) the people and tell (*higgid*) them the
mishpat hammelek. The command to obey the people is repeated, and,
in addition, Samuel is given another directive. Are the warning and
the telling the same act, i.e., does Samuel warn by telling the *mishpat
hammelek?* Or are the warning and the telling two separate acts, i.e.,
are we given details on the telling but not on the warning? From
another viewpoint, is the *mishpat hammelek* a warning or a telling, a
declaring? The Hebrew *higgid,* to declare, recalls Deuteronomy,
where Moses *declares* the Lord's word and where a judge *declares* a
decision (*mishpat*).

If the *mishpat hammelek* is not the warning (`ed), what could be? The
book of the law that is "by the side of the ark of the covenant of the
Lord your God" is an excellent candidate (Deut. 31:26); it is a witness
(`ed) and occurs in the context of Moses' appointment of Joshua as his
successor and replacement. Is it Deuteronomy 32 that is mentioned in
the same context and is also called a witness (`ed, Deut. 31:19)? Per-
haps it is the "justice of the kingship" (*mishpat hammelukah*) that Samuel later writes in the book "and deposits before the Lord" (1 Sam.
10:25). In the first two instances, the warning would have nothing
specific to do with "king" and "kingship" and would accord with the
interpretation that the Lord is referring to Israel's consistent and
ongoing rebellion against him.

However we interpret the Lord's directive to warn and to tell, Samuel carries it out, or at least he carries out the last half.

> Samuel told [`amar*] all the words of the Lord to the people who
> were asking a king from him, and he said, "This will be the justice/
> custom of the king who will rule over you." (1 Sam. 8:9–11)

Is Samuel warning and telling or just telling? The "justice," in vv. 11–
18, is a description of conscription for various forms of royal service
and of royal appropriation of land and produce. Is the description
part of "all the words of the Lord" that Samuel told the people? We
have a situation similar to that noted by Polzin in Deuteronomy, particularly from chapter 11 on, where the reported words of the Lord
and the reporting words of Moses are indistinguishable. In 1 Sam.
8:10–18, we cannot separate the Lord's original words from Samuel's
report and interpretation. One verse demonstrates the implications.
"You will cry out in that day because of the king whom you have

chosen for yourselves, but the Lord will not answer you in that day"
(1 Sam. 8:18). Is this a threat, a hope, of Samuel? Is it a warning, a
promise, of the Lord?

Finally, what of the *mishpat hammelek,* the justice/custom of the king?
Even though it is not a glowing picture of the benefits of a king, is it
therefore a condemnation of the king? It may be, but it may also be a
portrayal of the harsh aspects of the king's rule to offset the people's
enthusiasm. Stress is on the king's taking and tithing. He is being
compared to the priest, with the notation that the king will be far
more expensive to support. The ambiguity of the speech is evident in
v. 17—"You will be his *`abadim* [servants or slaves]."

However we understand the speech,

> The people refused to listen to the voice of Samuel; they said, "No!
> for there will be a king over us. Indeed, we will be like all the
> nations, and our king will judge us and go out before us and fight
> our battles."

The addition of the military function balances Samuel's talk of conscription in vv. 11–12. The people may be denying the accuracy of
Samuel's depiction—no, this will not happen—or its relevance—we
don't care; we still want a king! In either case, they do not heed
Samuel's words. "Whoever will not heed my words which he [the
prophet like Moses] will speak in my name, I myself will require it of
him" (Deut. 18:19). Will the Lord now require it of Israel? Has Israel
given heed to the word of the Lord? Is the Lord, and the narrator,
interpreting the Deuteronomic legislation on "king" and "prophet" in
such a way that it has a much different relevance and application to
the present situation?

Summary
The closing verses of chapter 8 play upon the verb *shama`,* to hear,
listen to, obey. Samuel hears the people's words, tells them to the
Lord, "and the Lord said to Samuel, 'Obey their voice and make them
a king.' " The reversal (interpretation?) of Deuteronomy 18 is repeated; the prophet must heed the words of the people. Does the
reversal extend so far that the words of the people are the words of
the Lord? The episode ends with the dispersal of the people from
Ramah; "Samuel said to the men of Israel, 'Go every man to his city.' "

> The Israelites departed from there at that time, each one to his
> tribe and family; they went out from there each man to his inheri-
> tance. In those days there was no king in Israel; every man did what
> was right in his own eyes. (Judg. 21:24–25)

In these days there is to be a king in Israel, and the matter is evil in the eyes of Samuel.

Chapter 8 closes with some points of clarity. There will be a king. This is in accord with the legislation, the "word of the Lord," in Deuteronomy and is supported by the Lord himself in this chapter. It is also in accord with the Deuteronomic legislation in that little or nothing is said of how the people should respond to the king. He is to govern them, but nothing is said of their obeying him and his words. Samuel will be instrumental, even if grudging and resentful, in the appointment of the first king. Samuel is caught in the middle. His authority is recognized and undermined at the same time by both the people and the Lord. The Lord's word to Samuel is to obey the people's words to him. Samuel is judge and prophet who obeys the people and appoints a king to judge in his place.

1 Samuel 9–11

"They Made Saul King"

1 Samuel 9–11 can be dealt with together, as all three chapters deal with Saul and present him in a positive light; they are also "framed" by chapters 8 and 12, which concern the king, although Saul is not named in them, in a more general sense. A major issue, or group of issues, that I follow in the reading is the manner in which the text dances around "king," "kingship," and "prophet." There are other topics but I do not trace them; the words are used and questions raised, but very little is said about them. Chapter 8 left us expecting the appointment of a king; we get that, in 1 Sam. 11:15, but only after some lengthy and detailed narrative that leaves us wondering what a king is, what a prophet is. In the reading, I attempt to demonstrate how "king" and "prophet" are in the text both directly (the words themselves) and indirectly (allusions and wordplay); I also discuss how the text raises expectations concerning the understanding of "king" and "prophet" and does not fulfill them, although the lack of fulfillment manifests itself in quite different ways.

Saul

As noted above, chapter 8 closes with an allusion to the end of Judges and with the prospect of the imminent appointment of a king. Chapter 9 opens, as 1 Samuel 1 does, with a four-generation genealogy, and earlier I noted the implication of Saul in the birth story of

Samuel. Perhaps the Lord will finally establish his word, and Saul will be another Samuel.

> There was a man of Benjamin whose name was Kish, son of Abiel, son of Zeror, son of Becorath, son of Aphiah, a Benjaminite, a man of wealth; he had a son whose name was Saul, a handsome young man. There was not a man among the people of Israel more handsome than he; from his shoulders upward he was taller than any of the people. (1 Sam. 9:1–2)

The link with Samuel through the birth story carries us back to Samson and Moses. Samson "began" to deliver Israel from the hand of the Philistines; Samuel carried the process further and achieved more success than Samson. Saul will likewise fight the Philistines to deliver Israel, but ultimately he will share more with Samson than with Samuel or Moses.

Saul, unlike Moses, Samson, and Samuel, does not have a birth story; the absence is marked by the chain of allusions to other birth stories. Saul's introduction is too good and does not fit the OT pattern for deliverance or heroes, which usually presents the leader as somehow unfit for leadership or at least as an unpromising candidate. Saul's ancestry and physical appearance make him a likely candidate. Saul is a candidate, and chapter 9 alludes to more than just the closing verses of Judges—it alludes also to the closing chapters 19–21. Benjamin is marked by ambiguity; Saul is marked by ambiguity. The excellent pedigree noted in 1 Sam. 9:1–2 can at the same time be ominous. Many of the elements of chapters 9–11 will similarly be double-edged.

As a Benjaminite, is Saul to be a man of misfortune, a man of vigor, or perhaps both? The allusion to Judges 19–21 inserts Gibeah, Jabesh-gilead, and Shiloh into the text; the first two play central roles in the story of Saul. Jabesh-gilead is a twofold symbol of Saul's finest hour and of his death.

Seeking and Finding

"The she-asses of Kish, Saul's father, were lost." Saul and his servant search for them in Ephraim, Shalisha, Shaalim, and Benjamin, "but they did not find them." Seeking (*biqqesh*) and finding (*matsa´*) or not finding include a constellation of texts and themes in 1 Samuel that may or may not involve the Hebrew words and themes of 1 Sam. 9:3–4. For example, on a thematic level, both the Israelites and the Philistines seek the word of the Lord in chapters 4–6. Israel asks for, seeks, a king. "The Lord has sought out [*biqqesh*] a man after his own heart" (1 Sam. 13:14) and has found him—David. Saul seeks and pursues David relentlessly; only when David flees to the Philistines does Saul "*seek* him no more" (1 Sam. 27:4). Thus there is an allusion to "king" in the opening verses of chapter 9, but nothing is said about any king, only the lost she-asses.

After a long, fruitless search, Saul is concerned that his father might be worried about them and not about the asses. We are given insight, although limited, into Saul's character. Saul's servant responds to the concern.

> There is a man of God in this city; he is a man held in honor; all that he says comes true [*bo´ yabo´*]. Let us go there; perhaps he can tell [*higgid*] us about the journey on which we have set out. (1 Sam. 9:6)

A man of God is associated with, if not defined as, a prophet, since "all that he says comes true" is listed or implied as a mark of a prophet (Deut. 13:1–2, 18:22; 1 Sam. 3:19–21). Both Deuteronomy texts use the Hebrew term *bo´* to mean "come true."

Higgid, to tell or declare, introduces the above discussion of Moses, judges, and Samuel into the reading, but what is at issue here would seem to have little to do with serious pronouncements of a judge or a Moses. The text, however, is beginning a series of allusions to and comments on "king" and "prophet" that raise our expectations for this tale of a search to end in the discovery of clarity on kingship and prophecy.

The *words* of 1 Sam. 9:6 are pregnant: "Perhaps he can tell [*higgid*] us about the journey [*derek*] on which we have set out [*halak*]." We know the outcome of this journey—Saul as *nagid* of Israel. *Higgid* is based on the same Hebrew root, **ngd*, and does double duty by alluding to declaring (Moses and Samuel) and to *nagid* (Saul). (*Nagid* is usually translated "prince," "leader," or such; I leave it untranslated, since a specific meaning could be misleading for my purposes.) We also know of that other fateful mission (*derek*) that Saul undertakes in 1 Samuel 15 and of the final way (*derek*) he goes on (*halak*, 1 Sam. 28:22). Both of the latter concern Saul as king, not as *nagid*.

The man of God does not speak without recompense. "What can we bring the man? There is no bread in our sacks, and there is no present to bring to the man of God" (1 Sam. 9:7)—a practical concern but literally a far-reaching statement. "Some worthless fellows . . . despised him and brought him no present" (1 Sam. 10:27); this occurs immediately after Saul has presumably been chosen king. "What can we bring?" in Hebrew is *mah nabi´;* out of context, the phrase can be translated, "What is a prophet?" "Prophet" is *nabi´*; the word is in v. 9.

Curtis notes that 1 Sam. 9:7–9 present a type of folk etymology based on the wordplay between *nabi´* and the causative stem of *bo´*, to bring—*habi'*. "There is no present *to bring* to the man of God." Shaviv picks up on this and considers it strictly wordplay, not a mistaken folk etymology; he ascribes the suggestion to Vischer and Buber. This accords neatly with the fact that the prophet's words are to come true, *yabo'*; Shaviv lists other parallels from Deuteronomy and Jeremiah. In addition, he comments on the wordplay of *nagid* and *higgid* with added examples.

Seer and Prophet

Saul's servant has a quarter of a shekel of silver to give to "the man of God to tell us about our journey." The narrator interrupts with an answer of sorts to "What is a prophet?":

> Formerly in Israel, thus said the man who went to inquire of God, "Come, let us go to the seer [*ro'eh*]" for he who is now called the prophet [*nabi'*] was formerly called the seer. (1 Sam. 9:9)

The comment offers some specific information on a change of names but adds nothing relevant to the context, whether chapter 9 or all of 1 Samuel. "Seer" is not a frequent term—in Genesis-Kings it occurs only in 1 Sam. 9:9–19; it is not a known entity employed to clarify an obscure term, "prophet."

Indeed, the comment in its immediate context tends to obscure an otherwise relatively clear term. The above analysis of Deuteronomy 18 and 1 Samuel 3 resulted in a limited, but fairly definite, picture of a *nabi'* as one who speaks a word of the Lord in the name of the Lord and who is to be obeyed. Deuteronomy 13 does note one major exception to this; not even a prophet can demand worship of other gods. 1 Sam. 9:9 severely limits this understanding; there is no mention of a word of the Lord, except indirectly through "inquire of God," or of obedience. Even if we assume that "seers" used to serve such a limited function, prophets in the rest of Samuel-Kings do far more. When, indeed, it this "now," when the former *ro'eh* is called *nabi'*? To summarize, 1 Sam. 9:6–9 raise the query of what a prophet is and what a prophet's relation to, or identity with, "man of God" and "seer" may be. I follow the beginnings of a grappling with the question in 1 Samuel; the grappling continues in Kings.

Over and above this, "seer" invokes earlier passages that play upon sight and blindness with an emphasis not on vision but on hearing and words. The emphasis continues in Saul's encounter with Samuel. The comment in v. 9 is not developed. Samuel identifies himself as the seer in v. 19, and the issue—the words "seer" and "prophet"—is dropped. The conversation between Samuel and Saul in vv. 19–21 concerns speech, not visions, even though it is night.

The Encounter

The discussion between Saul and his servant ends with Saul's assent to the servant's proposal. "Saul said to his servant, 'Your suggestion is good; come, let us go.' And they went to the city where the man of God was." Vv. 11–18 narrate the encounter between Saul and Samuel. The details and style build to a climax that never occurs.

> As they were going up the ascent, they found young girls coming out to draw water and they said to them, "Is the seer here?" They answered them, "He is. Look, he's right before you! Hurry now for he has just come to the city because there is a sacrifice for the people on the high place. As soon as you come to the city, you will find him before he goes up to the high place to eat because the people will not eat until he comes since he must bless the sacrifice. After that those invited eat. And now, go up for you can find him right now!"

Saul seeks the lost asses and seeks a word from the seer about them; he finds young girls who state that he can soon find the seer. Alter has noted the reflex of the OT betrothal scene, the "encounter with the future betrothed at a well." He focuses on the meetings with Rebekah, Rachel, and Zipporah in Genesis 24 and 29 and in Exodus 2. Two elements of the scene type are relevant. The traveler "encounters a girl . . . or girls at a well. Someone, either the man or the girl, then draws water from the well; afterward, the girl or girls rush to bring home the news of the stranger's arrival" (Alter 1981, p. 52). Saul meets the "young maidens coming out to draw water" who tell him to "make haste." Alter comments,

> This is probably a deliberate strategy of foreshadowing. The sense of completion implicit in the betrothal of the hero is withheld from this protagonist; the deflection of the anticipated type-scene somehow isolates Saul, sounds a faintly ominous note that begins to prepare us for the story of the king who loses his kingship. (Alter 1981, pp. 60–61)

A "deflected betrothal" is fitting for a man who has a "deflected birth story."

The echo of former meetings at a well of water, a symbol of life, particularly the meeting of Jacob and Rachel, is subsequently weakened by Samuel's prediction that Saul is to "meet two men by Rachel's tomb in the territory of Benjamin" (1 Sam. 10:2); "tomb" tips the ambiguous symbol of Benjamin toward the pole of misfortune and death. It invokes the memory that Benjamin's life is at the expense of the death of others, whether his mother or the inhabitants of Jabesh-gilead.

However, at this point in 1 Samuel 9, the girls' statement is noteworthy for its emphasis on haste and imminence; a decisive encounter
is about to occur. The description of the encounter scene uses participles to present the action as Saul and his servant see it and to
heighten the expectation that an important moment is now at hand.

> They went up to the city; they are entering the center of the city,
> and here is Samuel coming out toward them on his way up to the
> high place. (1 Sam. 9:14)

But the moment is delayed.

> The Lord had opened the ear of Samuel the day before Saul came:
> "About this time tomorrow I will send to you a man from the land
> of Benjamin, and you will anoint him *nagid* over my people Israel.
> He will save [*hoshi`a*] my people from the hand of the Philistines for
> I have seen my people because their cry [*za`aqah*] has come to me.
> When Samuel saw Saul, the Lord answered him, "Here is the man
> about whom I said, 'This one will rule [*ya`tsor*] over my people.' "
> (1 Sam. 9:15–17)

Two scenes follow—a flashback to the previous day and the meeting
with Saul from Samuel's viewpoint. Both are narrated in the past
tense, without participles. The immediacy of vv. 11–14 is deflected;
the encounter occurs, but it does not produce the information we
have hoped for. If anything, questions of "prophet" and "king" are
more clouded than before. Obscurity is present despite and because
of a revelation—an "uncovering of the ear"—from the Lord to Samuel. This would appear to mark Samuel as a prophet, yet the commissioning is the opposite of 1 Samuel 3. There a message was given
without action; here action appears—"anoint him"—without a message. The Lord explains his reasons to Samuel, but Samuel is given no
word of the Lord to proclaim. If Samuel is to be understood as prophet, then we must adjust our understanding of "prophet" to include
carrying out a directive of the Lord that does not involve declaring a
word of the Lord to be obeyed.

The Lord's statement itself deepens the problem. "King" may be
alluded to, but Saul is to be anointed *nagid*. Chapter 8 spoke of appointing (v. 5, *śim*), giving (v. 6, *natan*), choosing (v. 18, *bachar*), and
making (v. 22, *himlik*) a king. The Lord's statement in 1 Sam. 9:16 has
a ring of kingship about it, for Samuel will anoint (*mashach*) the man
from Benjamin. There is play in evidence on words in the *qatil* form—
nabi' and *nagid*—and the Song of Hannah introduced the anointed,
the *mashiach,* in parallel with the king (1 Sam. 2:10). Yet the ring of

kingship is faint, since the rest of the Lord's statement sounds like commissioning of a judge. "When the people cried [*za`aq*] to the Lord, the Lord raised up a savior [*moshi`aq*] for the people of Israel who saved [*hoshi`a*] them" (Judg. 3:9). Does this indicate some identity between king and judge? Finally, "when Samuel saw Saul, the Lord told him, '. . .he it is who will rule [*ya`tsor*] over my people.' " The root `*atsar*, to hold back or restrain, is not employed elsewhere to refer to reigning or ruling. The root *malak*, to be king and to rule, is studiously avoided.

The Banquet

> Saul approached Samuel in the gate and said, "Please tell [*higgid*] me where is the house of the seer?" Samuel answered Saul, "I am the seer; go up before me to the high place. You will eat with me today, and I will let you go in the morning, and I will tell [*higgid*] you all that is on your mind. As for your asses that were lost three days ago, do not set your mind on them for they have been found. And for whom is all that is desirable in Israel? Is it not for you and all your father's house?" (1 Sam. 9:18–20)

If v. 14 contains a note of surprise, "here is Samuel coming out toward them," it is not registered in v. 18. Saul speaks deferentially and does not equate Samuel with the man of God, the seer, whom he is seeking. I see no reason to assume, as many do, that Saul does not know who Samuel is; what is striking is that no reaction is reported. We do not know what Saul thinks of Samuel or of this meeting.

Apparently the lost asses are what is on Saul's mind, but Samuel informs Saul that they have been found. Samuel has something far different in mind to tell Saul. What that is will not be revealed until chapter 10, and Samuel concludes his statement with a "question" about all that is desirable in Israel. What does he mean by "all that is desirable"? How does he relate it to the divine revelation in 1 Sam. 9:15–17 and to the previous command in chapter 8 to make the people a king? Does he, in fact, have a king in mind here? This is one of several questions in chapters 9–11 that can unsettle the reading, since they come at points where we expect and would like a statement, a positive declaration. "Questions" can be unsettling because there is always the possibility, however slight, of answering them in a way that runs counter to the "obvious meaning" of the text. One could answer Samuel with a resounding, "No!"

Saul is not totally baffled by Samuel's question, since he has heard some sort of unexpected offer that he can object to with his protestation of unworthiness, which itself is expressed in a question.

> Am I not a Benjaminite from the smallest of the tribes of Israel? Is
> not my family the humblest of all the families of the tribe of Benja-
> min? Why then have you spoken to me in this way?

The claim of humble origins stands in tension with his introduction in
1 Sam. 9:1–2 but does fit with "the customary response of individuals
called into divine service" (McCarter 1980b, p. 179). McCarter cites
Exodus 3–4 as a parallel and quotes Gideon, "But my lord, how can I
free [*hoshi `a*] Israel? My thousand is the weakest in Manasseh, and I
myself am the humblest in my family!" (Judg. 6:15). As with the
Lord's statement in v. 16, the narrative accords with a Judges pattern.
Finally, I note the formal balance of Saul's objection; this is not a
stammering, hesitant reply. I pay attention to the form, not just the
content, of most of Saul's statements (cf. Alter 1981, pp. 62–87).
    Samuel, Saul, and his servant go to the banquet. The tale is nar-
rated with attention to detail. The text recalls Samuel's birth story
through the theme of eating and drinking and, at the same time,
anticipates both the later banquet to which Jesse and his sons will be
invited and Saul's final meal at Endor. Saul sits at the head of the
banquet as the honored guest and is served a reserved cut of meat
that was kept for the "appointed time." This implies considerable
significance, but what are we to make of it? More importantly, what
does Saul make of it? Is he impressed, amazed, perplexed, dumbfounded? How does he regard Samuel—as great man, as local judge
or seer, as established prophet of the Lord? The lack of information
on Saul's reactions and thoughts is central to my continuing reading
and is, in a sense, highlighted by the momentous events of that night
and the following day. (I assume that 1 Sam. 10:1–6 transpires on the
same day.) Thus "Saul" is added to "prophet" and "king" as a query in
the text, but as a query that is not pursued, let alone resolved. We
may be able to set our minds at rest that Saul's asses have been found,
but we then become anxious about "prophet," "king," and "Saul."

The Anointing
The next morning, Samuel finally seems to get to the point. He tells
Saul to let the servant go ahead,

> "but you stand here right now so that I may cause you to hear
> [*'ashmi`a*] the word of God." Samuel took the vial of oil, and he
> poured it on his head and kissed him and said, "Has not the Lord
> anointed you as *nagid* over his heritage?" (1 Sam. 9:27–10:1)

Whatever the point at which he has finally arrived, Samuel's way has
been circuitous and evasive; this contrasts with his much more direct

approach in chapter 16. The roundabout way continues. Samuel does not speak or declare, he causes to hear, and it is the word of God, not the word of the Lord, that is heard. "God" recalls the man of God and inquiry of God in 1 Sam. 9:6–10, not the Lord's revelation in 1 Sam. 9:16–17. In the anointing, Samuel does not declare or pronounce; he asks a "question." His "question" refers back to the Lord's revelation in 1 Sam. 9:16–17, where the Lord spoke of "my people Israel" three times; here Samuel speaks of "his heritage."

What is Samuel trying to do? Is he following some prescribed ritual? Is he proceeding willingly and perhaps savoring this elaborate and solemn exercise of his power? Or is he acting reluctantly and resentfully, dragging things out to delay the appointment of another leader, perhaps a successor? Regardless of Samuel's intentions, we can again ask what effect this has on Saul.

"Samuel took the vial of oil, and he poured it on his head." The statement is an excellent example of a two-edged allusion. Anointing with oil is associated with priests and kings and marks Saul as an important and recognized official. However, "vial" (*pak*) is a rare word. Elsewhere it occurs in Elisha's command to anoint Jehu king (2 Kings 9:1–3). Jehu fulfills the word of the Lord spoken by Elijah by annihilating the house of Ahab and by eradicating Baal worship from Israel, but he does it by a brutal purge. "Jehu was not careful to walk in the law of the Lord the God of Israel with all his heart; he did not turn from the sins of Jeroboam which he made Israel to sin" (2 Kings 10:31). When Samuel anoints David, it is with a horn (*qeren*) of oil. The term is in the Song of Hannah: "He will give strength to his king and exalt the power [*qeren*] of his anointed" (1 Sam. 2:10). *Pak* in 1 Sam. 10:1 dissociates Saul from David and from the closing statement of the Song of Hannah.

Signs
"Has not the Lord anointed you as *nagid* over his heritage?" No mention is made of salvation from the Philistines; no purpose is given for the anointing; no explanation is provided of what a *nagid* is or is to do. Instead, Samuel again veers off and describes three signs that will befall Saul when he leaves Samuel. The signs are described in v. 2–6; the second, in vv. 3–4, is a fine example of the detail.

> You will go beyond there and come to the oak at Tabor; three men going up to God at Bethel will find you there, one carrying three kids, another carrying three loaves of bread, and another carrying a skin of wine. They will greet you and give you two loaves of bread which you will take from their hand.

A parallel with the signs of Exodus, the plagues, suggests itself, but the parallel underlines the diminished stature of Samuel's proposed signs. A more cogent analogy is with Gideon and his demand for signs from the Lord to prove "that it is you who are speaking to me" (Judg. 6:17) and "that you will save [*moshi`a*] Israel by my hand" (Judg. 6:36). Again a theme or pattern reappears from Judges. The signs can have double meaning. They are to convince Saul that this is the word of God and that "he will save my people from the hand of the Philistines" (1 Sam. 9:16). The signs can also convince Saul of Samuel's authority since it is Samuel who is predicting them.

Samuel's prediction concludes, "Now when these signs come true [*bo*], do whatever you hand *finds* to do for God is with you"; appropriate action is left to Saul's discretion. Fulfillment is soon confirmed. "When he turned his shoulder to leave Samuel, God gave him another heart, and all these signs came true that day." It is uncertain whether being given another heart is the same as being turned "into another man," as predicted by Samuel in v. 6.

Words that "come true" (*bo'*) are a central criterion for recognizing the true prophet, the prophet who speaks a word of the Lord. But these words in 1 Sam. 10:2–6 are predictions, not directives or commands. Samuel does nothing but speak; the signs happen to Saul, he has to do nothing, he does not have to obey. Again we can ask, what is the effect of the signs? Do they convince Saul of his own position and authority? The signs have come true, and this should mark Samuel as a true prophet. But for what purpose? What of Samuel's status is at stake here? He is not proclaiming a word of the Lord that is to be obeyed; indeed, the word of the Lord has come to him commanding him to obey the people. There is a challenge to, a modification of, the Mosaic criterion of a true prophet. What a prophet says may occur and yet have little to do with the immediate situation. Moses himself had already registered a major exception in Deuteronomy 13.

Vv. 2–6 are predictions, but vv. 7–8 do contain directives of a sort. V. 7, cited above, authorizes Saul but does not give him a specific command; appropriate action is left to his discretion. V. 8 presents an ambiguous statement.

> You will go down before me to Gilgal; and look, I am coming [or, will be coming] to you to offer burnt offerings and to sacrifice peace offerings. Seven days you will wait until I come to you, and I will make known to you what you are to do.

The statement can be dissociated from its context, because it has more the character of a command or a statement than a prediction; it says nothing of God, and it does not leave things up to Saul. The statement, however, is equivocal. First, is this a direct command, or is it a request without imperative force? Second, the time when Saul is to go to Gilgal is not given. Is it before, immediately after, or any time after the fulfillment of the signs? Perhaps the signs are fulfilled while Saul is on his way to Gilgal.

Third, what will Samuel show Saul to do? It is generally assumed, and we will see that Saul so assumes, that the instruction has to do with offering sacrifices, since Samuel is coming to Gilgal to sacrifice. However, the verse permits a reading in which Samuel's offering sacrifices is one reason, or even the main reason, for his coming to Gilgal but has nothing to do with what he will show Saul to do. The reading of 1 Sam. 7:9–10 offers a parallel for a dual purpose in which sacrificing is an independent act. The deception of Saul by the Lord and Samuel in 1 Sam. 16:1–5 is another parallel. "You will say, 'I have come to sacrifice to the Lord.' *I will make known to you what you are to do*" (1 Sam. 16:2–3). This does not necessitate seeing any deception involved in Samuel's statement in 1 Sam. 10:8, we will return to it in the discussion of chapter 13.

The fulfillment of the signs is noted briefly. "When he turned to leave Samuel, God gave him another heart, and all these signs came true that day." The fulfillment of the third sign is then narrated in more detail. Saul meets a band of prophets, and

> The spirit of the Lord came mightily upon him and he prophesied among them. Those who knew him before looked and there was Saul prophesying with the prophets. They said to one another, "What has come over the son of Kish? Is Saul also among the prophets?" (1 Sam. 10:10–11)

Do the people regard Saul's behavior as something good or bad, or are they just surprised that Saul is with the prophets without judging the fact? The same questions are appropriate to Saul's being another man with another heart—is this good, bad, or just a fact?

The previous occurrences of the verb "to prophesy" (*hithnabbe'*) are in Num. 11:16–30. Seventy elders are appointed to help Moses bear the burden of the people. "When the spirit rested upon them, they prophesied, but they did so no more" (Num. 11:25). The prophesying is a sign of their appointment and not a permanent practice. Eldad and Medad prophesy in the camp, and Moses in response to Joshua's desire to stop them says, "Are you jealous for my sake? Would that all the Lord's people were prophets, that the Lord would put his spirit upon them!" (Num. 11:29). Here "prophet," "prophesying," and the Lord's spirit are associated with leadership of the people; Saul's possession by the spirit and his prophesying can be a sign that he is a

leader acceptable to the Lord. However, the band of prophets in
1 Samuel 10 with their musical instruments seems to be a permanent
fixture and seems to have little to do with leadership of the people.

Unlike the seventy elders, Saul prophesies again, but "after an evil
spirit from God" has come upon him; *RSV* translates, "He raved
[*yithnabbe'*] in his house" (1 Sam. 18:10). The prophesying has a de-
monic quality. Finally, Saul goes to Ramah, where "he too prophesied
before Samuel and lay naked all that day and all that night" (1 Sam.
19:24). This prophesying can be a sign that Saul has lost his kingly
status, that he is no longer another man with another heart.

This passage, like the comment in 1 Sam. 9:9, complicates the issue
of "prophet." The understanding of "prophet" that I have been developing with adjustments revolves around an authoritative figure
who commands, performs, and predicts; his speeches and actions
should concern serious matters. The prophetic bands (*nebi'im*) and the
prophet-seer (*nabi-'-ro'eh*) do not fit this understanding, since they do
not center on an authoritative figure concerned with serious matters.
This leads me to separate the concept of "a prophet" from the Hebrew term *nabi'*; this does not mean that they are mutually exclusive,
just that they are not identical. What is a prophet is a larger question
than what is a *nabi'*. However, we can rephrase the people's question,
"Is Samuel also among the prophets [*nebi'im*]?" since most of his statements and acts in chapters 9–10 accord as well with traveling show-
men as with a prophet like Moses.

From Nagid to Melek

Saul's uncle, probably Ner (1 Sam. 14:50), asks, "Where did you go?"
Saul's response is brief: "To seek the asses, and when we saw that they
were not [to be found], we went to Samuel." Play on the root **ngd*, to
say and declare, returns.

> Saul's uncle said, "Please tell [*higgid*] me what Samuel said to you."
> Saul said to his uncle, "He told us plainly [*higgid*] that the asses had
> been found." But the word [*dabar*] of the kingship [*melukah*] which
> Samuel had spoken, he did not tell [*higgid*] him. (1 Sam. 10:15–16)

We share a similar position with Saul's uncle. We both know that the
asses have been found, and none of us knows anything about "the
word of the kingship which Samuel had spoken." We, however, have
a privileged position vis-à-vis Saul's uncle, since we know that Saul
said nothing about it, i.e., we know that Samuel did tell Saul something about kingship. Saul knows something about the matter of the
kingship. But what? And what about himself as king? The "word"
concerns kingship, not king. Does Saul have any greater clarity on the

speeches and events of chapters 9 and 10 than we do? Perhaps he is even more confused and perplexed. Does he refrain from telling his uncle because it is an important secret, because the silence was demanded by Samuel, or because he does not understand it himself? These types of questions also apply to Saul and Samuel—how does Saul regard Samuel? How does Samuel want Saul to regard him?

Digression: King, Kingship, and Kingdom

There are several terms derived from the Hebrew root **mlk,* which concerns being king and ruling. *Malak,* to be king and to rule, and *melek,* king, present no problem for translation. *Malak,* in its causative form *himlik,* means to make king, to crown. Other nominal forms are more problematic.

Melukah is translated "kingship" (1 Sam. 10:16); others, e.g., *RSV,* translate it "kingdom."[1] I prefer "kingship," since in the large majority of times the word refers to the right to rule, to the power and authority of the king, and perhaps to the king's power as a sign of unity, a sign of the existence of an entity—the people and the kingdom. *Melukah* is comparatively abstract; it is something exercised, not owned or ruled over. Unlike *mamlakah,* it never occurs with a pronominal suffix.

Mamlakah is translated "kingdom" (1 Sam. 10:18) in accord with most other translations. In the majority of its occurrences,[2] the term refers to kingdom as a political-social entity, with frequent connotations of geographical expanse. Focus is more on what is ruled than on the king's power to rule. 1 Sam. 10:18 refers to kingdoms that oppress Israel; *mamlakah* is in parallel with the Egyptians. *Mamlakuth* is an infrequent term that occurs in 1 Samuel once, in 1 Sam. 15:28, where I translate it "kingdom." It appears to be a synonym for *mamlakah. Malkuth* is another rare word which occurs in 1 Samuel only in 1 Sam. 20:31, where it can mean "kingdom" or "kingship."

The varying use of the terms, especially *melek, melukah,* and *mamlakah,* can reflect variations in reference, but I do not offer this as the only explanation for every use of each term, particularly in chapters 10–11. Here it is not necessarily a different meaning at issue but an avoidance of another term; *melukah,* for example, not *melek,* appears in 1 Sam. 10:16, 25, and 1 Sam. 11:14.

[1]*Melukah* occurs in these places in Genesis-Kings: 1 Sam. 10:16, 25; 1 Sam. 11:14; 1 Sam. 14:47; 1 Sam. 18:8; 2 Sam. 12:26; 2 Sam. 16:8; 1 Kings 1:46; 1 Kings 2:15, 22; 1 Kings 11:35; 1 Kings 12:21; 1 Kings 21:7; and 2 Kings 25:25.

[2]Some representative occurrences of *mamlakah* in Genesis-Kings are: Gen. 10:10; Gen. 20:9; Exod. 19:6; Num. 32:33; Deut. 17:18, 20; Deut. 28:25; Josh. 10:2; Josh. 11:10; 1 Sam. 10:18; 1 Sam. 13:14; 1 Sam. 27:5; 2 Sam. 3:28; 2 Sam. 7:13, 16; 1 Kings 5:1; 1 Kings 9:5; 1 Kings 12:26; 2 Kings 11:1; 2 Kings 14:5; and 2 Kings 15:19.

Long Live the King!

1 Sam. 10:17–25 mark a change in setting and tone. Samuel, clearly the people's leader, gathers them at Mizpah, one of the cities where he judges Israel, to appoint a king. The story appears as the expected sequel to chapter 8; it is as though 1 Sam. 9:1–10:16 could be left out with their equivocations and deflections. But change in setting and tone do not necessarily signal change in clarity.

Samuel's speech, in vv. 18–19, bears comparison with the unnamed prophet's speech in Judg. 6:8–10 in terms of content and terminology. Both recite the Lord's gracious deeds for Israel and her ungrateful response. The prophet in Judges charges Israel with not obeying the Lord's voice by fearing the gods of the Amorites; Samuel picks up on the Lord's speech in 1 Sam. 8:7–9 and accuses Israel of having "this day rejected your God . . . and you have said to him, 'Set a king over us' " (1 Sam. 10:19). Neither speech is followed by judgment. The prophet's pronouncement in Judges 6 is followed by Israel's deliverance through Gideon; Samuel's is followed by the selection of Saul as king. Once more Saul and Gideon are placed in parallel.

Is Samuel making a specific and accurate accusation? If so, why is not there some judgment or punishment pronounced? Or is Samuel resentfully and grudgingly following the Lord's command to make a king? He will remind the people one more time of the gravity of their request.

A lot procedure is called for, which leads to the selection of Benjamin, then of Saul's family, and, finally, "Saul the son of Kish was taken by lot." Saul is sought for and is not found. "The people asked the Lord again, 'Is there yet a man to come here?' The Lord said, 'Look, he is hiding in the baggage.' " Why is Saul hiding? Is it because of fear and perplexity stemming from the preceding events, particularly a fear of Samuel? Was the hiding prearranged by Saul and Samuel, and the Lord, to impress the people? Samuel did make a serious accusation about the king and may wish to balance it.

The selection by lot marks Saul as the Lord's elect, but there is also a negative side to the procedure. First, there are only two other accounts of selection by lot in the OT. The first is in Joshua 7, the Achan episode; the other is in 1 Sam. 14:38–44, Jonathan's violation of Saul's oath. Neither is a "good story," and both contaminate the selection of Saul. He has hidden himself, as Achan had hidden the booty (Josh. 7:20–22). Second, the story in 1 Samuel 10 borders on the trivial, if indeed it is not a parody, particularly the detail of Saul's hiding among the baggage. This is not the depiction of the king that chapter 8 leads us to expect, nor is the comment on Saul's stature in accord with what 1 Sam. 9:2 leads us to anticipate. Is Saul remarkable—"There is none like him among all the people"—just because he is so tall?

Similar to 1 Sam. 9:11–14, 1 Sam. 10:20–23 build our expectation that a decisive event is imminent and then veer off. Saul is not explicitly established as king; remarkably, he is not even mentioned by name in v. 24, "the moment of decision."

> Samuel said to all the people, "Do you see him whom the Lord has chosen? There is none like him among all the people." The people shouted, "Long live the king!" Samuel told the people *the justice of the kingship* [*mishpat hammelukah*], and he wrote it in the book and laid it up before the Lord. Samuel sent all the people away, each one to his home. (1 Sam. 10:24–25)

"Long live the king!" Is this a specific wish for Saul or an affirmation about any king? Again I note that Saul is not named in these crucial verses.

This is the only mention in 1 Samuel of the Lord choosing (*bachar*) the king; this is in accord with the Mosaic dictum in Deut. 17:15. "You may indeed set as king over you him whom the Lord your God will choose." "Do you see?" in comparison with 1 Sam. 16:1—"I have seen [chosen, provided] for myself a king among his sons"—may be asking for the Israelites' assent to the Lord's choice. On the other hand, it may be another sign of Samuel's reluctance; he asks a question and does not make a declaration.

Samuel wrote the *mishpat hammelukah* in the book and deposited it before the Lord. This is a reflex of the Mosaic directive: "When he sits on the throne of his kingdom, he will write for himself in a book a copy of this law . . . and it will be with him and he will read it all the days of his life" (Deut. 17:18–19). However, in 1 Samuel 10, it is not Mosaic law but an undefined *mishpat hammelukah* that is written in the book; there is no mention that the king should read it. Nor is this necessarily identical with the *mishpat hammelek* of chapter 8. Perhaps Samuel is deliberately avoiding the word "king" (*melek*), or he may be stating fundamental principles before proceeding to set up an individual king. What is *mishpat* in this instance—justice, custom, or due? Is it meant to be a positive, negative, or neutral statement?

As at the end of the Ramah assembly in chapter 8, the people are dispersed from Mizpah. "Saul also went to his home at Gibeah." Saul is connected with and contaminated by the events of Judges 19–21. "With him went men of valor whose hearts God had touched." Is this similar to Saul's being given another heart by God? Do we assume that this divine "touch" increases their valor and loyalty to Saul? Do they stand in contrast to the "worthless fellows" (*bene beliyya`al*) who say,

"How can this one save us?" Gibeah has probably changed in many ways since the times depicted in Judges, but it is still inhabited by worthless fellows (Judg. 19:22).

"How can this one save us?"—in the mouths of these "worthless fellows," this is a rejection of Saul's ability to deliver Israel. Out of context, it is a pregnant question, "How, in fact, is Saul to save Israel?" The next chapter provides an answer of sorts but still leaves open the question of Saul as king, i.e., Saul can save Israel as "judge," but will he be able to as king? Or is there a hint here that "king" and "judge" share many characteristics and duties?

1 Samuel 11

Saul's Finest Hour

1 Sam. 11:1–11 mark another major shift in setting and tone. This time the narrative will be clear and definite; there is an obvious threat and a decisive resolution. Yet the story stands in strange isolation from its context, both preceding and succeeding. It shares much with the stories of deliverance by the judges, especially Jephthah, since he defeats the Ammonites (Judg. 11:1–33). It is the Philistines, not the Ammonites, who pose the serious threat to all Israel and Judah in 1 Samuel; Saul defeats a Transjordanian enemy in Trasnjordan. As in Judges, the people are faced with a foreign oppressor who is threatening to "put disgrace upon all Israel."

When Saul hears of the Ammonite challenge, "the spirit of God came mightily upon Saul . . . and his anger was kindled." He slaughters a yoke of oxen and sends the pieces to Israel—"Whoever does not come out after Saul and Samuel, so will it be done to his oxen!" Saul shows respect for Samuel, but he acts at his own discretion. Unlike as in Judges, Saul marshals the forces of Israel and Judah, not of just a few local tribes. "The dread of the Lord fell upon the people, and they came out as one man." Israel goes out "as one man," and the battle leaves the Ammonites in the opposite condition. The Israelites "cut down the Ammonites until the heat of the day; those who survived were scattered so that no two of them were left together" (1 Sam. 11:11). Saul can repeat Jephthah's military success over the Ammonites, and he can also repeat the needless vow that endangers his child's life.

1 Sam. 11:1–11 intone a pattern from Judges. Saul appears more as judge, i.e., a leader at a particular moment of crisis, than as king, i.e., a permanent, institutional leader. However, Saul is not explicitly

called "judge" or "king." The clarity and resolution of the story are notable, and I regard the story as a type of paradigm—the strong, successful Saul. (This quality is probably signaled by the fantastic size of Saul's army—330,000 soldiers.)[3] Practically, "paradigm" means that I will refer back to the story in the ensuing material, especially that on 1 Samuel 13–15.

The positive and decisive impact is offset by two points. Faced with the Ammonite challenge, the elders of Jabesh-gilead ask for a seven-day respite to seek help; "then if there is no savior [*moshi`a*] for us, we will come out to you." Saul's deliverance of Jabesh-gilead is remembered by them when they retrieve Saul's body and "fast for seven days" (1 Sam. 31:11–13). Thus Saul's greatest moment is marred by anticipation of his death. There is a savior for Jabesh-gilead when attacked by the Ammonites, but there was none when attacked by the Israelites. The Ammonites threaten to gouge out the right eyes of the people, but the Israelites smote "the inhabitants of Jabesh-gilead with the edge of the sword; also the women and the little ones" (Judg. 21:10). Saul's greatest moment is tarnished by an event from the past.

"Saul Will Reign over Us!"
1 Sam. 11:12–15 are troublesome, problematic verses that form a fitting close to chapters 9–11, themselves so troublesome and problematic. Vv. 12 and 14 are more difficult, with v. 12 the most difficult.

> The people said to Samuel, "Who is saying, 'Saul will reign over us'? Give us the men that we may put them to death." And Saul said, "Not a man will be put to death this day for today the Lord has wrought deliverance in Israel." (1 Sam. 11:12–13)

Two associated queries that I note and do not pursue—how does this stand in relation to the preceding in terms of time and place? "The people [*ha`am*]"—is this the whole people, or is this the army? *Ha`am* can mean *the people* or *the army*. If it is the army, the scene apparently follows close after the defeat of the Ammonites; if it is the people, the scene could be elsewhere and later.

V. 12 asks death for those who are saying, "Saul will reign [*yimlok*] over us." This is most difficult to square with the preceding and subsequent contexts, particularly 1 Sam. 10:24—"All the people shouted, 'Long live the king!' "—and 1 Sam. 11:15—"All the people . . . made Saul king [*himlik*]."

[3] It does not matter whether this is an accurate and exact number, i.e., 330,000 men, or whether it represents military units, i.e., "thousands," which may be far less in actual numbers. Three hundred thirty "thousands" is still 110 times more than three "thousands."

Most translations and commentaries take the statement as a question—"Shall Saul reign over us?" (*RSV*)—or add a negative particle on the basis of the Greek—"Saul shall not reign over us!" (McCarter 1980b, p. 199). The people's statement is a reference to the worthless fellows who said, "How can this one save us?" Saul has shown that he is the Lord's chosen by his victory; therefore the men have slandered the Lord himself and should be executed. The question is addressed to Samuel, not Saul, which accords with Samuel's status in 1 Sam. 10:17–25. Finally, I find the first proposal rhetorically satisfying in that a text so marked by questions that can be read as assertions has an assertion that can be read as a question.

In line with this particular reading, Saul is faced with a challenge to his rule at its inception, but responds magnanimously and thereby demonstrates his authority to pass judgment in a sacral matter. He agrees with 1 Sam. 10:24—"Long live the king!"—as he opts for life over death.

This is a plausible, but not necessary, reading. The "worthless fellows" say nothing of Saul as king (1 Sam. 10:27); the only ones who apparently do that are the people (1 Sam. 10:24). The worthless ones are explicitly questioning Saul's military leadership, his ability to save them, not his qualifications as king or leader beyond military issues. In addition, the people in 1 Sam. 11:12 use a participle, "Who is it who is saying"; they are not referring solely to a past event.

If we accept the Hebrew text as translated initially, then we are forced to reread 1 Sam. 10:17–27 and, indeed, all of 1 Sam. 9:1– 11:11 with a critical eye, looking for some possible explanation for this bizarre demand from the people. They make it of Samuel, not Saul; perhaps they have been impressed by Samuel, especially by the denunciation in 1 Sam. 10:17–19, and are now attempting to recognize his authority once more. 1 Sam. 11:1–11 is a demonstration of Saul's military ability, and that is sufficient. Who needs a king when the people have Samuel and General Saul? Saul as *nagid*, not *melek*, could be included in the discussion at this point.

"King" and "kingship" are here, but there is a serious question of proper procedure, of "the justice of the kingship," and channels, i.e., Samuel. The men of 1 Sam. 11:12 want to make Saul king prematurely and on their own. Thus, at the close of chapter 10, Samuel designates Saul as the Lord's chosen but not yet as *melek*. In any case, Saul intervenes on his own, perhaps in unauthorized fashion or in accord with 1 Sam. 10:7—"Do whatever your hand finds to do"—but not quite so magnanimously as in the previous interpretation, since now he spares those who support him. To those who once said, "Life for the king," he now says, "Life for you."

We can also introduce an element of personal competition here between Samuel and Saul. Full development of this line would add to the above readings and would not necessarily contradict or alter them. The people make their demand of Samuel, thereby ignoring Saul's feat in 1 Sam. 11:1–11. Saul is not to be ignored. He intervenes and shunts Samuel aside. Samuel does not take this lightly. He proposes to go to Gilgal, one of his "judge cities," to move the action to his home territory. The people speak of Saul reigning. Samuel speaks of renewing the kingship, thereby ignoring Saul and perhaps insinuating that Saul has damaged the kingship. I will trace the conclusion to this line of reading after discussing other possible readings of v. 14.

> (14) Samuel said to the people, "Come, let us go to Gilgal so that we may renew the kingship [*melukah*]." (15) All the people went to Gilgal, and they made Saul king there before the Lord in Gilgal. They sacrificed there peace offerings before the Lord, and Saul and all the men of Israel rejoiced greatly there.

Why Gilgal? I just noted one reading that is not flattering to Samuel. On the other hand, Samuel could be impressed with Saul's victory and demonstration of his authority and now be ready to declare Saul king. A king was demanded at Ramah and designated at Mizpah. Samuel is choosing yet another site to make Saul king; perhaps he is still smarting from the people's rejection of him at Ramah.

Why "renew" (*chiddesh*)? The word generally refers to rebuilding, restoring, and recreating after serious damage or total destruction. How has the kingship been damaged or destroyed? By Saul, as Samuel may insinuate? If so, how? Is it something to do with 1 Sam. 10:26–27, 11:1–11, or 11:13? Has Saul acted prematurely and out of order? By the people's demand in 1 Sam. 11:12? Or by the worthless ones' question, challenge, in 1 Sam. 10:27? Perhaps the term "to renew" here has a weaker sense of reaffirming and renewing at a later date; it is not a matter of damage but of time—let us again say that we will have a king. To pursue these questions more fully would take us again over the familiar (?) terrain of chapters (8) 9–11—what do we know about the "matter of the kingship"?

"They Made Saul King"

1 Sam. 11:15 closes the episode and chapters 9–11 with an allusion to and fulfillment of 1 Sam. 8:22: "Obey their voice and make them a king [*himlik melek*]." Finally Saul is explicitly made king; there is no doubt of this. But the verse is reticent about other issues. No further light is cast on renewal or on kingship. If Samuel was trying to shift

the action to his home territory, the result is ambiguous, since "all the people . . . made Saul king." Does this include Samuel or not? Is he being shunted aside, or is the emphasis being put on unity? Is this a subtle way of noting the transition from Samuel to Saul? The verse opens with Samuel distinct from the people and closes with Saul distinct—"Saul and all the men of Israel." The possibility of rivalry between Samuel and Saul is not resolved.

Conclusion

It is difficult to go beyond chapter 11, since the closing verses are so intransigent, so resistant to closure. And their resistance forces a continual and critical rereading of chapters (8) 9–11. However we understand v. 12, we justify the interpretation by referring back to specific passages that we then read in light of the reading of 1 Sam. 11:12–15. In respect to the king and kingship, chapters 9–11 have produced little certain extra knowledge. Saul is king, but we still have been told nothing about the "matter of the kingship" or the "justice of the kingship." Indirectly, the connection between "king" and military leadership, explicit in 1 Sam. 8:20, has been confirmed, and there have been hints that the king will be like a judge, as in Judges. The latter, however, may connote only military leadership.

In respect to Samuel and "prophet," there has been an increase even though the knowledge may be complex and not broken into definite categories. Much of the complexity and ambiguity stems from three elements—Samuel, prophet, *nabi´*—that are associated, although they are neither identical nor rigorously distinguishable. That is, Samuel is a powerful leader who fills various roles. Many of these can be attributed to a prophet in the sense of someone who can declare and interpret a word of the Lord to the people. The latter sense is not always associated with the *nabi´*; *nabi´* is in Deuteronomy 18, 34, and 1 Samuel 3 but not in 1 Sam. 9:9 or 10:5–13. 1 Sam. 3:20 calls Samuel a *nabi´*, but the statement about the *nabi´* and *ro´eh* (seer) in 1 Sam. 9:9 has little or nothing to do with most of the portrayal of Samuel.

Rather than focus solely on the incommensurability of these three, let us shift to a more positive note. Samuel is a decisive and powerful figure who mediates between the Lord and the people; he transmits the respective words of each to the other, particularly in chapter 8. He intercedes with God for the people; he judges the people, perhaps without the guidance of a direct word from the Lord. He is their recognized leader, even if it means appointing his own successor and thereby displacing himself. He can predict future events. He carries out the divine commission to appoint Saul and David, even though his motivation and purpose for the actions are not given.

Samuel can be called "prophet," with "prophet" defined as one who does what Samuel does; from another point of view, "prophet" must be redefined as we encounter the different aspects of Samuel. In the latter view, we begin with an understanding of "prophet" derived from previous books, especially Deuteronomy and the portrayal of Moses and the prophet like him, and adjust or interpret it. Whether Samuel, Moses, or this developed understanding of "prophet" is called *nabi'* is not crucial. Samuel is called *nabi'* once, while Moses, the "prophet of prophets" in that future prophets are like him, is called *nabi'* twice—in Deut. 18:15–18 and 34:10. That is, we have *nabi'*s who are prophets, *nabi'*s who are not prophets, and prophets who are not *nabi'*s.

The issue is not with *nabi'*, the concept of "prophet," or Samuel but with the question, "What is a prophet?" The "what is . . ." presumes a definable essence, a "what," i.e., a statement of the prophetic nature that will apply to figures such as Moses, Samuel, Nathan, Elijah, Isaiah, etc., and allow us to exclude other characters and other actions of a prophet that are deemed unprophetic, e.g., what may be Samuel's showmanship in chapters 9–10. However, what we have are characters—here Moses and Samuel—who speak and act in a variety of ways, with some shared and some not. They are prophets, and what they do is prophetic. Other prophets will arise, and what they will do is prophetic, although it may be different from, if not in sharp contrast to, what Moses and Samuel do.

Samuel is not a disembodied prophet or leader of whatever type. He is a human character whose "official" duties and authority will always be intermingled with "personal" emotions, opinions, and reactions. The mix cannot be undone so that "official" and "personal" aspects can be separated and described in isolation from each other. Since it is misleading to speak of the two as separate, I have put the terms in quotes. The same comments hold for Saul and for the relationship between Samuel and Saul; 1 Samuel 8–11 are not simply a treatise on "prophet," "king," and "kingship" but are a narrative involving Samuel and Saul. Their opinions of and reactions to each other, and to others, including the people and the Lord, have to be taken into account. However, the text frustrates any attempt to reach a definitive understanding, because it produces so little explicit information on either Samuel or Saul; my reading of 1 Samuel 8–11 is dotted with questions and with possible readings of the reactions and motivations of Samuel and Saul. I do not repeat them here, but will refer to them, re-ask them, in the analysis of 1 Samuel 12 and 13–15.

These concluding points are transitional. The last half of 1 Samuel narrates the stories of Saul, David, Michal, and Jonathan in the same mode as the first half. Attempts to take them as disguised treatises on "king," "kingship," and succession will be constantly frustrated. "What is a king?" will lead us into the same complexity and undecidability as "What is a prophet?"

1 Samuel 12

Samuel, The Orator

Chapter 11 closes with reference to the final verse of chapter 8; chapter 12 opens with reference to the same verse and then retraces much of the terrain of chapter 8—the elder Samuel, his sons, and the request for a king. Chapter 12, however, covers the ground in such a different fashion that we may wonder if it is the same ground. In the analysis, I emphasize the characterization of Samuel; Samuel's "review" of past history and his authority; the relations between Samuel, the king, the Lord, and the people; and the development of Samuel's speeches.

1 Sam. 12:1 stands in uncertain relation to 1 Sam. 11:14–15 in terms of time and setting but not of characters. Samuel stands alone and speaks to "all Israel," not just the people or the army; Saul is in the background and is not mentioned by name. Samuel's concerns are more general and longer-range than just Saul and his reign.

Samuel opens by informing the people that he has responded to their demand and to the Lord's command in chapter 8; he then turns to the present.

> Look, I have obeyed your voice in all that you said to me, and I have made a king [´amlik melek] over you. And now, here is the king going before you. I am old and grey. Here are my sons with you. I have gone before you from my youth until this day.

Although the statement seems straightforward, a variety of readings are possible in view of Samuel's motivation. I follow two different characterizations of Samuel, which I sketched in the reading of chapter 8; these "two Samuels" are poles, and possible readings of Samuel accord with either or with some mixture of them.

At one pole is the authoritative and stern prophet who declares his innocence and the people's guilt. They have requested a human king and have thereby rejected their true king, the Lord. Samuel's denunciation is severe but not unyielding. The people and their king will have a future—to be determined by their obedience to the Lord's word. This is the "good" Samuel, the Lord's and the people's established prophet and leader. At the other pole is the authoritarian, harsh, and bitter leader who is forced to appoint his own replacement. He does it with resentment and acrimony. The people's request is evil, because it is a rejection of him. His denunciation of them is more personal polemic than divine word. At relevant points I will note how the different views of Samuel can affect our reading of chapter 12.

The opening scene, 1 Sam. 12:1–5, can be read as an expression of Samuel's sarcasm and bitterness. He presents the people with their leaders—the king who will take much of what is theirs, an old man, and the old man's corrupt sons. Samuel declares his innocence of judicial fraud and bribery, and the people accept the declaration. Yet Samuel's declaration is irrelevant, since it is Samuel as "kingmaker," as prophet, as the one who speaks for God and to God on the people's behalf, who is at stake here. Samuel may be an honest judge who follows the word of the Lord in Deuteronomy 16–17, but this has nothing to do with the context, particularly the speech in 1 Sam. 12:6–17.

On the other hand, this is a solemn and proper transfer of power. The focus is on Samuel, since he is the kingmaker at this stage. His authority and tenure are affirmed vis-à-vis other leaders and the people. V. 5 is the climatic moment, as the king is called the Lord's anointed and is associated with the Lord over against Samuel and the people.

This distinction, this possibility of portraying Samuel in a variety of ways, could be traced throughout the chapter, but I note the "different Samuels" at only a few relevant points. Otherwise I restrict myself to a general observation. The overall interpretation or reading of chapter 12, particularly Samuel's speeches in vv. 6–17 and 20–25, is in large part determined by our understanding of Samuel. If he is the bitter old leader, then a good deal of these speeches, especially the denunciations of the people, can be ascribed to this character trait, i.e., their "meaning" is that Samuel is bitter. We then do not have to inquire further about their relevance to the narrative, e.g., has the Lord in fact been rejected, is the request a serious sin? However, these questions must be asked and pursued if we assume that Samuel is the Lord's austere and loyal prophet. As noted at the close of the discussion of chapter 11, we are not dealing with a disembodied prophet but with a human being whose every act and speech are to be read and judged from several vantage points. How are we to decide if the request is a sin if we cannot first decide whether the accusation is an accusation or an expression of bitterness?

First Speech (1 Sam. 12:6–17)

Samuel's first speech begins as an elaboration of his address to the people at Mizpah in 1 Sam. 10:17–19. He gives more detail on "all the kingdoms who were oppressing you" and quotes Israel's confession that the people have sinned by forsaking the Lord and serving the Baals and the Ashtaroth. The rehearsal is reminiscent of Judg. 10:10–16, especially the citation of the people's confession in 1 Sam. 12:10. However, in 1 Samuel 12, the plea is presented in a conditional mode, "Deliver us out of the hand of our enemies *so that* we may serve you." Samuel alters the Judges narrative and hammers home the point that he himself is one of the deliverers whom the people are putting aside. "The Lord sent Jerubbaal and Bedan and Jephthah and Samuel and delivered you from the hand of your enemies."

"Bedan," unknown to Judges, signals the alteration; this is not a literal and accurate summary of Judges, taking "literal and accurate" according to common usage. However, noting the alteration is not automatically accusing Samuel of willful deception, of distorting the "true story" solely to serve his own present purposes. No one, including Moses and the Lord himself, ever "literally and accurately" summarizes or reports the "true" or "original" story. For example, Moses' recital of the events at Sinai in Deuteronomy 5, 9, and 10 diverges significantly from the narrative in Exodus 19–24 by major and minor omissions and additions; even the Ten Commandments are altered. In Josh. 24:2–13, Joshua quotes the Lord, and the Lord's summary of the past is close, but not exact. Finally, the Lord's image in Exod. 19:4—"how I bore you on eagles's wings and brought you to myself"—does not accord with the events at Marah, Meribah, and Rephidim.

The result is not necessarily a questioning of a person's authority or reliability, his trustworthiness, for it can be the reverse. An important aspect of authority and reliability is the right to change and alter, to interpret, a preceding account, law, or whatever, in view of present circumstances. I employ "necessarily" and "can be," because we are in a zone attempting to work between the poles of literal accuracy (truth) and distortion (falsehood). Samuel's rendition of the past, particularly of the attack of Nahash the Ammonite, like the Lord's in Exodus 19 and Moses' in Deuteronomy, is told in such a way as to serve the speaker's present purposes; it is a tendentious distortion. Yet, in the examples cited, there is no challenge, explicit or implicit, to the Lord, to Moses, or to Samuel on the grounds that they do not have their facts straight. Thus "tendentious distortion" is too strong and is inappropriate, since it is not balanced in the OT text by the other pole of literal accuracy and truth. No one is praised for telling a story accurately. (This is separate from, although related to, the question of what Samuel's present purposes might be.)

This is not to declare the distinction between accuracy and distortion meaningless and false, since that would be judging one dichotomy by another. It is a questioning of the distinction's origin and its effect. Extensive pursuit of the dichotomy between literal and accurate representation and distorted and false representation would involve us more in the history and present status of biblical interpretation than in a reading of 1 Samuel. This is beyond our present scope.

The above point is the obverse of the earlier comments on the lack of relevance of a rigorous dichotomy between the literal and total fulfillment of a "prophecy" and its lack of fulfillment. In 1 Kings 2:27, the narrator informs us that "Solomon expelled Abiathar from being priest to the Lord, thus fulfilling the word of the Lord he had spoken against the house of Eli in Shiloh." Is this a reliable statement about the literal fulfillment of a prediction, or is this the narrator's interpretation of a particular event as the fulfillment of that prediction? I opt for the latter.

We are presented with powerful examples of the Derridean dictum that repetition produces alteration and alteration produces identity. There would be no concern with an "original" report, speech, law, etc., if there were no repetition. The repetitions of OT narrative, in all their variety, put into question the notions of "original," "first," "primary"; in this particular instance, we put into question the search for the word of the Lord if that search is undertaken in the hope of ascertaining the first or original word that was lost or distorted through time, tradition, or interpretation. The first word cannot be found, even though we may never cease to search for it.

> When you saw that Nahash king of the Ammonites came against you, you said to me, "No, but a king will rule over us," and the Lord your God was (is) your king. (1 Sam. 12:12)

Samuel changes the narrative of events in the distant past and even those of the recent past, perhaps only a day or two before. There are three divergences from the tale in chapter 11. Samuel does not mention Saul or his victory; indeed, he mentions no victory. Second, he associates the demand for a king with the incident, transferring the people's request from Ramah (1 Sam. 8:19). Finally, he asserts that "the Lord your God is your king," implying that the people have rejected the Lord through their demand.

In vv. 14–15, Samuel presents the people with the choice of obeying or not obeying the Lord; the king moves into the background and

merges with the people. Samuel now stands in association with the
Lord against the people and their king; this is a marked change from
v. 5—"If both you and the king who rules over you follow the Lord
your God" (1 Sam. 12:14). The choice is not presented in rigorous
terms. There is no "then" in the Hebrew text to balance the "if," "If
you will fear the Lord and serve him . . . if both you and your king . . .
follow the Lord . . . ." (*RSV* and other translations add, "it will be well"
or some similar phrase to produce a "then.")

The lack of an apodosis occurs again in vv. 20–25; Samuel offers no
specific benefit for Israel's serving the Lord with all her heart. Is
Samuel implying that the people will not fear and serve the Lord? Is
his resentment showing (he simply will not connect the king with
things going well)? Does Samuel presume that the people know the
benefits that will accrue from their obedience? He wants to stress
obedience, not reward.

The other pole of the choice—"But if you will not listen to the voice
of the Lord"—is followed not by a harsh and final punishment but by
the assertion, "then the hand of the Lord will be against you and your
fathers." With the closing phrase, Samuel returns to the Lord's response in 1 Sam. 8:7–8 and fits the request for a king and his establishment into the traditional history of disobedience—"According to
all the deeds which they have done, from the day I brought them up
out of Egypt, even to this day, forsaking me and serving other gods"
(1 Sam. 8:7–8). The king slips further into the background.

Samuel asks the people to stand to witness "this great thing which
the Lord is about to do before your eyes." It is the wheat harvest, and
Samuel calls upon the Lord to "send thunder and rain," which would
be extraordinary events at this time of year. Samuel accents the result
of the display and concludes his first speech. "Know and see that your
wickedness is great which you have done in the eyes of the Lord by
asking for yourselves a king" (1 Sam. 12:17). The full Judges
formula—to do what is evil (wicked) in the eyes of the Lord—is
intoned for the first time since Judg. 13:1, although Samuel speaks
almost immediately to cancel its application and relevance.

The Sign (1 Sam. 12:18–19)
The sign is fulfilled. "Samuel called upon the Lord, and the Lord sent
thunder and rain that day; all the people greatly feared the Lord and
Samuel." No mention is made of "king" or Saul, even though Samuel
just referred to the people's request for a king. This may be where
Samuel would like to leave things, i.e., with only himself standing
between the people and the Lord—"the people greatly feared the
Lord and Samuel"—but he cannot, because there is a king on the
scene.

The people confess. "Pray for your servants to the Lord your God that we may not die. We have added to all our sins this evil of asking for ourselves a king." The people do not entertain the option of taking back their request or of serving only Samuel and not a king. They include the king in the history of disobedience: "We have *added to all our sins* the evil of asking for ourselves a king." "Add to" (*yasap*) recalls the "continue to" (*yasap*) of Judg. 13:1, *et al.*

Second Speech (1 Sam. 12:20–25)
Samuel assumes the history of disobedience and looks to a future that is free of disobedience and evil. He begins with a paradoxical assertion. *"Fear not; you have done all this evil,* yet do not turn aside from following the Lord, but serve the Lord with all your heart." According to 1 Sam. 7:3, the people are doing the latter, at least in the sense of not worshipping the Baals and the Ashtaroth. Yet "all this evil" is in the past, and Samuel's concern is the future. In a rare use of the word *tohu*, Samuel admonishes the people:

> Do not go after vain things [*tohu*] which cannot profit or save because they are vain [*tohu*]. Indeed, the Lord will not cast away his people for the sake of his great name because it has pleased the Lord to make you a people for himself. (1 Sam. 12:21–22)

In context, "vain things" can refer to other gods, kings, or any type of human institution that "cannot profit or save."

Vv. 20–22 combine, in oxymoronic fashion, themes of justice and mercy. Israel has done all this evil, but the people are not to fear. They should serve the Lord and not go after vain things, because the Lord will not reject his people. Indeed, Samuel himself, in a twist of Eli's "question" in 1 Sam. 2:25, assures the people that he will not "sin against the Lord by ceasing to intercede [*hithpallel*] for them." Moreover, he will instruct [*yarah*] them "in the good and right way." Is Samuel attempting to hold on to some last vestiges of power? Is he stepping aside grudgingly and resentfully? Or is this a proper handing over of the reins? Does Samuel step aside gracefully? His work as a major political leader and kingmaker is now over, and he has declared the word of the Lord to the people and to the king. Nevertheless, he will continue as prophet and judge, in the judicial sense, by interceding for the people and by instructing them in the good and proper way (Deut. 17:10–13).

Samuel mixes justice—"Only fear the Lord and serve him faithfully with all your heart"—and mercy—"For consider what great things he has done for you." His final assertion "contradicts" the assurance of v. 22—"The Lord will not cast away his people"—by returning to the conditional pattern of vv. 14–15 and with a far harsher "then." "If

you still do wickedly, *then* both you and your king will be swept away."
Continuing to sin and adding to one's sins (*yasap*) will lead to being
swept away (*sapah*).

Summary
Samuel does not operate with a strict dichotomy between justice and
mercy; he mixes them as, indeed, most of 1 Samuel does. In contrast
to Judges, the "gap" we encounter in 1 Samuel with the people's
request and the establishment of a king is how it all appears in "the
eyes of the Lord"; is it good, bad, or indifferent? If the question
cannot be decided, then how are we to speak with confidence of
either justice or mercy? Samuel and the people, in 1 Sam. 12:17–19,
regard the request as evil—nothing is said of the king himself—and
then cancel its effect by including it in the already long history of sin,
thereby putting it behind them, then turning to the future for hope
and life. The people have sinned constantly and are told, "Fear not!"
Past sin can lead to life; past grace can lead to destruction. "See what
great things he has done for you, but if you still do wickedly you will
be swept away." To repeat, if we cannot decide whether what the
people are doing is good or evil in the eyes of the Lord, then how do
we decide whether God's further actions in 1 Samuel are just or
merciful? On the other hand, the text makes the attempt into a
theme. It talks too frequently of sin, evil, good, judgment, etc., for us
to ignore the questions even if they are unanswerable. "Unanswerable" does not mean "unaskable."

Digression: Succession and Successors
The theme of succession is prominent in 1 Samuel. Samuel succeeds
Eli; Saul succeeds Samuel. A central question for Samuel is the manner
of succession—the designation and final coronation of Saul. Was it
proper and effective even though multi-staged and time-consuming?
Was it unnecessarily drawn out and made ineffective by its obscurity? I
have alluded to the succession scene in Deuteronomy 31, where there is
talk of witnesses and a book and where Moses delivers a warning,
including a forecast of future judgment. The comparison with 1 Samuel 8–12 could be extended, but I focus on some differences that come
to light in view of Deuteronomy 31.

   Joshua is appointed Moses' successor while the latter is still alive and
actually succeeds him as leader only after Moses' death. He carries on
Moses' work. "Joshua the son of Nun was filled with a wise spirit for
Moses had laid his hands upon him; the Israelites obeyed him and did
as the Lord had commanded Moses" (Deut. 34:9). The line of command continues in Joshua. The Lord has commanded Moses; Moses

has commanded Joshua; Joshua commands the people; the people obey Joshua.

This is the picture of the book of Joshua; Judges presents the opposite. Here there is no succession to Joshua or to the individual judges. The disastrous attempt of Abimelech to succeed his father Gideon underscores the break in succession. Nor is there any clear line of command. People are frequently ignorant of what is going on and of who—the Lord or God?—is acting. The close, Judges 17–21, portrays a time when there are no individual leaders, judges, kings, or otherwise.

Joshua and Judges do share the theme of a great decrease in the importance of the cultic order, especially the importance of the priests. The house of Eli may linger on into 1 Kings, but neither it nor any of its members has a significant role to play. In this instance, it is preferable to speak not of successors to, but of replacements for, the priests who were so central to Exodus-Deuteronomy. Priestly functions, particularly those of a military and judicial nature, are transferred to others, including judges, prophets, and kings. The transfer is piecemeal and spread over time.

Joshua and Judges can be viewed as opposites, with 1 Samuel falling somewhere in between. Eli is a priest and also a judge who "judged Israel forty years" (1 Sam. 4:18). Samuel judges Israel and includes himself in the line of judges in 1 Sam. 12:11. He is closely associated with Eli and perhaps raised by Eli as a stepchild. Although he is a fitting successor to Eli, chapter 3—Samuel's call and its aftermath—deals with Samuel not as priest or judge but as prophet and mediator of the divine word. This makes Samuel more like a delayed successor of Moses. Like Moses and Joshua, Eli dies; Samuel is then primary as prophet and judge (1 Samuel 7–8). In this connection, the battle of Ebenezer in chapter 4 is decisive, since Eli and his sons die on the same day.

The succession from Samuel to Saul is much more complicated, since Samuel plays an active, although equivocal, role in the appointment of Saul and then remains on the scene. This results in the conflict of chapters 13–16. Additional complications arise, because three individuals or groups are involved in Saul's designation—the Lord, Samuel, *ha`am* (the people, Israel, the army); the relationships between them can vary and are not always ascertainable, and what Saul is designated as, *nagid* or *melek*, varies. Finally, there is the fact that Samuel plays several roles, particularly those of judge and prophet, and apparently Saul succeeds only as king (judge), although there is reason to think that "king" can include some of the roles of the prophet.

The situation is complicated even more when Samuel denounces Saul in chapters 13 and 15 and declares Saul's kingship at an end, i.e., he nullifies the succession. Another successor, David, is appointed, and for a while all three are on the scene. The line of command and process of succession are not always clear in 1 Samuel, even when determinable. This is important in the subsequent chapters.

· 4 ·

1 SAMUEL 13-15

What Have You Done?

I treat chapters 13–15 as a quasi-unit, since they can be grouped around the failure and rejection of King Saul. A "why" is provided that is, simultaneously, an explanation and a question—this is why Saul was rejected; why was Saul rejected? I note wordplay and allusions that point beyond the present narrative. They are not meant to resolve issues but to re-emphasize that the individual stories belong to larger networks of analogies. Texts disperse one into the other on both literal and thematic levels.

Much of my analysis of Saul presumes and frequently refers to the reading of chapters 8–12, especially chapters 9–11. What is Saul's reaction to the events and speeches in these chapters? What is his opinion of Samuel and of himself as king? I could develop a large number of different Sauls, depending on the answers to these questions; however, I generally restrict myself to two polar views, which are heuristic and not the only two characterizations of Saul available. The character of actors in the OT is best discussed in terms of a continuum or spectrum marked not by discrete and distinguishable points but by imperceptible changes—a flowing with gradations and mergings. The question is not either/or but both/and.

At one end is a "strong" Saul—the Saul in Chapter 11. He is an able and self-assured leader of the people who knows that he has been made king by Samuel at the people's request with the Lord's sanction. He acknowledges Samuel's continuing role vis-à-vis the people and himself. Confusion and conflict in his relationship with Samuel will cause Saul problems in chapters 13 and 15. On the negative side, the strong Saul can be arrogant and a "willful sinner." At the other end of the spectrum is a "weak" Saul—overwhelmed by Samuel and by Samuel's speeches and signs. This Saul is intimidated by Samuel and unself-confident as king. He is more the bungler than the sinner.

The division into two Sauls is complicated by the role of others. The "weak" Saul can be seen in at least two lights. He is a weak, ineffectual leader who cannot deal with the success and power of others, particularly Samuel, Jonathan, and David; he seriously underestimates his own position and authority as king. On the other hand, he is not so much weak as he is a man with too many powerful opponents—again Samuel, Jonathan, and David—and too few friends. He is overwhelmed by Samuel not because of his own weakness but because of Samuel's strength. An analogous situation, in reverse, is evident in the "strong" Saul's relations with others.

A Feat of Arms

1 Sam. 13:1 is textually troubled in the matter of Saul's age and perhaps in the length of his reign, although two years is not an unlikely figure and would add a precipitous quality to the nature of Saul's decline and fall. In contrast to the situation in 1 Sam. 7:13–14, a state of conflict between Israel and the Philistines is presumed; we may be in the waning days of Samuel, when the hand of the Lord is no longer against the Philistines. The situation was alluded to in 1 Sam. 10:5: "You will come to Gibeath-elohim where there is a Philistine prefect [*natsib*]." It is a Philistine prefect (*natsib*) whom Jonathan kills. (*RSV* and others translate *natsib* as "garrison.")

Saul is king, no longer the charismatic hero of chapter 11; he is now facing a long-term campaign, not a one-shot victory over the Ammonites. A battle will not win this war. The changed situation is clear from the numbers. Saul mustered 330,000 men against the Ammonites but only 3,000 against the Philistines—a decrease by a factor of 110. The decrease also marks this as a different type of narrative from the paradigmatic quality of chapter 11. Chapter 13 shares little with the progress of events in the defeat of the Ammonites; gone is the decisiveness of that victory.

The initial action is by Jonathan, not by Saul or the army. "Jonathan slew the Philistine prefect who was in Geba, and the Philistines heard." In response, Saul "sounded the trumpet throughout the land, 'Let the Hebrews hear.' " The statement is terse. Twice we have the verb "to hear" without a sound or report that is heard. Saul's sounding the trumpet is not an explicit call to arms and battle. The result is "all Israel *heard* it said that Saul had killed the Philistine prefect and also that Israel had become odious to the Philistines." Does this reflect the right of the king to claim credit for others' feats, the popular crediting to the king of such feats, the garbling of the report as it spread through the land, Saul's deliberate attempt to take credit for Jonathan's feat for his own aggrandizement, or his inability to accept the success of one of his generals, even if it is his own son?

With the introduction of Saul and Jonathan, we are presented with the possibility of strained relations between them, particularly the possibility that Jonathan resents his father's getting credit for his deed. Here we can glimpse a spectrum by noting the large number of possible readings of Jonathan's resentment—from nonexistent to powerful. I list above five ways of interpreting "all Israel heard it said that Saul had killed the Philistine prefect"; only the final two paint Saul in dark colors, but all five could lead to Jonathan's resentment. He can resent Saul's getting credit regardless of Saul's actual intentions and regardless of how Jonathan perceives those intentions.

Gilgal

"All the people were called out to join Saul at Gilgal." The formation is passive; it is not explicit that Saul calls the muster. This is a contrast with chapter 11, where he calls out the army "after Saul and Samuel." No mention is made of Samuel in 1 Sam. 13:4. Why Gilgal? Does Saul remember the joyous times there when he was made king and hope for a similar victory and joy? Does he remember Samuel's directive or command to go to Gilgal and to wait for seven days? Does he think of Gilgal as the old camp for the conquest of the land? Or is Gilgal as far away from the Philistines as he can get without crossing the Jordan? We can ascribe one or various combinations of these motivations to Saul; the narrative shows that Saul is motivated by at least the second.

We are reminded of Gilgal as the camp in Joshua for the conquest of Jericho and Ai, Joshua 6–8, and of the holy war themes associated with the conquest. For my purposes, I focus on the following—the ritual aspect, especially the role of priests and ark in Joshua 6; the explicit attribution of the victory to the Lord; the ban (*cherem*) and the possibility of exceptions so that some booty can be taken; and, finally, the actual taking or not taking of booty (cf. Polzin 1980, pp. 73–115). Since 1 Samuel 11 is a foil for the reading, I note that these themes do not occur there. Joshua's initial and unsuccessful attack on Ai has been implicated in the reading of 1 Samuel through the lot-casting procedure involving Achan (Josh. 7:16–21) and Saul (1 Sam. 10:20–24); the implication contaminates Saul with the violation of holy war, not its fulfillment.

The Philistines gather at Michmash, about ten miles west of Gilgal, and they outnumber Saul's army—"thirty thousand chariots, and six thousand horsemen, and troops like the sand on the seashore in multitude." The Israelites react in fear and hide "in caves and in holes and in rocks and in tombs and in cisterns." Mass panic is an appropriate description. "Because of Midian the people of Israel made for themselves the dens which are in the mountains and the caves and the strongholds" (Judg. 6:2). Once again, Gideon is involved in the story of Saul.

> Saul was still at Gilgal, and all the army followed him trembling. He waited seven days, the time appointed [mo`ed] by Samuel, but Samuel did not come to Gilgal, and the people were scattering from [Saul]. (1 Sam. 13:7–8)

Emphasis is expressed by "still," but is this a note of surprise or of commendation? Saul waits seven days, "the time appointed by Samuel." Is this a narrational comment with high reliability, i.e., Samuel did command Saul and set a time limit, or is it only Saul's description of Samuel's earlier statement (1 Sam. 10:8)? Saul remembers it as Samuel's command and respects it despite the straits that he is in; for him, the "still" is commendation. On the other hand, the final sentence, which is the narrator's reliable comment, makes no mention of an appointed time.

Saul's situation deteriorates, and he takes action without waiting any longer for Samuel. "Saul said, 'Bring to me the burnt offering and the peace offerings.' He offered the burnt offering." Saul has interpreted Samuel's utterance in 1 Sam. 10:8 as a command concerning sacrifice—Samuel is coming to show him something about proper sacrifice. Otherwise, Saul's sacrifice is surprising, since he felt no need for sacrifice before fighting the Ammonites; it is only after the victory and the crowning of Saul that peace offerings (but no burnt offerings) were given. Here, at Gilgal again, Saul prepares a burnt offering but no peace offerings, even though he called for them. Why does Saul not take matters into his own hands and immediately attack the Philistines as he did the Ammonites; indeed, why has he not attacked them before now? Why wait seven days? Is he afraid of the Philistines' huge numbers?

> While he was finishing offering the burnt offering, look, here's Samuel coming, and Saul went out to meet him and bless him. Samuel said, "What have you done?" And Saul said, "When I saw that the people scattered from me and that you did not come within the days appointed [mo`ed] and that the Philistines had mustered at Michmash, I said, 'Now the Philistines will come down upon me at Gilgal, and I have not entreated the favor of the Lord': so I forced myself, and I offered the burnt offering." (1 Sam. 13:10–12)

Saul employs *mo`ed,* strengthening the suggestion that the "time appointed by Samuel" in 1 Sam. 13:8 is his own interpretation, not the

narrator's assertion. Saul's response—twenty-seven words in Hebrew—
contrasts with Samuel's terse question, "What have you done?" (*meh
'aśitha*). Saul's explanation is the opposite of his laconic "Let the Hebrews hear" (*yishme'u ha'ibrim*); now it is the fullness of the statement
that raises queries. Why has Saul, the charismatic hero of chapter 11,
subordinated himself to Samuel? Against the Ammonites, he takes vigorous action—action independent of Samuel, perhaps even against
Samuel. In chapter 13, he talks and waits; why wait and not attack?
Even granting authority to Samuel, why does Saul pick out one statement by Samuel, that in 1 Sam. 10:8, and assume that it is a command
that applies to this situation and has to do with sacrificing or not sacrificing? Samuel's statement in 1 Sam. 10:8 is vague in terms of its status
as directive or command, in terms of its content and the specific times
that it is applicable to. Finally, even if taken as a command, why did the
events at Gilgal at the close of chapter 11 not count as fulfilling it?

One answer is the change of situation for Saul between the victory
over the Ammonites and the war with the Philistines; the change
would include the events in 1 Sam. 11:12–12:25. The different situations elicit different responses from Saul and partially account for the
events of chapter 13. By the end of chapter 11, Saul has been formally established as king; he is no longer just *nagid*. The people,
perhaps including Samuel, look to him for stable leadership that goes
beyond his achievement over the Ammonites, because Israel is faced
with a formidable enemy in her own land, not in Transjordan. One
swift, decisive victory will not win this war. Samuel's previous accom-
plishments provide confirmation, since the Philistines are again enter-
ing the territory of Israel.

For whatever reasons, Saul does not rise to the occasion; he does
not provide effective, stable leadership. He responds very differently
to the Philistine challenge than to the Ammonite challenge. 1 Samuel
13–15 catalog the various ways in which Saul fails to provide effective
leadership. My analysis discusses these ways in view of the "different
Sauls" presented above, with an eye on Saul's concern to acquire a
"word of the Lord" in the sense that he needs a specific guide for
what he is and is not to do. This involves a discussion of "words" of
the Lord, of Saul, and of Samuel, and a process of interpretation by
which we can arrive at the word of the Lord.

The Word of the Lord
To follow one line of reading, Saul is daunted by the office of king
and by the pressures of war, and he is overly impressed with Samuel
because of the events and speeches of 1 Samuel 9–10 and 12. He
longs for the simplicity and swift outcome of the Ammonite campaign

and turns to Samuel's speech to him in 1 Sam. 10:1–8 for a "simple answer." The signs of chapter 10 have come true, which proves, according to Deuteronomy 13 and 18, that Samuel is a true prophet and that therefore the people should fear him and should take his word as a word from the Lord. So there is good reason for Saul to interpret 1 Sam. 10:8 as a command. In contrast, to pursue a counterinterpretation, Samuel says nothing about the Lord in 1 Sam. 10:8, and the statement itself lacks the tenor of a command, because it is so vague.

Even if we consider the statement a command, there is no compelling reason for Saul to assume that it applies to this trip to Gilgal and not to the one after the victory over the Ammonites. And, more importantly, there are no compelling reasons, i.e., other texts, for Saul, or for us, to presume that sacrificing or not sacrificing, with or without Samuel, is the point of 1 Sam. 10:8. There are no OT parallels that strictly support Saul's assertion that he has to "entreat the favor of the Lord," especially by sacrifice, before going into battle against the Philistines, unless the emphasis falls on the distress and not on the military situation; it is the latter that Saul stresses. There is no substantial reason for Saul to regard sacrifice as a necessary prelude to battle. Ritual acts, personnel, and objects may be involved before and during battle, e.g., Deuteronomy 20 and Joshua 1–11, but not specific sacrificial acts. Finally, there is no reason, beyond the statement in 1 Sam. 10:8, to regard Samuel—as priest, prophet, or judge—as a necessary officiant at any sacrifice.

This elaborate process of interpretation and counterinterpretation is called for by Saul's detailed response. He does not just cite Samuel's statement as motivation but explains how it applies to the present situation and why he felt compelled to violate it. He even quotes his own thoughts. His response is polished, not marred by faltering or stammering; this time his oratorical skill may get him in trouble. Brevity could have helped him here.

Are we compelled to accept his explanation? Is Samuel? Saul's polished explanation contrasts with Samuel's terse charge, "You have done foolishly!" (*niskalta*), which, in turn, is followed by a balanced, formal accusation and announcement. By using specific terms and themes the denunciation intones preceding texts.

> You have done foolishly. You have not kept the commandment [*mitsvah*] of the Lord your God which he commanded [*tsivvah*] you for now the Lord would have established your kingdom [*mamlakah*] over Israel forever. But now your kingdom will not rise up [*lo' taqum*]; the Lord has sought out a man after his own heart, and the Lord has appointed [*tsivvah*] him *nagid* over his people because you have not kept what the Lord commanded [*tsivvah*]. (1 Sam. 13:13–14)

Retributive justice is central. Saul has sinned and will be punished. The denunciation fits the pattern of the speeches against the house of Eli in 1 Sam. 2:27–36 and 1 Sam. 3:11–14. The speeches are dispersed throughout the text and here can be attached to the house of Saul. Both Eli and Saul hear pronouncements of judgment, but in Saul's case, the sin which precipitates the punishment is not so clear.

How has Saul done foolishly? What is the commandment that he has not kept? Saul's explanation in 1 Sam. 13:11–12 takes 1 Sam. 10:8 as a command that he feels he has not kept. Samuel's denunciation shows that he may agree, but he says nothing of waiting, of *mo`ed,* of sacrificing, or of fighting. The denunciation can be read in a different mode.

Saul's foolhardiness, in this light, has nothing to do with sacrificing, since it is the product of his overall understanding of the situation and how he should respond to it. The commandment is not in Samuel's assertion in 1 Sam. 10:8, but in his statement in 1 Sam. 10:7— "When these signs come true, do whatever your hand finds to do for God is with you"—and in the Lord's commission to Samuel in 1 Sam. 9:16—"He will save my people from the hand of the Philistines." The king is to govern Israel and go out before them and fight their battles (1 Sam. 8:20); he should continue the state of affairs as it was under Samuel (1 Sam. 7:13–14). Saul is anointed *nagid* to save Israel from the Philistines; Samuel's denunciation speaks of the Lord seeking out another to appoint (*tsivvah*) *nagid,* because Saul has not done what the Lord commanded (*tsivvah*) him. Samuel's words invoke the narrative of chapter 9 and lend credence to this interpretation of what the commandment of the Lord is.

Samuel simply cannot believe that Saul is still at Gilgal preparing burnt offerings rather than engaging in full battle with the Philistines. Saul has blundered and has revealed himself as unfit, because he does not act on his own as king (1 Sam. 10:7); he assumes that Samuel has told him exactly what to do and that he must do it without question. He arrives at the wrong word of the Lord in his interpretation, and, as I have shown in my counterinterpretation, he should not have. That is, there are few texts to support Saul's rationale in 1 Sam. 13:11–12.

The "word of the Lord" is dispersed throughout the text of the OT. To speak of the word or commandment of the Lord is to initiate a process of interpretation and argumentation. I refer to texts that would support parts of Saul's interpretation and note the absence of texts that would support other crucial parts, especially sacrificing before battle. I marshal other texts to support the counterinterpretation. However, my interest is not the "true interpretation"; rather, it is to

show how the text itself calls for and fuels the process, the search, and
leaves it open—how it both supports and undermines the very notion
of a "true interpretation." There are tension and interplay between
details and terseness, between explicitness (Saul's explanation) and
generality (Samuel's denunciation). What a difference if Samuel denounced Saul for sacrificing too soon and without him!

Saul does not, or is not given the opportunity to, respond: "Samuel
rose and went up from Gilgal to Gibeah of Benjamin." The story is
truncated. We are given no further information on what the commandment of the Lord is, on who the other man is whom the Lord
has appointed, or on Saul's reaction to the denunciation. The narrative might not be truncated—Saul may be so in awe of Samuel that he
says nothing; he cannot challenge or question the great man. He
accepts the condemnation even though he is not sure what he has
done wrong or what it means that his kingdom will not be established
and that he has been replaced by another.

The lack of response allows us to develop another reading. Samuel
is not flabbergasted when he comes to Saul in Gilgal. He is a little
surprised, but not troubled, since this is a golden opportunity for him
to denounce Saul. This still leaves open the question of what Saul has
done wrong and how serious his error is (if indeed there is any wrong
or error). Such a reading produces a different understanding of the
dynamics between Saul and Samuel. Saul is not paranoid if he thinks
Samuel intends to destroy him. Samuel's denunciation is very stern
but general enough to leave Saul wondering; Samuel refers to "kingdom," not "king," in connection with Saul. Is Saul a sinner, an ineffectual bungler, or a good leader who is being pushed toward disaster?

At Michmash

The narrative provides no resolution and shifts to a matter-of-fact
report of the situation before the battle in chapter 14. The reports are
analogous to 1 Sam. 6:17–18, which speak of Philistine cities and a
stone rather than of the consequences for the Philistines of the return
of the ark. Samuel goes to Gibeah of Benjamin, Saul's home, rather
than back to Ramah. In the meantime, Saul's army has shrunk from
the 3,000 of 1 Sam. 13:2 to 600. "Saul, Jonathan his son, and the
army that was with them were in Geba of Benjamin, and the Philistines were encamped in Michmash" (1 Sam. 13:16). Jonathan is explicitly called Saul's son and will be frequently from now on, even if it
is superfluous from the point of view of information. Family relationships are a major topic in 1 Samuel.

"Geba of Benjamin"—is this the same as Gibeah of Benjamin? If so,
Samuel and Saul are together. As Saul's tribe is marked by contradic-

tions—vigor and misery—so is his home. As Benjamin, Gibeah is contaminated by the sordid events of Judges 19–21. "Gibeah"—is this a place name as in 1 Sam. 10:26 and 1 Sam. 13:2 and 15, or does it at times just mean "hill," as it may in 1 Sam. 10:5—Gibeath-ʹelohim, or the hill of God? Are Gibeah of Saul (1 Sam. 11:4) and Gibeah of Benjamin the same place? Is Geba identical to Gibeah? This ambiguity is not a major issue, but it is a good illustration of the ambiguity that pervades the narratives of Saul, Jonathan, and David.

The Philistines are at Michmash, less than two miles northeast of Geba. The scene is now set. The Philistines send out three raiding parties in different directions that are precisely indicated. The ability to send out raiding parties may reflect the situation described in 1 Sam. 13:6–7. 1 Sam. 13:19–22 describes the Philistine prohibition of Israelite ironsmiths: "No ironsmith was *found* in all the land . . . 'lest the Hebrews make themselves swords or spears.'" The policy is effective. "On the day of the battle there was neither sword nor spear *found* in the hand of any of the army with Saul and Jonathan, but they were *found* with Saul and Jonathan his son." The Israelites are in desperate straits.

The details of the description demonstrate an exact knowledge of the area and of Philistine practice. The narrator knows what is happening not just in Israel but also in Philistia; he knows specific practices, not just generalities. Such knowledge reminds us that the lack of details, relevant information, etc., in other situations is deliberate and not the result of a gap in the narrator's knowledge. Any narrator who knows what the Philistines charged for sharpening plowshares and axes should know whether Samuel and Saul are together at the same place and whether Saul wanted to respond to Samuel's denunciation. I do not write off such details and lacunae as merely OT narrative style.

1 Samuel 14

A Hasty Vow

Two characteristics of chapter 14 differentiate it from the preceding one—the presence of Jonathan and the absence of Samuel as major characters. Indeed, Samuel and Jonathan are never together. Samuel's dealings are with Eli and Saul, not with their sons. He pronounces to both the end of house and kingdom; children, therefore, are of no interest to him. On the other hand, Samuel is absent from a story that presents Saul's failures, if not sins, more clearly than chapter 13, where Samuel was present.

Chapter 14 is marked by the absence of the word of the Lord as it concerns Saul, even though we are informed that the initial rout of the Philistines is the work of the Lord (1 Sam. 14:23). Saul's interruption of an inquiry makes the absence a theme (1 Sam. 14:37). The absence of both Samuel and a word of the Lord about Saul is noteworthy because of the greater clarity of the narrative. At the end, Israel will have good reason to ask, "How can this one save us?"

The narrative divides into stories about Saul and Jonathan that merge at the end in the confrontation. The division occurs in the opening verses. Jonathan proposes to his armor-bearer that they attack the Philistine garrison, "but he did not tell his father." The scene shifts to Saul.

> Saul was staying in the outskirts of Gibeah under the pomegranate tree which is at Migron; the army with him was about six hundred men. (Ahijah the son of Ahitub, Ichabod's brother, son of Phinehas, son of Eli, the priest of the Lord in Shiloh, was there wearing an ephod.) (1 Sam. 14:2–3)

The narrator shows detailed knowledge of the locale and characters, including the physical setting of the garrison (1 Sam. 14:4–5).

An ominous note is sounded by the presence of Ahijah, a descendant of the cursed house of Eli. The judgment on the house contaminates Saul's house. Ahijah is the nephew of Ichabod, and the story of Saul is an excellent demonstration that "glory has departed from Israel." Ahijah is wearing an ephod, which is associated with inquiry of the Lord in the rest of 1 Samuel.

Jonathan

The narrative follows Jonathan through his defeat of the garrison and turns back to Saul in v. 16. Jonathan is a capable warrior who, accompanied only by his young armor-bearer, threatens and defeats the garrison. The feat can be understood as an act of bravery, of foolhardiness, and even of arrogance. In his speech to his armor-bearer, Jonathan invokes the Lord's help—"It may be that the Lord will work for us for nothing can hinder the Lord from saving by many or by few." This may be a sincere belief of Jonathan's that is motivating and giving him confidence, it may reflect only his attempt to motivate and encourage his young armor-bearer, or it may be a little of both.

I develop different, and contrasting, views of Jonathan to portray the range of his character and to illustrate what I mean by saying that character is portrayed on a continuum, a spectrum, and not as separate and discrete possible descriptions. I am not trying to demonstrate that a new, more sinister understanding of Jonathan should be followed but that such an understanding is *possible* and that this possibility infects every other possible reading of Jonathan. It is not a simple choice between a Jonathan who is sincere and brave—"good"—and a Jonathan who is ambitious and arrogant—"bad." These are only heuristic poles to show the range of possible portrayals of Jonathan; they and the various attributes associated with each tend to flow, to move toward each other. For example, a pious, brave Jonathan can still be ambitious and arrogant in some respects. This is not to argue finally for a view of Jonathan as a complex, multi-faceted character as a solution to the ambiguity of the text, although that is certainly one possibility. The text supports a "good" Jonathan and a "bad" Jonathan; it supports "in-between" and complex views. My contention is that it supports the different readings in such a way that we cannot prove or disprove any one of them as the only or the best understanding of Jonathan.

The reader can ask whether Jonathan's assertion about the Lord's ability to save by many or by few is a profound theological insight or a pious platitude. We have encountered this before and will encounter it again—explicit and specific statements about the Lord and his activity hover somewhere between profound truth and trite truism. The text provides enough to support both interpretations but not enough to choose one and reject the other. The defeat of the Philistines by Saul and the army is ascribed to the Lord—"The Lord delivered Israel that day" (1 Sam. 14:23)—but the slaughter of the garrison is ascribed not to the Lord but only to Jonathan and his armor-bearer. Nothing may hinder the Lord from saving by many or by few, but a weary army does hinder him from total destruction of the enemy.

Jonathan does not leave the issue with a proclamation of the Lord's power, he proposes a sign to reveal whether or not the Lord is with them in battle.

> Jonathan said, "Look, we are going over to the men, and we will show ourselves to them. If they say to us, 'Wait until we come to you,' then we will stand still in our place, and we will not go up to them. But if they say, 'Come up to us,' then we will go up for the Lord has given them into our hand. This will be the sign for us." (1 Sam. 14:8–10)

The latter occurs:

> The men of the garrison hailed Jonathan and his armor-bearer and said, "Come up to us, and we will show you something." Jonathan said to his armor-bearer, "Come up after me for the Lord has given them into the hand of Israel." (1 Sam. 14:12)

The sign can be understood as a commonsense proposal and not a test of the divine will. It is unlikely that the garrison would come down, because they would fear an ambush and because the rocky crags on which they are perched would prevent a surprise attack. Jonathan might be aware of this, so that his proposal is not a true sign; the text leaves it unclear.

If Jonathan is not certain of the Philistine response, then his is a serious and pious proposal on which their next move hinges. Moreover, this understanding of the proposal is possible even if Jonathan is certain of the reply; such certainty could indicate divine action. On the other hand, given the certainty of the Philistines' reply, it could be a ploy to bolster his armor-bearer; Jonathan points out to him that the sign has been fulfilled positively. Jonathan would be a formidable warrior and an excellent judge of people. Finally, one last alternative is that the proposal could be a demonstration that Jonathan has a flair for the dramatic—a penchant for doing things with ceremony and show. The three expositions of the proposal can be taken as mutually exclusive, or two or all three can be combined in various ways into a more complicated view of Jonathan. The text supports the wide range of possibilities but does not authorize one of them or some particular combination of them.

The effect of the defeat of the garrison is earthshaking.

> There was a panic in the camp, in the field, and among the entire army; even the garrison and the raiders trembled; the earth quaked; it was a very great panic [*cherdath 'elohim*]. (1 Sam. 14:15)

The Lord may be working for them, since the result is far out of proportion to the feat. "A very great panic" can be translated "a panic of God," which would support the interpretation, although not conclusively, since *'elohim,* God/god, can be used as a superlative. The issue is left open as the narrator turns to Saul's camp to report the effect of the panic on Saul.

The Vow: A Word of the Lord?
Saul, as in chapter 13 and now without Samuel's presence explicit or assumed, is unable to respond immediately, as he did to the Ammonites. Instead of mustering the army, Saul calls the roll to see who is absent; it is Jonathan. Is Saul pleased or shocked to learn that his son has again performed a feat of individual daring? Saul commands Ahijah, "Bring hither the ark of God"—not the ephod but the ark. Its presence is striking, and Saul's cavalier treatment of it is even more striking. This is not "the ark of the covenant of the Lord" coming to

save Israel from the Philistines, as the elders once hoped (1 Sam. 4:3). Apparently Saul is having Ahijah inquire of the Lord, although about what is not stated. It does not matter, since Saul stops the process, "Withdraw your hand." How, indeed, is Saul to save Israel if he does not immediately field the army and instead wastes his time on a pointless roll call and on incomplete inquiry of the Lord? In a more positive light, he perhaps realizes that the roll call is futile and stops a pointless inquiry to turn his attention to the battle.

Saul finally rallies the army, and the ensuing battle is marked by "very great confusion," not by a "panic of God." Hebrews who had previously deserted to the Philistines join in the battle; potential Philistines learn well from this turn of events (1 Samuel 29). Other Israelites who had fled or were in hiding (1 Sam. 13:6–7) return and join in the pursuit. "The Lord saved Israel that day" is an important theological comment and a note that "this one" did not save Israel.

Saul, like Jephthah, crushed the Ammonites. Saul, like Jephthah, makes a hasty, stupid vow that threatens, and in Jephthah's case takes, the life of a child. Saul's oath, in some ways, makes even less sense than Jephthah's. At least Jephthah's vow was explicitly designed to ensure victory. The association of Saul's curse—"Cursed be the man who eats food before it is evening, and I am avenged on my enemies" (1 Sam. 14:24)—with victory is not obvious. Does he consider it a form of fasting? Is he convinced that some ritual is necessary? Saul's motivation for the vow is unclear. How serious is the error of the oath? Is this sin? Has Saul wittingly done what is evil in the eyes of the Lord? Or is Saul out of control—either harried by others or weak and unable to respond in a consistent manner?

Saul claims personal vengeance—"and I am avenged on my enemies." No mention is made of the Lord or of Israel. In chapter 14, Saul has a problem with "timing"; he acts at one time hesitantly and at another precipitously. More important, he has a problem with the "word of the Lord" in the sense that he takes a single statement as a specific and irrevocable guide for his behavior; this was at issue in chapter 13. At the same time, Saul can falter in a formal attempt to ascertain the "word of the Lord." Saul cannot get things right. He hesitates when he should act resolutely; he acts precipitously or resolutely when he should finish a given action or refrain from it altogether.

Saul is in the company of both Jephthah and Samson; the latter makes a claim to personal vegeance, although with more attention to the role of the Lord: "O Lord God, remember me and strengthen me this one time, O God, so that I may be avenged for just one of my two eyes" (Judg. 16:28; cf. Judg. 15:7). Saul, like Samson, is a character ruled by strong and violent emotions, a man with a one-track mind.

Saul's parallel with Samson is complicated by the one between Samson and Jonathan. Jonathan did not tell his father of his venture against the Philistines, and he eats honey; Samson did not tell his parents he had killed a lion or that the honey they were eating came from the lion's carcass (Judg. 14:5–9). In addition, Saul is associated with "the men of Israel" in Judges 21 who will hold to their oath not to give their daughters in marriage to the Benjaminites even though this can lead to the extinction of an Israelite tribe and even though they have no problem giving their daughters in marriage to the Canaanites.

Jonathan, not having heard Saul's oath, eats honey that had dropped on the ground, "and his eyes became bright [*Qere*: *ta´ornah*]." This is an ironic fulfillment of Saul's original "cursed be"—"light" (*'or*) and not "curse" (*'arur*). A soldier informs Jonathan of the oath. He omits Saul's claim to personal vengeance, drawing attention to its presence in Saul's curse. We are informed, by the soldier or the narrator, that "the army was faint." Jonathan's response is harsh, and he stresses the dire consequences of the vow. Eating just a little honey has strengthened him; imagine the tremendous slaughter of the Philistines if the people had been able to eat freely of the booty of their enemies (1 Sam. 14:29–30).

The usual order of defeat and the taking of booty or spoils is reversed. Jonathan interprets holy war rules according to the situation, interprets them so that they produce victory, not defeat. Jonathan thereby plays part of the role Samuel could have played. Saul has produced a "word" in his curse, and he will adamantly refuse to interpret it according to the situation, in spite of the disastrous consequences that it brings. Saul acts resolutely and single-mindedly when he should admit the error of the vow and rescind it; at a later time, David recognizes the error of an analogous vow and rescinds it (1 Samuel 25). Saul, however, is in the company of Jephthah and Samson. Saul would agree with Jephthah. "I have opened my mouth to the Lord, and I cannot take it back" (Judg. 11:35). Why not?

Not only does Jonathan reverse the usual order of defeat and the taking of booty, he also alters the relation, found in Josh. 7:22–26, of troubling (`akar`) and booty. Achan takes booty from Jericho and brings trouble on Israel; Saul prevents booty from being taken and eaten and "has troubled the land" (1 Sam. 14:29). Nor is the parallel with Jephthah far, since he, in a perverse statement, accuses his daughter, "Alas, my daughter! You have brought me very low, and you have become the cause of great trouble to me" (Judg. 11:35). Saul is in despicable company—Achan, Gideon, Jephthah, and Samson.

Because of Saul's vow, the army does not eat and is too weak to crush the fleeing Philistines. "The army flew upon the spoil [*shalal*] and took sheep and oxen and calves and slew them on the ground, and the army ate them with the blood" (1 Sam. 14:32). Nourishment comes too late, and "the army is sinning against the Lord by eating with the blood." Saul's oath has disastrous consequences, yet he makes no connection between his oath and these events.

Faced with the army's "sin," Saul responds quickly. A great stone is brought as an altar on which the people can slay the cattle and "not sin against the Lord by eating with the blood." In fact, "Saul built an altar to the Lord; it was the first altar that he built to the Lord." Saul's act by itself may be proper, but the compelling situation would not have existed except for his oath. According to Jonathan's interpretation, the stone should have been brought out long ago. Building an altar is Saul's attempt to correct a bad situation while the original vow remains in effect. Saul can do the "right thing" at the "wrong time," making it the "wrong thing."

The famished people are finally able to eat at night, and Saul proposes to pursue the Philistines that same night. The army agrees or accepts with resignation Saul's blunders. "All that is good in your eyes do" (1 Sam. 14:36). This is repeated in v. 40. Is Saul just blundering, or is he willfully doing what is evil in the eyes of the Lord?

Before the pursuit begins, the priest, apparently Ahijah, urges that they draw near to God. "Saul inquired of God, 'Should I go down after the Philistines? Will you give them into the hand of Israel?' But he did not answer him that day" (1 Sam. 14:37). No reason is given for God's not answering Saul, but Saul quickly provides his own, "Come here, all you leaders of the army, and know and see how *this sin* has arisen today." In a demonstration of religious fervor or of his own dramatic flair, Saul proclaims, "For as the Lord lives who saves Israel, though it be in Jonathan my son, he will surely die." Given Saul's claim to personal vengeance, the opening phrase is ironic. This time, "there was not a man among the entire army that answered him," since many, if not all, are aware that Jonathan ate honey and violated Saul's oath.

Saul is a study in blunders and errors in this chapter—a man who cannot get things right. He begins to inquire of the Lord before the battle but stops the process in midstream; after the battle, he inquires but receives no answer. He truncates an inquiry and clings to a fool-hardy oath to the very end. Inquiry, holy war, booty, blood, altars—all are important issues that Saul cannot get straight, that he either does not do at the proper time or does not carry through to completion.

The Confrontation

Saul proposes a lot-casting procedure to choose between the army on one side and he and Jonathan on the other. Saul and Jonathan are taken; then Jonathan is taken. What, exactly, is happening here? Many points are unclear. Saul's inquiry of God is not answered; why does he assume that the lack of response is due to "this sin"? Why does he automatically pronounce the death penalty upon the sinner? In the story in 1 Samuel 28, when he is not answered by the Lord, he does not make such an assumption, since he consults with a medium at Endor. Perhaps, near the end of his life, he is in circumstances that he is not in 1 Samuel 14, or he may have learned from the events of chapter 14. When he says "this sin," does he have some transgression in mind, particularly one related to his previous oath? Why does he not relate it to the army's eating flesh with the blood in it, since the latter is a sin against the Lord? Why does he not ask the army what sins have been committed? If Saul has a specific sin in mind, the lot-casting could be superfluous. Finally, why does Jonathan's name come so readily to his lips in his initial acclamation?

Saul's casting of lots can be a formal, sacred affair, an attempt to identify and eradicate sin from within Israel. Achan is again implicated. On the other hand, the procedure can be an overreaction of Saul, melodrama, or, in a related vein, a dramatic act to cover up his earlier blunders, notably his oath. The parallel with Achan's trial highlights the melodramatic aspect of the trial of Jonathan. The battle of Michmash was not a holy war declared by the Lord himself (cf. Josh. 6:1–5), and Jonathan did not, like Achan (Josh. 7:1, 20–21), deliberately and secretly take silver and gold in violation of the divine ban, for he unwittingly and publicly tasted some honey with his staff in violation of his father's oath. And it is Saul, not Jonathan, who is accused of troubling the land.

Another possibility suggests itself. As with his previous vow, Saul precipitously binds himself with an oath when he receives no answer to his inquiry. He jumps to the conclusion that sin—indeed, "this sin"—is the cause and that the sin, even in Jonathan his son, deserves the death penalty. No one responds to the oath, because the army is dumbfounded by this second display of irrationality. Once he has spoken, Saul carries through by calling for the lot procedure.

Once Jonathan is taken by lot, Saul asks, "Tell me what you have done [*meh `aśitha*]" (1 Sam. 14:43). Samuel's question of Saul at Gilgal sounds in the distance (1 Sam. 13:11). Jonathan replies, "I tasted a little honey with the tip of the staff that was in my hand; here I am, I will die." Is this a pious Jonathan who will accept his father's decision whether it is wise or not? Or is this a more astute Jonathan who, by his statement, brings the issue to a brutal climax, forcing the army to step in to prevent an even more serious blunder? Or is he to be seen as a confident, arrogant Jonathan who defies and even scorns his father, certain that the army will rescue him? In any case, there is now more reason for Jonathan to resent and to be angry at Saul and to fear him.

Saul has both condemned him to death for eating a little honey and ignored his defeat of the garrison, a marvelous act that initiated the defeat of the Philistine army. The Israelite army does not ignore the feat and tells Saul what Jonathan has, in fact, done. "Should Jonathan then die who has wrought [`aśah] this great victory in Israel . . . he has wrought [`aśah] with God this day." The army ransoms Jonathan and plays the role that Saul played in chapter 11.

The narrative concludes quickly. "The army ransomed Jonathan, and he did not die. Saul went up from pursuing the Philistines, and the Philistines went to their own place." The pursuit of the Philistines is forgotten in Saul's resolve to execute his own son. The question of the men of Gibeah can be asked with serious import—"What has come over the son of Kish?"

The great confrontation that began in 1 Sam. 13:2 has come to an inconclusive end; the Philistines are not defeated. To this extent, Saul has failed; he has not destroyed the enemy. The question is, why not? However we wish to understand and evaluate Saul in chapters 13 and 14, he does not act as quickly and decisively as in chapter 11, and his hesitation is associated with sacrifice and other ritual matters, especially inquiries and oaths. Regardless of how we assess fault, Saul, particularly in chapter 14, gets in his own way. Instead of battle, we have roll calls, inquiry, and trial by lot. If the first inquiry is proper, why does he stop it, only to press on with a foolish curse; if he stops the first inquiry because it is irrelevant, why does he not likewise rescind the curse? Compared to chapter 13 and even chapter 15, chapter 14 presents the least appealing, the "worst" Saul; he does not defeat and crush the Philistines when he has the opportunity. The opportunity was not yet present in chapter 13, and he does defeat and crush the Amalekites in chapter 15. Yet there is no denunciation to match those in chapters 13 and 15; instead, chapter 14 closes with a positive summary of Saul's reign.

1 Samuel 14:47–52

The summary description of Saul's battles, in vv. 47–48 and 52, frames the list of his family in vv. 49–51. This is a checklist for 1–2 Samuel in that we can enumerate the members of Saul's house as they die. The description opens in v. 47, "Saul had taken [or, took] the kingship [*melukah*] over Israel." Is this a reference to the past ("had taken") or to the time immediately after the events of chapter 14 ("took")? Is it a complement to 1 Sam. 11:15, a note of fulfillment—Saul is king (*melek*) and has the full authority of the king (*melukah*)? In any case, the description and military summary are impressive and underscore the absence of a denunciation for Saul's military failure.

A closer reading, particularly in comparison with the summaries on

Samuel in 1 Sam. 3:19–4:1a and 1 Sam. 7:13–14 and the comment on
Saul in 1 Sam. 10:26—"With him went men of valor whose hearts
God had touched"—reveal major qualifications. First, a summary here
and not at the end of his reign hints that his reign is already over.
Second, there is no mention of the Lord or of God in 1 Sam. 14:47–
52; Saul is on his own. Saul still gathers to himself any strong and
valiant man, but God does not touch their hearts. "There was hard
fighting against the Philistines all the days of Saul" contrasts with "the
hand of the Lord was against the Philistines all the days of Samuel"
(1 Sam. 7:13). Third, the summary concerns wars and hard battles;
only v. 48—"He smote the Amalekites and delivered Israel from the
hands of those who plundered them"—speaks of victory. It is ironic,
given chapter 15, that it is associated with the Amalekites.

1 Samuel 15

The Lord Changes His Mind

The chapter is climactic. Saul's loss of kingship and kingdom are
irrevocable; the rest of 1 Samuel details how in fact he does lose it all.
David is soon introduced, and Samuel recedes as a central character.
The relationship between Samuel and Saul is replaced by those between Saul and David, David and Jonathan. I read chapter 15 closely
to reveal its structure and content and to show how it brings together
and presages many texts, words, and themes.

The Mission

> Samuel said to Saul, "Me the Lord sent to anoint you king over his
> people Israel; and now [*we`atah*] listen to the voice of the words of
> the Lord.

Samuel puts himself first—in Hebrew his first three words are "me
sent the Lord"—which can be a proper focus on himself as the vehicle
for the word of the Lord or an egotistical statement, a reminder to
Saul that Samuel is his superior. The speech is formal. After the
initial reference to the past comes *we`atah*—"and now" or "but now"
(see 1 Sam. 2:30 and 1 Sam. 12:13)—introducing the command.
"Listen/obey," "voice/sound," and "word(s)" are major terms of the
entire chapter (Alter 1981, p. 93); the motif is underscored by the
redundant "voice of the words."

For the first time, we are informed that Saul has been anointed
king. Previously he was anointed *nagid* and was set, given, or chosen

king or made king. Saul is anointed king, and the command is urgent. In contrast to chapter 13, there is no doubt as to the statement's status or context; it is unequivocally a command.

> Thus says the Lord of hosts, "I will punish what Amalek did to Israel in opposing them on the way when they came up out of Egypt. Now [`atah`], go and attack Amalek and utterly destroy [*hacharamtem*] all that they have; do not spare them, but kill man and woman, infant and suckling, ox and sheep, camel and ass." (1 Sam. 15:2–3)

"Thus says the Lord of hosts." Samuel is delivering a formal command from the Lord. This is an unequivocal command with motivation and background; there is no need to gather a word of the Lord dispersed through the text. Both Exod. 17:8–16 and Deut. 25:17–19 agree that the Amalekites' memory is to be blotted out because of their attack on Israel in the wilderness. Saul has already engaged them in battle (1 Sam. 14:48). The command goes beyond Saul to the army, since "utterly destroy" is in the second person plural.

V. 2 speaks of blotting out the memory. V. 3 clarifies that the memory is to be blotted out by the holy war ban and execution. All the Amalekites and their possessions are to be devoted to the ban (*cherem*). 1 Samuel 15 is frequently cited as a classic holy war narrative along with the stories in Joshua 6–8—the destruction of Jericho, the violation of the ban by Achan, and the destruction of Ai. The latter have been implicated in the reading of chapters 13–14; chapter 14 introduced the theme of taking, or not taking, booty.

A major rule of holy war, the application of the ban (*cherem*), is intoned, which is otherwise applicable only to peoples and places within the land (Deut. 20:10–18). In addition, the severity of the stricture is increased by the imperative to show no mercy or compassion, which is not used elsewhere in a holy war context. "Do not spare" (*lo´ tachmol*) does accord with the full application of the death penalty, e.g., Deuteronomy 13. The legislation on holy war has patently been interpreted. One question is, who is doing the interpreting? The Lord? Samuel? Both? As so frequently with the words of the Lord and Moses in Deuteronomy, I find the words of the Lord and Samuel here indistinguishable; both are interpreting. The word to Saul leaves little room for equivocation or wondering, but it does leave room for further interpretation.

I take the latter possibility, the room for interpretation, as an opening to develop two radically divergent readings of the entire chapter. The first is a standard interpretation with some important modifications—Saul has willfully violated a direct command from the Lord and is therefore rejected as king by the Lord and by Samuel. This is a "retributive justice" view. The second is a "power politics" view; I am indebted to Polzin for basic insight on it (especially Polzin 1980, pp. 74–80). I phrase his statement in terms suitable to a reading of 1 Samuel 15.

A paradigmatic theme that runs through these books—Polzin has Joshua through 2 Kings in mind—is that the people's or an individual's prosperity "will result from the diligent observance of 'all the law which my servant Moses has given you' (Josh. 1:7)." In example after example, Polzin demonstrates that such diligent observance implies interpretation of "all the law;" it is not to be applied in a strict literalist sense. Joshua can exempt Rahab from the ban on Jericho, and the Lord exempts the booty from Ai. The law of total ban is not applied in an unyielding manner without regard for the circumstances. Joshua can so interpret and apply the law on his own without divine sanction. In contrast, in 1 Sam. 15:1–3, the Lord and Samuel expand and stiffen the total ban so that it is applied in an unyielding manner—slaughter all without mercy.

If the Lord and Samuel can interpret the word of the Lord, why cannot Saul? Thus arise my two readings—as retributive justice, the arrogant sinner is punished; as power politics, Saul loses a crucial argument about who can interpret this word of the Lord. I note, but do not develop, the relevance of the two readings for chapter 13.

Exemptions

The campaign, like that against the Ammonites, gets off to an excellent start, since Saul can muster 210,000 men; this is far more than his previous 600 (although fewer than the 330,000 he had against the Ammonites). Chapter 15 is granted a paradigmatic quality similar to that of chapter 11 and is thereby distinguished from chapters 13 and 14. Saul goes immediately to the city of Amalek; before attacking them, he allows the Kenites to leave.

> Saul said to the Kenites, "Go, depart, go down from among the Amalekites, lest I destroy you with them; you showed kindness to all the people of Israel when they came up out of Egypt." The Kenites departed from among the Amalekites. (1 Sam. 15:6)

Saul's exemption of a group from death comes before the battle; in chapter 11, it followed the battle. Saul is capable of interpreting the word of the Lord in a specific situation. The Amalekites opposed Israel; the Kenites showed her kindness (`aśah chesed`). Only the Amalekites are mentioned in vv. 2–3. Saul exempts the Kenites as Joshua and Israel had exempted Rahab and her family, who had showed kindness (`aśah chesed;* Josh. 2:12–14) to the spies. Does this proper exemption underscore the improper exemption of the cattle? Or does it indicate that the latter is proper? Saul can interpret and apply the word of the Lord. He has learned a valuable lesson from chapter 14; a word, whether a command, law, vow, or whatever, is not to be adhered to in a strict, literalist sense. It is to be interpreted and applied according to the circumstances. Kenites are exempted for past good, cattle for future sacrifice.

> Saul smote Amalek from Havilah as far as Shur which is east of Egypt. He took Agag the king of Amalek alive and utterly destroyed all the people with the edge of the sword. (1 Sam. 15:7–8)

So far, so good. There is an analogy for taking the king alive: "The king of Ai they took alive and brought him to Joshua . . . and he hanged the king of Ai on a tree until evening" (Josh. 8:23-29). Saul is not denounced by Samuel for this exemption; it is not explicitly or implicitly stated, as so many commentaries assert, that this is a major violation of holy war rules by Saul. The issue of violation concerns what else is left alive.

> Saul and the people spared Agag and the best of the sheep and of the oxen and of the fatlings and the lambs and all that was good. They were not willing to destroy them utterly; all that was despised and worthless they utterly destroyed. (1 Sam. 15:9)

The verse is important, since it is the narration of the event that Saul will twice "repeat." The sparing (*yachmol*) is contrary to the command in v. 3 not to spare (*lo' tachmol*). Agag is not alone in being spared; they were not willing to destroy the best of the animals, only the despised and worthless. It is not just that they do not destroy but that they are not willing to. This is deliberate, but for what purpose? We are told what they do not do, not why they do not do it or what they in fact do. Both Saul and the army are explicitly involved.

"I Repent"
A word of the Lord comes to Samuel; it concerns only Saul.

> The word of the Lord came to Samuel, "I repent that I made Saul king because he was turned back from following me, and my words he has not raised up." (1 Sam. 15:10-11)

The army is not included in the judgment, and the accusation of sin does not refer specifically to the Amalekite episode. The judgment is reminiscent of Gen. 6:6–7. God repents (*nacham*) that he ever created humanity, because "the wickedness of humanity was great in the earth." Elsewhere God repents because of compassion; he changes his mind about a specific punishment or judgment (Exod. 32:11–14; Deut. 32:36; Judg. 2:18; 2 Sam. 24:16). Here he changes his mind about having made Saul king, not that he has anointed Saul, "for he has turned back from following me." Samuel's warning in 1 Sam. 12:12–20 echoes in the background. "My words he has not raised up" alludes to Elkanah's invocation in 1 Sam. 1:23.

The retributive justice interpretation, which is supported by the text, is that Saul has violated a divine command by exempting the cattle; because of this, the Lord nullifies his establishment as king. The text, however, does not support only this interpretation.

"My words"—Samuel has spoken of God's voice (1 Sam. 12:14–15), mouth (1 Sam. 12:14–15), and commandment (*mitsvah*) (1 Sam. 13:13–14). (In the last, because Saul has not kept the commandment of the Lord, his kingdom will not arise.) "My words" is not followed by a phrase such as "which I have commanded him," and the plural is unexpected, unless we take it as referring specifically to Samuel's pronouncement, "Listen to the voice of *the words* of the Lord" (1 Sam. 15:1). Is the Lord repenting because of Saul's particular transgression against the Amalekites or because of a series of sins, e.g., Saul's failures in chapters 13–15, with the Amalekite issue the most recent, if it is a failure? This is analogous to the possible interpretations of the Lord's response to Samuel in 1 Sam. 8:7–8. Or is this analogous to the Lord's statement about his rejection of Eliab, David's brother, in 1 Sam. 16:6–7? The Lord has rejected Eliab, and we are given no reason. The Lord offers Samuel a general motivation relating to sin; perhaps the narrator is more accurate. "The Lord repented that he had made Saul king over Israel" (1 Sam. 15:35). No motivation is offered.

If it is the particular transgression, it is surprising that the army is not also indicted, since both "Saul and the army spared Agag and the best of the sheep." The army's exemption can be understood according to the parallel with Achan.

> The people of Israel broke faith in regard to the devoted things for Achan . . . took some of the devoted things, and the anger of the Lord burned against the people of Israel. (Josh. 7:1)

Achan has sinned, therefore all Israel has sinned and feels the effect. The execution of Achan results in the Lord's turning from his anger and the subsequent punishment of Ai. 1 Samuel 15 presents a twist of the Achan episode in that both Saul and the people—the army—have committed the sin, yet only Saul is condemned; the people are exempted. It is possible that Saul alone is condemned because he is king, the representative of the people. 1 Samuel :15 is a study in possible exemptions—the Kenites, Agag, the cattle, the army, and even Saul, since he is not executed liked Achan.

A final question—does this "word of the Lord" in vv. 10–11 follow directly upon vv. 1–9, or is there a break? Does it introduce a new episode presenting Samuel's reaction and the subsequent encounter between Samuel and Saul? Analogous to 1 Sam. 8:7–9, the Lord is not offering Samuel a "true explanation" for his change of mind; he is trying to support his prophet, i.e., the Lord knows what Samuel's response will be.

"Samuel was angry, and he cried to the Lord all night." This is susceptible to different interpretations, depending on our view of Samuel and his opinion of a king and of Saul in particular. I see two divergent possibilities. If Samuel is sympathetic to Saul and his plight, then he is angry with the Lord's change of mind about making Saul king; Samuel cries to the Lord to forgive Saul his sin and to retain him as king. On the other hand, if Samuel is antagonistic toward Saul because Saul represents a challenge, then Samuel is angry with the Lord because his change of mind can further undermine Samuel's own position with the people. Samuel has recently proclaimed Saul king, and what will the people think if he now "dethrones" him? Samuel prays for the lord to retain Saul or to maintain, in some other way, Samuel's credibility. Whatever reading we follow, Samuel does carry out the Lord's commission, his "change of mind," by reporting and interpreting it to Saul; Samuel says far more to Saul than what is included in the word of the Lord in v. 11.

The Confrontation (1 Sam. 15:12–21)

"Samuel rose early in the morning to meet Saul." We are not informed of Samuel's location; he is told that Saul went to Carmel and "set up a monument for himself." This can be an acceptable act or an attempt by Saul to claim personal victory, as in 1 Sam. 14:24. Saul has gone from Carmel to Gilgal. Why Gilgal? Had this been prearranged? Is Saul still under the influence of Samuel's statement in 1 Sam. 10:8, as he was in chapter 13? He will soon link Gilgal with sacrifice (1 Sam. 15:21).

Three times Saul explains to Samuel what happened in the battle with the Amalekites—vv. 13 and 15, 20–21, and 24. I analyze the statements and compare them with each other, with Samuel's statements, and with the narration in v. 9. Again there are two possible readings. Saul increasingly implicates himself in sin as he talks himself into a corner; Saul repeatedly declares his innocence, since he has "raised up the word of the Lord."

> Samuel came to Saul and Saul said to him, "Blessed be you to the Lord; I have raised up [*qum*] the word of the Lord."

Saul unwittingly contradicts "the word of the Lord" reported in vv. 10–11; however, he refers to "the word," not "the words," which the Lord spoke of. The Lord's proffered motivation for his change of mind may not be germane to the rest of the chapter.

Saul's statement is brief and to the point. Samuel's response continues the aural imagery—he hears the voice of the sheep and the oxen. If Saul has listened to the voice of the Lord, why is Samuel listening to these voices? Saul explains and begins to implicate himself through his eloquence; Saul may be eloquent, but he is not prudent in speech (*nebon dabar*) like his neighbor; his words are not effective and beneficial. Alternatively, Saul's words are accurate—there was an acceptable reason to exempt the cattle—although not effective, since Samuel does not accept them.

In contrast to v. 9, Saul speaks of the army sparing the cattle; he repeats the opening phrase of v. 9 but leaves himself out.

> *They* have brought from the Amalekites that which the army spared, i.e., the best of the sheep and of the oxen, to sacrifice them to the Lord *your God;* the rest *we* have utterly destroyed. (1 Sam. 15:15)

(He omits mention of Agag, but Agag's exemption is not at issue in Samuel's denunciation.) Is Saul here trying to shift blame to the army, i.e., I have been obedient, but they have not, or is he legitimately giving them credit for the sacrifice?

Saul does not say that both he and the army "were not willing to destroy" the best cattle and changes the previous "all that was despised and worthless" to the inclusive and colorless "the rest." On the other hand, Saul replaces the negative "and they were not willing to" with a positive purpose—"to sacrifice to the Lord your God." Was this omitted by the narrator in v. 9, or is it an afterthought or rationalization on Saul's part? Do "best" and "good" imply illegal booty or fitting sacrifice? "The Lord *your God*"—Saul is presenting his case in flattering terms, ending with the focus on Samuel and "us." "*They* spared . . . the Lord *your* God . . . *we* have utterly destroyed." In whatever way we understand Saul, "the Lord your God" expresses the Lord's rejection of Saul and the eventual departure from him of the spirit of the Lord (1 Sam. 16:14).

"Samuel said to Saul" (1 Sam. 15:16)—both men are named. The detail marks a break between Saul's explanation in v. 15 and Samuel's utterance; this is serious. "Stop!"—literally, "Drop it!" The terse imperative is analogous to "you have done foolishly" (1 Sam. 13:13). "Stop! I will tell [*higgid*] you what the Lord said to me this night." There is an allusion to Saul's first encounter with Samuel in the term *higgid* and in the talk of night and morning (1 Sam. 15:12). "And he said to him, 'Speak.' And Samuel said . . . ." Saul is referred to by pronoun and not even by that in the latter phrase as the focus shifts to Samuel's word, the word of the Lord, spoken "this night."

"And Samuel said, 'Though you are little in your own eyes, are you not head of the tribes of Israel?' " Another allusion is made to their first meeting—"Am I not a Benjaminite from the smallest of the tribes of Israel?" (1 Sam. 9:21). Saul is charged with not taking his position as king seriously enough; he may be subordinating himself to Samuel when he does not need to. The charge renders hollow Saul's attempt to shift the blame to the people.

Samuel repeats and rewords the command of vv. 1–3:

> The Lord anointed you king over Israel. The Lord sent you on a mission, "Go, utterly destroy the sinners, Amalek, and fight against them until they are consumed."

Samuel speaks only to and of Saul in the second person singular; he does not mention the army. This is a one-to-one confrontation. Samuel briefly reviews the past in v. 18 before accusing Saul in v. 19; there are three accusations. The first is general: "Why did you not obey the voice of the Lord?" The second is specific: "Why did you swoop upon the spoil?" The previous episode is alluded to—the army swooped upon the spoil" (1 Sam. 14:32; *Qere*). This is the first reference to spoil (*shalal*) in chapter 15. The third accusation is general and damning: "Why did you do what is evil in the eyes of the Lord?" 1 Sam. 12:17, Judg. 13:1, etc., ring in the distance. Saul refutes the first two charges and does not mention the third; he probably feels that his two responses negate Samuel's third charge.

"Saul said to Samuel" (1 Sam. 15:20)—both men are named. A break is indicated between Samuel's utterance—"What the Lord said"—and Saul's response; attention is drawn to the response and to Saul. He repeats his explanation, or excuse, at greater length and with a well-balanced rhetorical structure. Saul again shows that he is a master of rhetoric, tailoring his speeches to the context, but he is ineffective; his speeches do not serve their purpose. Samuel is not persuaded; Samuel does not change his mind.

Saul's statement emphatically protests his innocence, proclaims his fulfillment of the mission, and denies that anything was taken as booty. The army took some things to sacrifice to the Lord. Does Saul remember the battle of Michmash and the total rout that would have been possible if the people had eaten of the booty, i.e., if he had paid attention to the army's needs and not just his own oath? In v. 15, Saul spoke of the army and "we"; in vv. 20–21, he speaks of "I" and the army. The order of v. 15 is reversed; gone is the inclusive "we," and "your God" comes at the end.

> *I* have obeyed the voice of the Lord; *I* have gone on the mission on which the Lord sent me; *I* have brought Agag king of Amalek, and
> .   Amalek *I* have utterly destroyed. *The army* took of the spoil, sheep and oxen, the best of the things devoted to destruction [*cherem*], to sacrifice to the Lord *your God* in Gilgal.

The first sentence opens and closes with a first person verb—"I have obeyed . . . I have utterly destroyed." The obedient "I" is central.

The differences between vv. 15 and 21 are instructive. Saul uses "spoil," which was introduced by Samuel in v. 19, and it is the first word of Saul's description of what the army took. After "spoil," he lists "sheep and oxen" and, third, "the best" (*re'shith*). This is a different term for "best" from that employed in vv. 9 and 15 (*meytab*). Saul's new word may reflect Samuel's use of the related "head" (*ro'sh*) in v. 17. Finally, Saul lists "the things devoted to destruction [*cherem*]", which is an addition to v. 15. "To sacrifice to the Lord your God" is the same as in v. 15 except that it is in last place, focusing on Samuel. "In Gilgal" is an addition. This too may be an attempt to flatter Samuel, who is associated with the place, but it also recalls the events of chapter 13.

What do we make of this? Is Saul attempting an even more radical distinction between himself (obedient) and the army (disobedient)? This certainly follows from the details. Saul has utterly destroyed Amalek, but the army kept booty, "the best of the things devoted to destruction." On the other hand, Saul responds to Samuel's charges emphatically and with detail and clarity.

Listening, Sacrifice, and Delight (1 Sam. 15:22–23a)
Samuel will have none of this. He will not accept Saul's explanation or excuse. Saul is a sinner who must be denounced; Samuel is the interpreter of the word of the Lord and will brook no rival. "And Samuel said" (1 Sam. 15:22)—no mention is made of Saul by name or by pronoun; the focus is on the pronouncement. Samuel begins with a question and does not leave its status open; he answers it.

> Has the Lord as great delight in burnt offerings and sacrifices as in
> obeying the voice of the Lord? Pay attention! to obey is better than
> sacrifice, and to hearken than the fat of rams.

The statement accords with the two readings I have been developing.
In regard to retributive justice, there is nothing wrong with sacrifice
in its own time and place, but Saul is unable to identify that time or
place. He consistently confuses the time and place of sacrifice with
that of war, the time to save Israel from her plunderers. He too
quickly identifies sacrifice and other ritual, e.g., not eating, as the
primary aspect of a word of the Lord; it is to be adhered to despite all
contrary circumstances. Saul assumes, in chapters 13 and 15, that
Samuel shares his concern with sacrifice. Samuel does not. "You have
done foolishly." 1 Sam. 15:22 can be read in a similar vein. Even if
Saul and the army have spared the best to sacrifice to the Lord—and
doubts can be raised that this was their intention—it is still disobedience to the Lord's word—"Utterly destroy . . . do not spare." There is
not a hint of sacrifice.

As for "delight" or "desire" (*chepets*):

> "If a man sins against a man, God will mediate for him, but if a man
> sins against the Lord, who can intercede for him?" But they would
> not listen to the voice of their father for it delighted [*chapets*] the
> Lord [or, it was the Lord's desire] to kill them. (1 Sam. 2:25)

The allusion brings important themes into play—(dis)obedience, retributive justice, sacrifice and ritual, life and death. 1 Sam. 15:22 has a
different application to the house of Eli, since, for a priestly house,
"obeying the voice of the Lord" is precisely a matter of "burnt offerings and sacrifices." For the priest, to obey is to sacrifice.

Hophni and Phinehas are doing nothing wrong or questionable in
their concern with sacrifice; it is their actual practices that are sinful,
disobedient to the word of the Lord. Saul, in one sense, is the opposite. His actual practices are not in question. Whether or not they are
legitimate is irrelevant, since his very concern with sacrifice is illegitimate and misplaced.

Power Politics

Saul's concern with sacrifice is not the issue. Samuel denounces Saul
for daring to interpret the command against the Amalekites in a way
that does not fully agree with Samuel's interpretation. He employs a
common debating technique. He shifts from a particular situation—
Saul's detailed response—to an authoritative pronouncement of a
principle and closes with a declaration that the debate is over, that the

decision has been reached. Saul can argue no more; he can only accept or reject Samuel's pronouncement. He can only accept Samuel's authority or assert his own against it.

To return to Samuel's pronouncement, he answers his own question in v. 22 or at least states a principle—introduced by the particle *hinneh*, "look," "pay attention"—that could serve as an answer. Both the question and the principle are in a comparative mode—"as . . . as" and "better than." The implied answer is that the Lord has greater delight in obedience than in burnt offerings and sacrifices; this is not to say that he has little or no delight in the latter.

"Indeed the sin of divination is rebellion, and iniquity and idols are stubbornness" (1 Sam. 15:23a). Samuel moves from the comparative mode, which leaves open the status of sacrifice, to the declarative mode, introduced by the emphatic particle *kiy*, "indeed." It can connect the declaration to the preceding as an explanation, since *kiy* also means "for" and "because," but the explanation says nothing about sacrifice.

It implies that Saul is a stubborn rebel. There is a willfulness to his errors. As rebel, Saul joins the people of Israel who questioned Moses and the Lord in Numbers 16–17, especially Num. 17:25, and Deut. 31:24–29. The texts associate rebelliousness and death. The Deuteronomy text was alluded to in the reference to the book containing the justice of the kingship (1 Sam. 10:25). Moses' law is written in a book and placed by the side of the ark, and Moses concludes his statement about the book:

> I know how rebellious and stubborn you are; look, while I am yet alive, today, you have been rebellious against the Lord; how much more after my death! . . . After my death you will surely act corruptly and turn aside from *the way which I have commanded you.* In the days to come, evil will befall you because you will do what is evil in the eyes of the Lord, provoking him to anger through the work of your hands. (Deut. 31:27–29)

In one reading, this is the point at issue. What is "the way which I have commanded you"? Who has the right to decide it, to interpret it, to apply it?

What is to be made of "divination" and "idols"? Saul may be a bungler and a rebel, but there is no hint that he has turned to divination and idolatry. There is a foreshadowing of his journey to the witch of Endor when he relies on divination. Divination returns us to Deuteronomy 16–18, which frequently appears to be "the text" of which much of 1 Samuel is the paraenesis or sermon. A diviner is spoken of in Deut. 18:9–14. Diviners, soothsayers, etc., are not allowed in Israel, because their practices are abominations of the nations being driven out by the Lord. Before and after this section, Moses speaks of priests and sacrifices (Deut. 18:1–8) and of a "prophet like me" (Deut. 18:15–22); both are germane to 1 Samuel 15. In 1 Samuel, diviners are mentioned in 1 Sam. 6:2: "The Philistines called for the priests and the diviners" to tell them what to do with the ark. The diviners are associated with the priests and with determining the word of the Lord, with establishing "why his hand does not turn away" (1 Sam. 6:3).

Once Samuel appears to Saul at Endor, Saul explains, "I have summoned you to tell me what I must do" (1 Sam. 28:15). With Philistines and with Saul, divination is joined with being told what to do; the Hebrew terms in chapters 6 and 28 are the same—*qara´* (call, summon), *hodi`a* (tell, inform), and `*asah* (do). This is in consonance with one portrayal of Saul; he fails because he seizes one statement, whether Samuel's or his own, as an infallible guide to what he should do. On the other hand, the web of allusions accords with the other portrayal. The conflict revolves about leadership and interpretation, i.e., what to do and who is to declare and do it.

Rejection (1 Sam. 15:23b–31)
"Because you have rejected the word of the Lord, he has rejected you from being king." Retributive justice becomes poetic justice when the punishment fits or matches the sin. "They have rejected me from being king over them" (1 Sam. 8:7). The people, however, are not rejected in return. The same occurs in 1 Samuel 12. The people have done what is evil in the eyes of the Lord by asking for a king and are told to fear not; future judgment is threatened if they continue in their wicked ways, but no judgment is pronounced for the request.

Samuel presents Saul with an unequivocal pronouncement that allows only two positions—obedience or disobedience, accept Samuel's position or assert his own. There is no room here for interpretation or application. You obey me or you do not; you acknowledge me or you rebel. The emphasis is so sharp that in v. 22 "obey" and "hearken" appear without objects; obedience comes close to existing separate from a command or word that is obeyed.

Is the final, definitive statement of Samuel—a prophet like Moses, who cuts through all of Saul's technicalities, his rationalizations, to get to the core of the debate—that Saul has disobeyed the Lord's word by not destroying all the cattle of the Amalekites? This is Samuel the stern, faithful prophet who will not turn from the way of the Lord despite personal feelings and the arguments of others. Or is the final, definitive statement of Samuel that I declare and interpret the word

of the Lord, not you? This is Samuel, the stern, harsh prophet who
will tolerate no opposition to his interpretations, who demands Saul's
acknowledgment of his authority.

> Saul said to Samuel, "I have sinned for I have transgressed the
> commandment [literally, mouth] of the Lord and your words be-
> cause I feared the army, and I obeyed their voice. Now therefore
> [*we`atah*] please pardon my sin and return with me so that I may
> worship the Lord." (1 Sam. 15:24–25)

Saul confesses his sin and accepts his punishment—"I have trans-
gressed the commandment of the Lord." Saul acknowledges Samuel's
authority and realizes that he has lost the debate—"and your words"—
realizes that his authority as king has been seriously undermined. "I
have sinned"—does this phrase refer to moral transgression or to political reality (i.e., I have blundered and lost)? "I feared the army
[*ha`am*] and I obeyed their voice"—excuse and self-incrimination? Saul
fears those he is to rule. Explanation? As Samuel obeyed the people's
voice, so did Saul. Fear means respect, and Saul respects those he is to
rule.

"Now therefore" is followed not by an announcement but by a
request for forgiveness by Samuel, not by the Lord. The significance
of Samuel's returning with Saul to worship the Lord is not apparent.
Is Saul attempting to placate Samuel and, through him, the Lord?
Does Saul make any distinction between Samuel's speech and the
word of the Lord? Saul's request leaves open whether he is appealing
to Samuel, to the Lord, or to both. Samuel's response in v. 26 reas-
serts Saul's rejection. "I will not return with you because you have
rejected the word of the Lord, and the Lord has rejected you from
being king over Israel." Saul unwittingly provides Samuel an opportunity for a more dramatic denunciation.

> Samuel turned to go, and Saul laid hold of the skirt of his robe, and
> it tore. Samuel said to him, "The Lord has torn the kingdom of
> Israel from you this day and has given it to a neighbor of yours who
> is better than you. Also, the Glory of Israel will not lie or repent
> because he is not a man that he should repent." (1 Sam. 15:27–29)

The robe (*me`il*) may be Samuel's or Saul's. Samuel's robe is the pro-
duct of maternal love (1 Sam. 2:19), although now it is a sign of
judgment; later, it is a sign of recognition in the scene at Endor that
repeats this judgment speech (1 Sam. 28:14). The robe is a link bind-
ing judgment on the house of Eli to that of Saul, linking chapters 2
and 15. The ambiguity of whose robe it is points to chapter 24; the

sight of "the skirt of the robe" in David's hand leads to Saul's admission that David will be king and that the kingdom of Israel will be established in his hand.

The robe (*me`il*) can symbolize the kingdom, judgment, and death through the following linkage. Jonathan strips (*pashat*) himself of his robe and presents it to David (1 Sam. 18:4), symbolizing a transfer of royal power (Jobling) in accord with Mosaic practice. Moses transfers Aaron's authority to Eleazar his son by stripping Aaron of his garments and giving them to his son (Num. 20:26–28). Saul acts out a loss of the spirit by stripping off his garments, prophesying (raving?), and laying naked for an entire day (1 Sam. 19:24). This is the final fate of Saul and Jonathan on Mt. Gilboa. The Philistines strip Saul of his armor and cut off his head.

Samuel repeats and changes not his preceding announcement but that in 1 Sam. 13:13–14, since it is the kingdom that Saul has lost, and it is the kingdom that is to be given to Saul's neighbor who is better than he. Does Samuel have someone particular in mind? Because Saul regarded sacrifice as better than (*tob min*) obedience, God regards another as better than he. "There was not a man among the people of Israel more handsome than [*tob min*] he."

"The Glory of Israel will not lie or repent because he is not a human that he should repent." As with other "theological statements," we can regard this as a profound insight or as a pious platitude. There is an allusion to Num. 23:19—"God is not man that he should lie, nor a human that he should repent"—that supports both readings. The Lord has just repented, changed his mind about making Saul king; cannot he repent of this repenting? "Glory of Israel" (*netsach yiśra`el*) occurs only here as a divine title. Why does Samuel not use "the Lord"? Does the title mark his statement as a maxim, as a rhetorical flourish, or as emphasis for its seriousness?

Is this the stern, true prophet of the Lord declaring the Lord's word versus a sinner, or is this a stern, unrelenting prophet denouncing a rival? The dramatics and generalities recall chapters 9–10 and support either reading. No specifics are given there about *nagid* and *melukah;* none are given here about rejection or Saul's neighbor. Nothing is said about how and when the rejection will manifest itself. Samuel focuses on the present situation, the fact of irrevocable rejection, and not on future events. But why?

> And he said, "I have sinned. Now please honor me before the elders of my people and before Israel. Return with me, and I will worship the Lord your God."(1 Sam. 15:30)

Saul acknowledges his sin, his defeat. This time his response does not pick up any new term or theme introduced by Samuel despite the number employed by Samuel. This lends a tone of finality and resignation to Saul's admission; there is no mention here of the word of the Lord or of Samuel or of obeying the army.

Saul realizes the gravity of his sin and the judgment; he realizes the gravity and the far-reaching implications of his defeat by Samuel. However, he wishes to save face before the leaders of "my people" (or, "my army") and before Israel. He has been rejected, his kingship has been undermined, but he will remain king in the eyes of the people for some time. The honoring is perhaps related to the worship of the Lord "your God." This is no longer flattery but acceptance of the Lord's rejection of him. "Samuel turned back after Saul, and Saul worshipped the Lord." Does he thereby honor Saul, or does the focus on Saul in the latter phrase emphasize his isolation from Samuel?

Agag
The honoring may come through the ritual execution of Agag, i.e., Samuel acknowledges that Saul was right in bringing Agag to Gilgal to be executed. On the other hand, the execution could be an implied censure of Saul, since only the king, not the animals, should have been kept alive; Agag is executed, not sacrificed, "before the Lord in Gilgal" (1 Sam. 15:33). Finally, Agag is executed by Samuel and not by Saul; the king of Ai was executed by Joshua (Josh. 8:28–29).

"Samuel said, 'Bring here to me Agag king of Amalek.' " Saul's demand is alluded to. "Saul said, 'Bring here to me the burnt offerings and the peace offerings' " (1 Sam. 13:9). Once more the charge is intoned that Saul places sacrifice ahead of a martial obligation. "Agag came to him *ma`adannoth*. Agag said, 'Surely the bitterness of death has turned away' " (1 Sam. 15:32). His statement can be read in two ways. He expects release from agonizing doubt about his fate by either a swift death or a reprieve from the death sentence. *Ma`adannoth* is the source of the ambiguity. Does Agag approach *fearfully* (*NAB*) or *hopefully* (*RSV*)? There is a parallel with Phinehas' wife, who may or may not have quietly accepted her death because of the birth of a son (1 Sam. 4:20).

Samuel replies to Agag with a poetic expression of justice: "As your sword has made women childless, so will your mother be childless among women." This is followed by an act, not a statement, of judgment: "Samuel hewed Agag in pieces before the Lord in Gilgal." The death penalty that might have befallen Saul because of sparing the animals is displaced unto Agag. Yet death, the word (*maveth*) and the theme, is associated with Saul. He will experience the bitterness of death. It does not turn away (*sur*) from him, but the spirit of the Lord and the Lord himself turn away (*sur*) from Saul (1 Sam. 16:14, 18:12, 28:15–16).

Conclusion

I refer several times to the final chapters of 1 Samuel, the last days and the death of Saul; chapter 30, David's campaign against the Amalekites, is implicated. In its diverse form and content, chapter 15 is a conclusion, a climax, to 1 Samuel 1–15, 9–15, 13–15, and, at the same time is an anticipation of the end of 1 Samuel, the end of Saul and Jonathan.

> Samuel went to Ramah; Saul went up to his house in Gibeah of Saul. Samuel did not see Saul again until the day of his death for Samuel grieved/mourned over Saul and the Lord (had) repented that he had made Saul king over Israel. (1 Sam. 15:34–35)

A definitive separation is shown by "until the day of his death." We are taken to the closing chapters, the deaths of both Samuel and Saul. "Grieved/mourned" is another double reading of Samuel's feeling toward Saul. Samuel is grieved, distressed, by Saul's failures and rejection, because Samuel expected so much from Saul; Samuel mourns Saul as one dead, possibly with personal satisfaction that he has failed. Samuel does not see Saul again because of the grief, the mourning, or the fear. He knows what Saul's reaction is to being bested in the "hermeneutical debate" at Gilgal. "If Saul hears, he will kill me" (1 Sam. 16:2).

1 Samuel 15 is similar to 1 Samuel 11 in that it ends with clarity amid ambiguity. Saul is made king by Samuel and the people (army) with the Lord's sanction; Saul is rejected as king by the Lord and by Samuel. What of the people (army)? Has the clash between Saul and Samuel been conducted in private or in public? There are many simultaneous ways of reading the events, the characters, and the implications for the future. For example, different understandings of why Saul is rejected have counterparts in the rest of 1 Samuel. Sin—Saul sins by destroying the house of Ahimelech in chapter 22; weak leader—Saul responds to Goliath's challenge with fear and trembling; conflict with another—Saul dissipates his and the kingdom's resources in his jealous pursuit of David.

1 Samuel 15 is a focal point, a clustering site, for many of the issues, themes, words, etc., of 1 Samuel. I have noted many in the reading and here isolate, as a summary of chapters 13–15, the question of the word of the Lord and obedience and interpretation. What is the word of the Lord? Where is it to be found? Who declares it? Who can

declare that it has or has not been obeyed in a given situation, i.e., who can interpret it? (Declaring and interpreting are different perspectives on the same process.) The reading of chapters 13–15 has traced various answers to these questions and has come to the conclusion that they have no definitive answer. There are no absolute criteria for deciding the questions.

1 Samuel 15 certainly offers one. The prophet declares the command of the Lord and its observance or violation; this is solidly supported by texts on prophets and on Samuel reaching back to Deuteronomy and before. Saul falls because he has violated a commandment of the Lord. Yet 1 Samuel 15 has already withdrawn the offer. The king can equally so declare. Saul falls because he is bested by Samuel; his authority is undermined. He has not sinned against the Lord in the matter of the Amalekites; he has yielded his power to Samuel. This also is solidly supported by texts reaching back into Deuteronomy and before. The word of the Lord is dispersed and is to be gathered rather than simply found. The word is to be interpreted, taught, applied, and not simply declared and pronounced. Asses may be easily found, but the word of kingship, of prophecy, of the Lord is not so easily found. Yet there are always those who wish to have it found easily; there is always that desire to locate a definitive word of the Lord. If we read on, we may locate such a word; someone may declare it. 1 Samuel 16 does get off to a clear, definitive start with another word of the Lord declared to Samuel.

· 5 ·

1 SAMUEL 16-18

---

1 Samuel 16

The Lord's Anointed and the King's Musician

1 Samuel introduces David, the anointed, the king-to-be. The narrative has an ordered plot, memorable characters, clearly stated themes, and a well-delineated setting. It offers reliable and essential knowledge of who David is, why he is anointed, and what it means to be anointed. There are statements about the Lord and his plans and actions. Yet the text has already withdrawn the offer in a series of feints and dead ends. Explicit details have indeterminate significance. The plot is opened by gaps, and it cannot be closed. The characters are elusive and cannot be univocally described at any level. Themes are expressly stated and then emptied of content by undecidability and equivocation. Settings are precisely delineated, but their significance is indeterminate.

The Anointing
The chapter divides into two parts. Vv. 1–13 are the anointing of David to replace Saul as king; vv. 14–23 are David's introduction into Saul's court as musician and armor-bearer. Since 1 Samuel 16 introduces David, is his "call narrative," it is surprising that he stays in the background; he does little and says nothing. 1 Sam. 16:1–13 is better termed a call narrative of Samuel.

> The Lord said to Samuel, "How long will you grieve/mourn for Saul; I have rejected him from being king over Israel. Fill your horn with oil and go; I send you to Jesse the Bethlehemite because I have seen [ra'ithi] for myself among his sons a king."

The Lord sends Samuel to the one to be anointed, rather than sending the one to be anointed to Samuel (cf. 1 Sam. 9:16); soon David is sent to Saul (1 Sam. 16:19–20).

Reminiscent of Moses in Exodus 3–4, Samuel carries out the commission only after an objection that Saul will kill him if he hears of it. The Lord responds,

> Take a heifer in your hand and say, "I have come to sacrifice to the Lord." Invite Jesse to the sacrifice, and I will make known to you what you are to do. You will anoint for me him whom I name for you.

This implies that Saul will know of Samuel's visit to Bethlehem, regardless of what he thinks of it; Samuel probably fears that Saul will retaliate for the events of chapter 15.

The narrative tells more of the relationship between the Lord and his prophet than of the one between the Lord and his anointed. 1 Samuel 3, the call of Samuel, contains the Lord's message without commission. In 1 Sam. 16:1–13, it is the opposite; Samuel is given a commission without explanation. 1 Sam. 16:1 matter-of-factly states that the Lord has provided, "seen," for himself a king. David is anointed, but why it is David is never addressed. Samuel says nothing to David when he anoints him. The matter of the significance of king(ship) is not raised here. Saul was anointed *nagid* to save Israel from the Philistines; no purpose is given for the anointing of David as king.

Jesse the Bethlehemite is introduced. He is evidently well-known since, in vv. 1 and 18, neither Samuel nor Saul asks for further identification once Jesse's name is mentioned. It is possible that he is an elder, since vv. 4–5 associate Jesse with the elders of the city who meet Samuel. Three of Jesse's sons are introduced—Eliab, Abinadab, and Shammah, apparently in order of birth. Jesse has four more sons and an eighth, the youngest, out tending the sheep. He is named in v. 13 at the end of the episode—David.

In his charge, the Lord informs Samuel that the new king is one of Jesse's sons but does not say which one. When Samuel sees Eliab, he immediately concludes that this is the anointed. Although no basis for the conclusion is stated, the Lord's response implies that Samuel has judged too quickly on the basis of physical appearance: "Do not look on his appearance or on the height of his stature, because I have rejected him." The echo of Saul's rise to kingship supports the implication, and the Lord's statement makes an indirect, negative comment on Saul, who is "a handsome young man . . . from his shoulders upward he was taller than any of the people" (1 Sam. 9:1–2).

"Man looks into the eyes, but the Lord looks into the heart" (1 Sam. 16:7). This is generally interpreted as an explanation for the Lord's rejection of Eliab, an explanation which engages the dichotomy of "true inner self" versus external and frequently false appearances—

"The Lord does not look upon what is external and visible, but upon what a man is like within" (Hertzberg 1964, p. 138). This goes beyond what the Lord says, since he does not state what he sees in the heart or that what he sees differs from what Samuel sees. Nor is the opposition operative elsewhere in Genesis-Kings; God does not choose a person because he knows that person's "true inner self." The statement that "man looks into the eyes, but the Lord looks into the heart" may be accurate theologically, but like other "theological statements," it is a platitude with little determinable relevance to the context. It is a feint of the text, an already withdrawn offer of reliable and significant truth.

I read the statement with Isa. 55:8—"My thoughts are not your thoughts, neither are my ways your ways, says the Lord." God's ways are not human ways, and neither Samuel nor we are to know why the Lord has rejected Eliab or why he has chosen David. The people reject the Lord, but he does not reject them; Saul rejects the Lord, and the Lord rejects Saul; the Lord rejects Eliab. "Do not look on his appearance or on the height of his stature" is not necessarily a rebuke of Samuel but a command—"Don't even glance at him, for I have rejected him"—without explanation. As a rebuke, it could be for transgressing the explicit command to "anoint for me him whom I name to you." Samuel correctly states that Jesse's next six sons are not the chosen, waiting for the Lord's assertion, "Arise, anoint him for this is he" (1 Sam. 16:12).

David is anointed at the Lord's command, "and the spirit of the Lord came mightily upon David from that day forward." Nothing is said of what David understands all this to mean, of how he reacts to it, or of whether he has perceived that the spirit has come upon him. When Saul was anointed king, "the spirit of the Lord came mightily upon him," and he became another man with another heart who prophesied with the prophets (1 Sam. 10:6–10). The spirit came upon Saul, and he defeated the Ammonites and was declared king by the people. The spirit came upon Samson, who performed feats of strength and destroyed Philistines (Judges 14–16). Is something similar, something new and decisive, to happen with David? Will he soon be king? Are defeat and destruction of the Philistines to occur? What is the significance of "from that day forward"? Is it a sign of permanence, a sign that David's possession by the spirit is to be qualitatively different from that of Samson and Samuel?

David and Saul

1 Sam. 16:14–23 narrates David's introduction to Saul's court as a skilled musician whose music soothes Saul when he is tormented by "an evil spirit from the Lord." "Whenever the spirit of God was upon

Saul, David took the lyre and played it with his hand; Saul was re-
freshed and well, and the evil spirit departed from him." Not only is
Saul deserted by the Lord (v. 14), but he is actively tormented by an
evil spirit (cf. 1 Sam. 18:10–11). However, the extent of the evil
spirit's influence is not stated. Is Saul only tormented or disturbed by
it, or do all the acts of the rest of his life flow from it? Does the evil
spirit come upon Saul "from that day forward"? What is the Lord's
role in the remainder of Saul's days?

1 Sam. 16:14–23 apparently occurs after the anointing of David,
although this is not stated, nor is there any indication of elapsed time.
David is the king's armor-bearer. Being a musician and an armor-
bearer does not correspond to the experiences of Samuel and Saul
when the spirit of the Lord came upon them. David is apparently a
permanent resident of the court: "Saul sent to Jesse, 'Let David remain in my service for he has found favor in my eyes' " (1 Sam.
16:22). The theme of finding occurs; David finds favor, but Saul is
not to find David. 1 Samuel 16 leaves room for conjecture about
David. He has been anointed and the spirit of the Lord has come
upon him, but no explanation or purpose is given.

1 Samuel 16:7: Appearance and Perception

1 Sam. 16:7, the Lord's statement to Samuel, emphasizes the theme of
seeing. One Hebrew root to see (*ra'ah*) occurs four times—three verbal and one nominal—and another root (*nbt*) occurs once, for a total
of five references to seeing and appearance in one verse. There is
patent allusion to Samuel, the seer (*ro'eh*; 1 Sam. 9:3–21; Alter 1981,
p. 149–50). The theme is reiterated in 1 Sam. 16:18, which presents
one perception of David; there will be others. 1 Sam. 16:12 describes
David—"He was ruddy and had beautiful eyes and good looks [*tob
ro'i*]."

1 Sam. 16:18 is detailed and concerns David's character; Saul asks
his retainers to find him a musician.

> One of the young men answered, "Look, I have seen [*ra'ithi*, cf. 1
> Sam. 16:1] a son of Jesse the Bethlehemite who is skillful in playing,
> a man of valor, a man of war, prudent in speech, and a man of
> good presence; and the Lord is with him."

Regardless of what the young man makes of his description of David,
whether he knows or believes this of David or whether he is trying to
present David to Saul in the best possible light, the text of the speech
offers an initial description of David that the narrative should confirm
or disprove.

"Skillful in playing" is confirmed in 1 Sam. 16:23, when David's playing gives Saul relief from the evil spirit, but 1 Sam. 18:10–11 and 1 Sam. 19:9–10 raise doubts about, if not deny, David's skill, since his playing fails, on three occasions, to give Saul relief. "A man of valor, a man of war" is part of David's character in 1 Samuel, since he is a successful warrior and general; he retains this in 2 Samuel, but his success can be questioned, particularly after the Bathsheba incident. War, regardless of how David is associated with it, is characteristic of almost all parts of the David story. "Prudent in speech" (*nebon dabar*) stresses the theme of speech/words and hearing so familiar from 1 Samuel 1–15. The phrase has been interpreted as meaning that David is an effective speaker; his speeches are wise, accurate, and beneficial (Rose 1974, pp. 63–65). It can also be taken in an ironic sense; David knows well the public and political effect of speech and therefore chooses his words carefully, wisely, for maximum public and political benefit. His speeches are wise, accurate, and beneficial, but for himself, not necessarily for others or for the nation; David does not incriminate himself in his speeches as Saul can. "Man of good presence or of good looks" serves no obvious function in the story, although there are allusions to it in 1 Sam. 16:12 and 1 Sam. 17:42, Goliath's first impression of David.

"The Lord is with him" is repeated by Saul and the narrator.

> Saul was afraid of David because the Lord was with him and had departed from Saul. Saul removed him from his presence and made him a commander of a thousand; he went out and came in before the people. David had success in all his undertakings, and the Lord was with him. Saul saw that he had great success and he stood in awe of him. . . . Saul saw and knew that the Lord was with David. (1 Sam. 18:12–15)

"The Lord is with him" is related to David's military success and to Saul's fear of him, but no further significance is stated. "Related to"— "David had success . . . *and* [not *because*] the Lord was with him."

Alter has noted the parallel between David in 1 Samuel 18 and Joseph in Genesis 39; the Lord is with both, and both prosper (Alter 1981, pp. 117–18). Potiphar and the prison keeper both ascribe Joseph's success to the Lord being with him (Gen. 39:3, 23), just as Saul is with David. Moreover, in Genesis 39, the narrator relates at least some aspects of Joseph's prosperity to the Lord.

> The Lord blessed the Egyptian's house on Joseph's account, and the blessing of the Lord was upon all that he had in house and in field. . . . The Lord was with Joseph, and he extended him steadfast love, and he gave him favor in the eyes of the prison keeper. (Gen. 39:5, 21)

There are no such statements in 1 Samuel 18. The Lord is with David, but to what effect and for what reason? The assertion approaches a statement of plain fact without implication or consequence.

1 Samuel 17–18

A Summary

1 Samuel 17–18 are analyzed in detail in *The Workings of Old Testament Narrative*. Here I summarize some of the major parts and do not include or repeat the analyses, because they are in that book and because some of their important aspects do not fit with the goals and make-up of this work. In those analyses, I give considerable attention to the split and undecidable view of David, which, like most of my character portrayals, is placed upon a continuum or spectrum with two poles. First is the familiar portrait of the pious and innocent young shepherd who is deeply shocked by Goliath's challenge and feels impelled, perhaps with divine backing, to act. Opposed to that portrait is the intelligent and cunning armor-bearer who knows Saul's weaknesses and sees in Goliath a perfect opportunity for personal fame and advancement. The analysis is tied in with the detailed description of Goliath and his armor. Is this a powerful and fearsome warrior or a big oaf weighed down with armor and with little mobility? Does David approach Goliath fearfully or confidently? Is he gambling, or is he sure of the outcome? He claims to have fought lions and bears (1 Sam. 17:34–36); can Goliath be worse?

Another example is David's proclamation of the Lord's power and intervention in the duel with Goliath.

> I come to you in the name of the Lord of hosts, the God of the armies of Israel, whom you have defied. This day the Lord will deliver you into my hand . . . so that all the earth may know that there is a God in Israel and that all this assembly may know that the Lord saves not with sword and spear for the battle is the Lord's, and he will give you into our hands. (1 Sam. 17:45–47)

Is this the sincere statement of a pious believer or the political speech, delivered in the open before both Israelite and Philistine armies, of a cunning schemer? The parallel with Jonathan's proposed sign (1 Sam. 14:6–12) is manifest. David demonstrates that he is a man prudent in speech (*nebon dabar*); I note this character trait of David throughout 1 Samuel. Finally, there are the relationships with Saul's children, Jonathan and Michal, which are presented in chapter 18. Does David love them? Does he appreciate the friendship and marriage for themselves or for their political utility? He is a royal son-in-law, and his friendship and covenant with Jonathan make him a "substitute son" of Saul.

Particularly in the discussion of chapter 17, I place emphasis on the ambiguity and undecidability of almost every segment, including the closing scene of the chapter, the "Whose son are you?" episode. I note and trace networks of parallels reaching back into Genesis, Exodus, and Judges and ahead into 2 Samuel; this is done more extensively with chapter 18. A great deal is made of the parallels with Jacob, including his encounter at the Jabbok (Genesis 32), his marriage to Leah and Rachel (Genesis 29), and Shechem's rape of Dinah (Genesis 34). The procedures by which I establish and trace the parallels are the same as used here, although the analogies are pursued more intensely and with less direct application to the 1 Samuel texts being read.

Violence and its attachment to David and his descendants are a theme common to chapters 17 and 18. This was encountered in 1 Sam. 16:18—David is a "man of war." I connect a series of texts through the word *sur, to depart and to remove. David removes Saul's sword (1 Sam. 17:39), a classic symbol of violence and blood, and then accepts Jonathan's sword (1 Sam. 18:4). Nathan the prophet assures David that the Lord will never remove his steadfast love (*chesed*) from him and his house (2 Sam. 7:8–15) and, after the Bathsheba and Uriah debacle, assures him that the sword (*chereb*) will never depart from his house (2 Sam. 12:9–10). Shimei, "a man of the family of the house of Saul," speaks accurately when he calls David a "man of blood" (2 Sam. 16:5–8). David is marked by war, violence, and blood, but his association with them can be ambiguous. Is he a good man forced to violence by the times and by others, or is he an unscrupulous man who will do anything to further his aims? The theme of violence and the question will be often repeated.

Despite the ambiguity and undecidability that are hallmarks of my reading of 1 Samuel 16–18, things do happen, the story does advance. What has occurred; how has the story moved; what has been added, dropped, or refocused? Samuel is gone as a central character after 1 Sam. 16:1–13 and is "replaced" by David. The varied relation between Samuel and Saul gives way to the relationship between Saul and David; what that is will occupy the rest of 1 Samuel. The relation between Saul and Jonathan is complicated by that between Jonathan and David.

The Word of the Lord

Samuel's departure marks three changes. First, the prophet is no longer an explicit issue. Second, associated with the first, there is a

significant shift in the appearance and role of the word of the Lord.
Finally, questions about Samuel and about Saul and Samuel are put
aside. The latter is of importance in regard to Samuel's status and
authority as prophet and interpreter of the word of the Lord. To this
point in 1 Samuel, the Lord himself has spoken at relevant points; his
action and intervention are occasionally noted by the narrator; and
others, especially Samuel, have quoted a word of the Lord or at least
have claimed to. Generally, these words of the Lord have been some
sort of command that has to be listened to and obeyed.

Regardless of how we read chapter 15, there are statements of the
Lord, in vv. 2–3 and 11, that stand at the center of the reading. It is
around them that we debate whether Samuel is a prophet or a jealous
leader and whether Saul has sinned or lost a power struggle. With
David we have few such words, whether from the Lord or from someone else, with which to evaluate his behavior. The reading of the last
half of 1 Samuel is not centered on a specifically given word of the
Lord, although it frequently reverts to the question of the significance
and implications of David's anointing and success. It is not that all
mention of the Lord and his word disappears, it is that the mode of
reference that changes. For example, David refers to the Lord several
times in chapter 17, chiefly in his grand proclamation, but the issue is
the Lord's acts, past and future, and the knowledge of the Lord that is
to result. There is no pronouncement of a word that is to be listened
to and obeyed. This will generally be David's and others' mode of
speaking of the Lord throughout 1 Samuel 17–31, e.g., chapters 24
and 25.

Prophets and citations from the Lord are not gone for good, since
both return in 2 Samuel and 1–2 Kings, where we can again discuss
the issue of the prophet and the cited word. In such an analysis,
Samuel's absence, for whatever personal reasons, from the latter half
of 1 Samuel would be significant. Whatever a prophet may be, he is
not one who is constantly present; we have already encountered this
in reading 1 Samuel 4–6. The absence of specific citations from the
Lord is significant. We can read, judge, and evaluate without them. I
made a special point of this in reading chapter 14. The "worst" Saul is
not denounced. No judgment is pronounced within the narrative, but
we the readers can certainly judge and denounce Saul.

Indeed, we read, judge, and evaluate even when presented with a
word of the Lord. The man of God's speech against the house of Eli
was a word of the Lord that was "fulfilled" by being literally dispersed
into the text to be attached, in a myriad of ways, to others and to
other houses, e.g., Saul and David and their descendants. 1 Samuel 13
presented the other end of the process, since the reading gathered a

word of the Lord that was already dispersed into the text in an attempt to understand Saul's failure at Gilgal. 1 Samuel 15 opened with a clear and focused word against the Amalekites; the question shifted to who can interpret and apply such a word—Samuel (the prophet) or Saul (the king)? Even the Lord's assertion that he had repented of making Saul king was ambiguous in regard to his motivation. A cited word of the Lord may be an explicit guide, but it is not an unequivocal and definitive law or explanation. As in 1 Sam. 15:1–3, the word in itself can already be an interpretation of a preceding word or words. Absence of such citations makes a difference; it does not introduce a completely new order.

1 Samuel 17–18 has presented *in nuce* the questions and issues that our reading and evaluation will deal with. How do Saul and David regard Samuel and their respective rejection and anointing? What do they make of the role of the Lord in their lives? What do they believe about their future? Is either taking steps to forestall or advance his future? How do they view and understand each other? How do we as readers regard all these questions and views? Does the Lord have anything to do with these events? If so, what? Why? To what effect?

The tangled, involuted reading will continue as we attempt to make sense of the undecidable, as we attempt to discern who is doing what and why. The putting into question of retributive justice is important; this is not to deny or nullify it. The text has upset and undermined the certitude of the formula or equation that good leads to reward and success and that evil leads to punishment and failure, i.e., we cannot predict an outcome on the basis of behavior, whether the latter is thought of as moral, religious, or worldly. The reverse is also upset. We cannot automatically assume that success or failure indicates that good or evil, in whatever sense, has preceded. For example, David's killing of Goliath can be explained in a variety of ways, including an element of chance, i.e., David gambles and wins. Throughout the remainder of 1 Samuel, David will generally succeed, but we can only ask, and then ask again, why? Is his success due to the Lord's intervention, and, if so, does this have anything to do with David's character or behavior? Or is it due to his own ability and sagacity, to Saul's incompetence, to the help of others, or to just plain luck? The same applies to Saul's failure.

Digression: Succession and Successors II
I previously discussed succession in relation to Eli, Samuel, and Saul and noted the complication of the issue and the process with Samuel and Saul, since Samuel designates Saul and remains on the scene to conflict with him and finally to denounce him and declare his kingship

over. Saul and David represent an even more complicated "succession," with an opaque chain of command. Saul is the actual king but is "illegitimate," since he has been rejected by the Lord and by Samuel; David is a successful general who is the "legitimate" king, since he has been chosen and anointed by the Lord and by Samuel. In both chapter 15 and chapter 16, we have direct quotes of the Lord's speech to Samuel and at least partial confirmation by the narrator. But in chapter 16 the anointing has been done in private, as Saul's was in 1 Sam. 10:1–8, and in chapter 15 the denunciation and rejection may well have been in private, since it is not explicit that the army sees and hears the encounter between Samuel and Saul. In each instance—anointing and rejection—we await an external and public confirmation or illumination similar to the battle of Ebenezer and Saul's battle against the Ammonites. The expectation is not quickly met, since the succession is complex and does not simply and immediately happen; it is a long, drawn-out process that takes the remainder of 1 Samuel to work itself out—King Saul dies and is succeeded by King David. It is accurate to refer to all of 1 Samuel as a succession narrative.

The complex and lengthy process is highlighted by the text, which delays or withholds resolution and definition at those points where they can be most expected. The analysis is indebted to the studies of Alter (1981, pp. 147–52), Gros Louis, and Knierem. David's anointing is a private matter; only Samuel and his family are there. We may wonder what they make of the affair, but there is no match for the public proclamations of Saul as king at the close of chapters 10 and 11. Even though David goes public as Saul's armor-bearer, this does not involve his status as king and anointed. Gros Louis, in fact, refers to this as "a private and personal relationship with Saul" and sees David going public in chapter 17 (Gros Louis 1977, pp. 21–22).

Although chapter 16 closes without clarifying the ramifications of Saul's rejection and David's anointing, chapter 17 opens with a very public battle scene that offers an excellent occasion for such clarification. Two armies face each other across an intervening valley that serves as an open, public platform for battle, for Goliath, and for David. Despite the opportunity for a decisive confrontation parallel with the battles of Ebenezer and with the Ammonites, nothing so decisive happens here. The Philistines flee, and many of their army fall, but this is not presented as a significant defeat or rout. This is not reminiscent either of Saul's finest hour or his worst. Eli and his sons die on the one day; nothing untoward happens to Saul and his sons on this day. The import of Saul's rejection is not to be immediately manifest. The battle of Michmash is a better parallel; Saul blunders, the battle is indecisive, and nothing is made of it.

Before the battle, Jonathan defeats the Philistine garrison, but the feat is ignored; no praise or reward is forthcoming. David defeats the Philistine Goliath, but no praise or reward is forthcoming; no decision is reached. David proclaims the Lord's intervention (1 Sam. 17:45–47), but this is not subsequently confirmed by the Lord or the narrator. David is promoted because of his later success, not because of his killing of Goliath (1 Sam. 18:5, 12–16); the women praise David for killing myriads, not for killing Goliath (1 Sam. 18:6–7). Saul offers his daughters' hands to David not as a reward for killing a Philistine (1 Sam. 17:24–27) but on the chance that the Philistines might kill David (1 Sam. 18:17–25). (I have already discussed the limited information granted by the note that the Lord is with David in 1 Sam. 18:12–16, 28–30.)

· 6 ·

1 SAMUEL 19-23

1 Samuel 19

Flight and Escape

Chapter 18 closes with an assertion of David's success: "The leaders of the Philistines attacked, and as often as they attacked David succeeded more than any of Saul's servants, and his name was very honored" (1 Sam. 18:30). Saul's plan has backfired, since no violence befalls David because of his marriage to Michal. Saul returns to the direct approach similar to his spear throws in 1 Sam. 18:10–11, but this plan is canceled because of Jonathan's intervention. "Jonathan, Saul's son, had great delight [*chapets*] in David." Jonathan is certain that Saul seeks to kill David; the subsequent reconciliation between Saul and David may obscure this for Jonathan, since he apparently has to re-learn it in chapter 20. David must hide "in a secret place" (1 Sam. 19:2), which foreshadows his sin with Bathsheba "in a secret place" (2 Sam. 12:12).

> Jonathan spoke well of David to Saul his father and said to him, "Let not the king sin against his servant David because he has not sinned against you and because his deeds have been of very good service to you. He took his life in his hand, and he slew the Philistine; the Lord wrought a great victory for all Israel. You saw it and rejoiced. Why then will you sin against innocent blood by killing David without cause?" (1 Sam. 19:4–5)

Jonathan uses "sin" three times and speaks of "innocent blood" and "killing without cause." Such issues have not been raised since chapter 15; they will be raised again in the encounter between David and Jonathan in chapter 20. Nevertheless, the issue of "sin" is not developed in either place; it will be raised again in 1 Samuel 24–26.

Jonathan refers to Saul seeing and rejoicing over David's defeat of Goliath. The statement offers added information about the battle and

Saul's reaction to it, but there is no confirmation that Jonathan is giving an accurate account. "Saul listened to Jonathan's voice and Saul swore, 'As the Lord lives, he will not be put to death' " (1 Sam. 19:6). The narrator withholds comment on Saul's feelings and thoughts, and Saul offers no explanation for his oath. Is Saul convinced by Jonathan's argument or by some part of it; if so, which part? Is it the talk of sin, the victory over Goliath, or some subtle reminder of the possible consequences of such a violent deed as killing David, his successful and respected army commander? Or are the oath and the reconciliation a fraud, a means to get David back to court, where Saul can make another attempt "to pin David to the wall with the spear"? Did Saul, in fact, see and rejoice over David's victory, or is this an embellishment by Jonathan?

1 Sam. 11:12–13 and 1 Sam. 14:45 emphasize the opacity of the present text, since they contain the information "missing" here. Saul rejects the army's demand that some be put to death: "Not a man will be put to death this day for *today the Lord has wrought victory in Israel.*" In chapter 14, the army pleads with Saul to give up his vow that Jonathan die, since it is he *"who has wrought this great victory in Israel . . . as the Lord lives, there shall not one hair of his head fall to the ground for he has wrought with God this day."*

Saul tries a third time to "pin David to the wall" (1 Sam. 19:10); this time David realizes the seriousness of the attempt and "flees and escapes." Up to this point, I assume that David has stayed at least in the vicinity of the court. Much of the remainder of 1 Samuel is occupied with the stages of David's "flight and escape" and Saul's pursuit. It ends with David's escape to Achish of Gath in 1 Sam. 27:1–3. "When it was told Saul that David had fled to Gath, he sought for him no more" (1 Sam. 27:4).

Michal, Saul's daughter, helps in David's initial flight. She deceives her father's men by putting *teraphim* in David's bed, making them believe that David is there. Michal, younger sister to Merab, is David's wife; marriage to a younger sister draws a parallel between Michal, David's wife, and Rachel, Jacob's wife. Rachel is ill-fated. She is barren for a long period, then gives birth to only two sons and dies while giving birth to Benjamin, who is marked by ambiguity—vigor and misery, life and death. The only mention of Rachel by name in 1 Samuel intones death: "You will meet two men by Rachel's tomb in the territory of Benjamin" (1 Sam. 10:2). When Jacob and his family are fleeing from Laban, Rachel steals Laban's *teraphim* and lies about the theft. Alter has noted the particular parallel and thinks that it may "foreshadow a fatality shared by Michal with Rachel" (Alter 1981, p. 120).

"David fled and escaped and he came to Samuel at Ramah and told him all that Saul had done to him" (1 Sam. 19:18). Samuel says nothing in response; Samuel never speaks to David, here or elsewhere. We are not given a hint of what he thinks of David. The incident at Naioth in Ramah in 1 Sam. 19:18–24 is an example of a story told literally and in detail but a story whose significance in itself and for its context is clouded. There is no narrational comment on either the action or the characters. Nor is any reaction—physical, verbal, or emotional—of Samuel or David reported; Jonathan is not mentioned. We cannot tell whether Saul's prophesying/raving has changed the state of affairs in effect after David's flight from Saul's house. The main comment by the narrator is the impersonal and enigmatic question, repeated from 1 Sam. 10:12, which closes the episode: "Is Saul also among the prophets?" We still know nothing definite about the significance of either anointing or rejection.

Realpolitik

Although Saul attempts to kill David three times while possessed by an evil spirit, most of his schemes are hatched rationally and coolly, whether they involve an indirect approach through his daughters or a direct approach through his men. Such naked displays of power and force dominate the final chapters of 1 Samuel. As noted, previous issues such as the word of the Lord, the prophet, and the king have been dropped or de-emphasized for the time being. The narrative continues with its concern for the portrayal of characters and of the various relations, stormy or friendly, clear or undecidable, between them and grants an increased intensity to relations that are exploitative, violent, and deadly. This is what I intend by the term *realpolitik,* and a large portion of the rest of my reading of 1 Samuel will deal with the violence and force, including massacres, that seem to come so naturally to both Saul and David. Power and its veiled or naked exercise will concern us. Who exercises it? Upon whom? For what purpose or lesson? Who, if anyone, learns a lesson?

Shifting Sands

"The point of view shifts; the prose style shifts and its tone . . . sequences of events abruptly vanish. Images clash; realms of discourse bang together" (Dillard 1982, p. 24). This is an apt description of what we have encountered in reading 1 Samuel; themes shift and abruptly vanish as well. Reassuring interpretative dichotomies—e.g., the distinction between form (the narrative) and content (the themes and issues)—are not effective. 1 Samuel is not a narrative presentation of otherwise distinct concepts or offices, whether the word of the Lord, interpretation, "prophet," or "king."

The word of the Lord must be interpreted and applied, but the word of the Lord is not a simple and definite entity. It is always already an interpretation. It must be arrived at through a process that combines interpretation and application, that merges the past text with present texts and circumstances, but this process is not a simple and definite procedure. There is no one set of rules that will account for the multiple ways of understanding the divine word in Deuteronomy, Joshua, and 1 Samuel, let alone the other books of the OT.

It is attractive to think that we can subsume the variety, the shifts, and the repetitions of the narrative into a theological thesis that can speak of God's "mysterious ways" and of the unresolvable tension between the divine will and plan (these are our terms and not those of the biblical text) and human wills and plans. The former is unitary, monotheistic; the latter is diverse, because of the multiplicity of characters. This is a seductive thesis, since it allows us, simultaneously, to posit a divine will and plan and to keep it beyond the reach of a full human understanding. For me, 1 Samuel (and most of the OT) is wrestling with a more radical thesis that renders God's role, his will and plan, undecidable. It is not just that we cannot fully know his will and plan, for 1 Samuel gives us no assurance that there is any such thing as a divine will and plan. This is another way, a more "theological" or "philosophical" way, of stating my oft-repeated point that divine statements and comments on divine activity are very limited in their information and in their relevance to the context.

The Lord anoints and rejects Saul and anoints David. He gives a reason for the anointing—to save Israel from the Philistines—and one for the rejection—Saul has not followed him or raised up his words—although the latter is ambiguous. No reason or purpose for the anointing of David is given, which leaves us in a twilight zone wondering if the reason is not given or if there is no reason. Are David's ways in conflict with the ways of the Lord? Are there any special ways of the Lord that are to be David's? Saul dies and David becomes king—is this divine judgment/reward? A divine act of any type? We will continue to ponder these questions as we read of the *realpolitik* of characters such as Jonathan, Nabal, Abigail, Achish, Saul, and David.

1 Samuel 20

A Summary

1 Samuel 20 is also dealt with at length in *The Workings of Old Testament Narrative,* and, as with chapters 17–18, I summarize some of the analysis, since it is contained in the other work and since much of it does not accord with my present purposes. The chapter opens with a

lengthy conversation between David and Jonathan, ostensibly concerned with Saul's reasons for wanting to kill David. "What have I done [*meh `aśithi*]? What is my guilt? What is my sin before your father that he seeks my life?" Saul begins, spends, and ends his royal career seeking something. The conversation and narrative shift from determining such sin or cause for Saul's plan to determining whether Saul, in fact, is set on killing David. A plan is concocted so that Jonathan can determine, at the new moon festival, whether Saul is indeed so inclined. David is absent from the feast, and Saul is enraged at both David and Jonathan, at whom he throws a spear. David and Jonathan agree upon an elaborate sign system, involving arrows shot and a lad sent, to inform David secretly that Saul is bent on killing him. The sign is acted out, but David and Jonathan meet and talk anyway.

My analysis focuses on the discrepancy between determining Saul's reasons for wanting to kill David and determining whether Saul wants to kill David at all. Similar discrepancies are located in the initial conversation between Jonathan and David (1 Sam. 20:1–23) so that at points it is difficult to call it a conversation; it appears that the two may have their separate purposes for this encounter, purposes that are at odds with one another. The final discrepancy noted is the secret sign that is performed and then treated as superfluous.

Several interpretations are proposed that can be simplified by being put on the familiar spectrum. At one end, David and Jonathan are concerned with determining Saul's resolve and the reasons for it; they find that Saul's resolve is inflexible, and David continues his flight. Jonathan and David have to part, but they part as friends and allies. At the other end, the concern with Saul's resolve is a camouflage for other political intentions. These may be various. David's chief one is to find if Jonathan may be of some help to him in spying on Saul and in thwarting Saul's attempts on his life. Jonathan may have several intentions. If he is consumed by his anger toward Saul, he may be actively trying to oust Saul or to get revenge by supporting David. On the other hand, he may be caught between his loyalties for father and for friend and may be making an effort to reconcile them or at least to keep them from killing one another. Finally, Jonathan wants to stay in the good graces of David and Saul so that he will be in a good position regardless of the outcome of the conflict between the two.

Jonathan and David are close friends and are bound by a covenant that extends to descendants (vv. 12–17, 42). Jonathan demands an oath from David sealing the covenant because of his sincere love for his friend or because of his fear of David's violence. Jonathan has sufficient experience to know the violence and irrationality that his father is capable of and may fear the same of David if David prevails in the conflict with Saul. "And he [David] rose and left, and Jonathan went to the city" (1 Sam. 21:1). "Sequences of events abruptly vanish" (Dillard 1982, p. 24). We will read of Jonathan twice more—in chapters 23 and 31, each of which will be dealt with in context.

1 Samuel 21

Ahimelech and Achish

After departing from Jonathan, David goes to the sanctuary at Nob, where he meets with the priest Ahimelech; the majority of chapters 21–22 is concerned with the meeting and its after-math, concluding with the destruction of the house of Ahimelech (cf. Alter 1981, pp. 64–67, 70–72). The chapters employ several modes of repetition, which should elucidate the narrative and some preceding material. The main events of Nob, which are narrated in 1 Sam. 21:2–10 (Eng., 1 Sam. 21:1–9), are referred to in retrospect by the three characters who were there—David, Ahimelech, and Doeg the Edomite (1 Sam. 22:9–23). There is a reference to David's defeat of Goliath and to the song sung to David and Saul as they returned from the battlefront. David's flight to the Philistines in Gath, Goliath's city, is surprising, but the Philistines may provide clarification of their view of David and of the duel with Goliath.

Ahimelech, priest of Nob, is the third person David encounters in his flight from Saul. The story is reminiscent of Samuel's trip to Bethlehem to anoint David. Both incidents involve deception, trembling at the meeting of a lone figure, consecration, and sacrificial food. 1 Samuel 16 is followed by the Goliath story; 1 Sam. 21:2–10 alludes back to it. Just as chapter 17 did not clarify the questions left by chapter 16, chapters 21–22 do not resolve the problems left by chapters 17–20. The chain of events that revolve around Ahimelech involves references and allusions to the past, but it lacks the specificity or trustworthiness needed to reconstruct a narrative of the past from it.

"David came to Nob to Ahimelech the priest; Ahimelech came to meet David trembling and said to him, 'Why are you alone, and no one with you?' " The trembling may be appropriate in the presence of authority, as the elders of Bethlehem tremble at Samuel's approach (Smith 1899, p. 197). Or Ahimelech may suspect that David is in flight because he is alone and therefore in some danger (McCarter 1980b, p. 349). Ahimelech's questions presume earlier contact with David when David was accompanied by others; Ahimelech tells Saul that

David has come to Nob previously (1 Sam. 22:14–15). David's reply is a lie—Saul has sent him on a secret mission, he is to meet his men soon, and he left with such urgency that he brought no food or weapons with him. Although David's alibi is false, his need for food and weapons is real. The narrative can, in this regard, be broken into two parts, obtaining the bread and obtaining the sword of Goliath, with the break in v. 8, the notice of Doeg's presence at Nob.

Bread

David asks first for bread. "Now then, what have you at hand? Give me five loaves of bread or whatever can be found." Ahimelech has no ordinary bread, only holy bread, the bread of the Presence, which he can give to David provided the men have had no sexual contact with women. David replies directly to the restriction with forceful assurance that the men are holy, consecrated. David continues his lie; as a man prudent in speech, he is not caught in the lie.

Ahimelech gives him the holy bread, "for there was no bread but the bread of the Presence which is removed from before the Lord to be replaced by hot bread on the day it is taken away" (v. 6). Is this detail stressing that "this sacred bread is appropriate for the chosen king" (Ackroyd 1971, p. 171)? Is David taking the bread that has been removed and therefore "is not taking bread actually needed for cultic purposes" (Alter 1981, p. 65)? Is it, and the taking of Goliath's sword from the sanctuary "from behind the ephod," emphasizing that David recognizes neither secular nor sacred constraints? Could there be a comment on Ahimelech's competence and his (im)proper maintenance of the sanctuary?

The narrative notes that "a certain man of the servants of Saul was there that day detained before the Lord; his name was Doeg the Edomite, the chief of Saul's shepherds." The significance of "being detained [`atsar`] before the Lord" is not apparent; there is a play on David's statement that "women have been kept [`atsar`] from us." There is an ironic allusion to the Lord's assertion that Saul will rule [`atsar`] his people (1 Sam. 9:17) and to David as shepherd in Doeg, chief of shepherds.

David makes a more urgent request, "Have you not here a spear or a sword at hand?" Ahimelech presents him with "the sword of Goliath the Philistine whom you killed in the valley of Elah." Did Ahimelech see the duel or only hear of it? His statement is tantalizing, but he says nothing more of the event or its aftermath. The sword is "behind the ephod," a foreshadowing of Abiathar's escape to David "with an ephod in his hand." David accepts the sword, and violence is reintroduced and attached to David. Bloody violence soon transpires as Doeg massacres the priests of Nob and the entire city, and David accepts the blame (1 Sam. 22:22).

Achish: A Second Deception

"David rose and fled that day from Saul; he went to Achish the king of Gath" (v. 11). David encounters the fourth person in his flight. Why does he go to Gath? Is this the next stage in his flight? Does he leave Nob and its vicinity because he knows that Doeg will tell Saul that he was there (cf. 1 Sam. 22:22)? Does he go certain that Saul will not and cannot pursue him there? At the news of David's second escape to Gath, Saul definitively ends his pursuit (1 Sam. 27:4). The first trip does not have that effect, because David soon leaves and returns to Judah.

Achish's servants ask, "Is not this David king of the land?" This foreshadows David's later status, but here it is a mistake, an overevaluation. The servants continue, "Did they not sing to one another of him in dances, 'Saul has slain his thousands and David his ten thousands'?" When this was first sung in 1 Sam. 18:6–7, Saul reacted with anger and jealousy; this time David reacts with fear. "David took these words to heart and was very much afraid of Achish the king of Gath." He relies on deception and pretends to be mad; Achish is gulled by the pretense. "Do I lack madmen that you have brought this one to be mad in my presence? Will this one come into my house?" Is he gulled? *RSV* translates, "You have brought this fellow to play the madman." Does Achish see a madman or only one playing at being mad? His final question is an ironic forecast of David's return to Achish, when he may again be gulled by David. The couplet is then quoted for a third and final time by the Philistine commanders when they react with distrust of David, and he is again dismissed (1 Samuel 29).

David's second flight to Achish follows readily upon his experience in his first visit. The Philistines are no threat, since they can apparently be tricked. They overestimate his position in Israel and, for some reason, do not connect him with the slaughter of hundreds of their own, including Goliath. Indeed, David may have Goliath's sword with him as a visible reminder.

1 Samuel 22

A Massacre (Holy War?)

"Saul was sitting at Gibeah under the tamarisk tree on the height with his spear in his hand, and all his servants were standing about him."

He upbraids his servants for not informing him of the pact between David and Jonathan.

> No one discloses to me when my son makes a covenant with the son of Jesse; none of you is sorry for me or discloses to me that my son has raised up my servant against me, to lie in wait, as at this day. (1 Sam. 22:8)

Doeg the Edomite is present at the court. He has nothing to report about David and Jonathan, but he can inform Saul that

> I saw [ra'ithi] the son of Jesse coming to Nob, to Ahimelech the son of Ahitub; he inquired of *the Lord* for him, and gave him provisions, and gave him the sword of Goliath the Philistine. (1 Sam. 22:9–10)

The details are striking, particularly as they relate to the narrative of David at Nob.

Doeg refers to Ahimelech as "the son of Ahitub." The genealogical information was not presented with Ahimelech's introduction, when it would have been appropriate. The information is confirmed by the narrator in vv. 11 and 20. I previously discussed the possibility that Ahimelech is of the house of Eli.

"He inquired of the Lord for him." The action is not reported in 1 Sam. 21:2–7 but is confirmed by Ahimelech himself. "And gave him provisions"—in the ensuing dialogue, no one—Doeg, Saul, or Ahimelech—refers to the fact that the provisions were holy bread. If this omission indicates that taking the holy bread was not a serious transgression, then why is it mentioned in the preceding narrative? Or, if it was important there, why is it glossed over here? Could it be that Doeg did not realize what the provisions actually were and that Ahimelech is not going to incriminate himself by mentioning the holy bread? It may support Alter's contention that David was given used, not fresh, bread. Finally, it may relate to Saul's consistent failure to properly evaluate things sacral or to his present resolve to wipe out the priests as an example; he has an excuse for that in the inquiry. The "omission" of this portion of the narrative in 1 Sam. 21:2–7 is "balanced" by the "addition" of the charge that Ahimelech inquired of the Lord for David.

"And gave him the sword of Goliath the Philistine"—this seems to be a serious charge, yet Saul makes little of it. "Why have you conspired against me, you and the son of Jesse, in that you have given him *bread and a sword* and have *inquired of God* for him?" The Edomite speaks of the Lord; the Israelite king speaks of God. Saul is so consumed with his fear and hatred of David that he shows no concern for the Lord or the word of the Lord. This is not the Saul of chapters 13–15. Saul may be so set on revenge against David through the priests of Nob, on making an example of them, that he is not concerned with solid charges as holy bread and Goliath's sword.

Ahimelech rejects Saul's accusation that he himself did anything wrong in consulting God on David's behalf. He replies directly to Saul's charge and speaks of God, not the Lord. The text of the reply is susceptible of at least two different translations; neither denies that Ahimelech did consult God, and both can refer to the fact that Ahimelech has done this for David.

> Is today the first time that I have inquired of God for him? No! (*RSV*)

> Have I on this occasion done something profane in consulting God on his behalf? God forbid! (*NEB*) (1 Sam. 22:15)

Doeg said nothing of having seen David at Nob until Saul rebuked his servants; perhaps he thought there was nothing amiss with David's presence at the sanctuary. Doeg may have fabricated the charge to make the accusation as damaging as possible. Ahimelech does not deny the charge, since he sees nothing wrong with the action, even though he had not actually consulted the Lord for David. His defense is a positive assertion of his innocence, not a denial that he has done something.

Ahimelech closes his defense with a request that the king not accuse him or his family of anything, "for your servant has known nothing of all this, much or little." Whatever Ahimelech did for David, he did it in ignorance of any break or of any hostility between David and Saul. Saul pronounces judgment, "You will surely die, Ahimelech, you and all your father's house." Whether or not Saul has accepted Ahimelech's defense, his sentence means death for the priest and his entire family. Saul may be interested not in punishing an act of treason—he ignores the bread and the sword—but in eradicating a group of potential enemies and in making an example of them for the Benjaminites gathered at Gibeah. This is supported by Saul's initial summons, not just of Ahimelech, but of all his family. Further, when Saul orders his guard to kill all of them, it is "because their hand also is with David, and they knew that he was fleeing and did not disclose it to me." He had accused the Benjaminites of not informing him of the covenant between his son and David.

At the same time, Saul's stated reason renders Ahimelech's defense superfluous, since now it does not matter what Ahimelech did or what he knew—he told Saul nothing of David. Saul defines such silence as treason, in the cases of both Ahimelech and the Benjaminites. The condemnation contrasts with the praise that Saul bestows on the Ziphites for telling him of David's whereabouts: "May you be blessed by the Lord for you had compassion on me" (1 Sam. 23:21). They and the men of Keilah derive the proper conclusion from the example of the house of Ahimelech (1 Sam. 23:6–13, 19–24).

> Saul said to the guards about him, "Turn and kill the priests of the Lord. . . ." But the servants of the king were not willing [*lo' 'abu*] to put forth their hand to attack the priests of the Lord. The king said to Doeg, "You turn and attack the priests." Doeg the Edomite turned and attacked the priests, and he killed on that day eighty-five persons who wore the *linen ephod*. Nob, the city of the priests, he put to the sword; both men and women, children and infants, oxen, asses and sheep, he put to the sword. (1 Sam. 22:17–19)

"The priests of the Lord"—this is the only time in the episode that Saul mentions the Lord. Through the hand of a foreigner, Saul perpetrates upon Israelites, priests of the Lord, what he himself did not perpetrate upon foreigners, the Amalekites.

> Saul and the people spared [*chamal*] Agag and the best of the sheep and of the oxen and of the fatlings, and the lambs, and all that was good; they were not willing [*lo' 'abu*] to destroy them utterly. (1 Sam. 15:9)

In chapter 22, Saul exhibits no concern for a word of the Lord. The "perverse holy war" continues: "You have had compassion [*chamal*] on me" (1 Sam. 23:21).

Saul's crime in this episode is blatant. He massacres the innocent Israelites for his personal ends; he destroys a priestly family to make an example of them for any others who might consider aiding David. Yet, as with his obvious failures in the battle of Michmash (chapter 14), there is no explicit denunciation of Saul. The analogy with chapter 15, however, reminds us that this is the king who has lost his kingship and kingdom and is demonstrating the loss by acting in a way unbefitting any king.

Nuances in the analogy with chapter 15 have to be analyzed, since that chapter was susceptible of at least two separate readings. If we assume that Saul blatantly sinned in sparing Agag and the cattle, then the parallel between chapters 15 and 22 emphasizes the extent of the crimes in both. Saul does against the Israelites what he did not do, but certainly should have, against the Amalekites. If, on the other hand, we read chapter 15 as a clash over the right to interpret the Lord's word and conclude that Saul was justified in sparing the king and cattle, then the parallel emphasizes the crime in chapter 22, since sparing some was acceptable even with the Amalekites, Israel's hated enemy.

Abiathar: A Sole Survivor

> One son of Ahimelech the son of Ahitub, named Abiathar, escaped and fled after David. Abiathar told David that Saul had killed the priests of the Lord. David said to Abiathar, "I knew on that day when Doeg the Edomite was there that he would certainly tell Saul. I have turned upon all the people of your father's house. Stay with me; fear not; for he that seeks my life seeks your life. With me you will be in safekeeping." (1 Sam. 22:20–23)

David accepts the blame, and the violence of the sword remains attached to him. His acceptance is a statement of fact, not necessarily an admission of guilt, since he says no more of it, nor does he bewail the catastrophe. Whatever David's opinion of his involvement in the slaughter of Abiathar's family, the episode ends with Abiathar bound to David for his protection.

David's Support Groups

The people whom David meets in his flight, beginning with Samuel in 1 Sam. 19:19–24, are often interpreted, in various ways and to varying degrees, as pointing to support for David coming from all parts and levels of society. McCarter's comment on 1 Sam. 19:19–24 is thorough and representative of the approach:

> Once he is safely out of Gibeah, David makes his way to the prophetic encampments near Ramah where he confers with Samuel. This is the first in a series of interviews between David and various individuals who assist his escape, viz. Samuel, Jonathan, and Ahimelech of Nob, to each of whom he goes in turn. All of them are important people—Ahimelech and Jonathan may be said to represent "church and state" to some extent—so that their support of the fugitive hero is especially significant. A new theme, for which we were prepared by Michal's part in the preceding incident, is introduced here: David is protected from Saul by the leading citizens of Saul's kingdom. (McCarter 1980b, pp. 329–30)

My reading of the texts demonstrates that David's protection from Saul can be one of their themes, but not always a definite and certain theme and never the only theme, the "meaning" of the series of meetings. Ahimelech helps David with the provision of bread and a sword, but the narrative does not unequivocally state that either Samuel or Jonathan actually aids David.

McCarter's explication can be expanded into a continuum. At one end is the reading of McCarter and others. 1 Sam. 19:9–22:23 is concerned with a group of people who, with one exception, aid David—Michal, Samuel, Jonathan, Ahimelech, a band of outlaws, the kind of Moab, the prophet Gad, and the priest Abiathar. David is supported by representatives of various parts of "church and state," both upper and lower classes. The one exception is Achish, king of Gath.

The other pole—Michal does help David escape. Samuel turns out to be of little or no use; Saul may prophesy in his presence, but he does not yield in his relentless pursuit of David. Jonathan proves to be of no help for one or more reasons. Ahimelech can give David succor in his immediate flight but not in the long term. David must flee from Nob to Gath; he has to leave his own land and go to the Philistines for relief. Nor do the Philistines provide support; indeed, they themselves present a danger to David. Ironically, the Philistines do, at one time, help David escape (1 Sam. 23:26–28).

After fleeing from Gath, David returns to Judah—to the cave at Adullam, where his brothers and family join him (1 Sam. 22:1).

> Everyone who was in distress, and everyone who was in debt, and everyone who was discontented gathered to him; he became their leader. There were with him about four hundred men. (1 Sam. 22:2)

If this is support, it is ironic. "Saul went to his home at Gibeah and with him went men of valor whose hearts God had touched" (1 Sam. 10:26). "When Saul saw any strong or any valiant man, he attached him to himself" (1 Sam. 14:52).

David's family, at least his parents, are more of a hindrance than a help, since David leaves them in the custody of the king of Moab "until I know what God will do for me" (1 Sam. 22:3–4). Nothing more is said of David's parents or of his brothers. David leaves his stronghold at the behest of a prophet. "The prophet Gad said to David, 'Do not remain in the stronghold; depart and go into the land of Judah.'" Do his parents accompany him on his return? Has the Lord sent Gad? Has Gad helped David? No reason for his command to David is given. Is David in some danger in Moab, as he felt he was in Gath? Gad's only other appearance is in 2 Samuel 24, where he brings a message of judgment to David and presents David with a choice of three punishments—famine, flight, or pestilence (2 Sam. 24:11–14). Future reading will have to develop the parallel further in light of the unsettling effects of other incidents in 2 Samuel 21–24 on the reading of the David story.

Finally, Abiathar comes to David with an ephod. He will be with David for the rest of David's life and will be of some aid, but he is a member of the doomed house of Eli. The judgment speech against the house of Eli now contaminates David and his house. Abiathar joins David, and David offers him asylum and protection. Who is helping whom?

1 Samuel 23

David Narrowly Escapes

David's offer of protection to Abiathar accords with his independence in chapter 23, since he attacks the Philistines with his own army. David may be independent, but his situation is precarious. Saul's pursuit is relentless; the people of southern Judah do not shelter David and are willing to hand him over to Saul. They may be motivated by loyalty to Saul (Gunn) or by fear of a reprisal akin to that which befell Nob; David is certain that Saul will destroy Keilah on his account (1 Sam. 23:10).

The analysis of chapter 23 focuses on two related issues—inquiry of the Lord, including the use of the ephod, and the Hebrew word *yad*, which means "hand" and "power." I begin with the latter. *Yad* occurs nine times in the chapter—vv. 4, 6, 7, 11, 12, 14, 16, 17, and 20. Seven times it refers to giving (*natan*) or handing over (*sagar*) into someone's control and whether the giving over is accomplished or not. The Philistines are given into David's hand, but David is not surrendered into Saul's hand. In v. 16, Jonathan strengthens David's hand in God. V. 6 combines the two issues—Abiathar comes to David "with an ephod in his hand."

The use of *yad* as "power" occurs elsewhere in 1 Samuel, notably in chapter 24, where the term occurs eleven times—vv. 5, 7, 11–14, 16, 19, and 21. The issue is more of restraint than of (in)effective exercise of power. Saul has been given into David's hand (1 Sam. 24:5, 11), but David will not put forth his hand against the Lord's anointed (1 Sam. 24:7, 11). The restraint is anticipated, in an ironic mode, in 1 Sam. 22:17: "The servants of the king were not willing to put forth their hand to kill the priests of the Lord." There is a double twist of power and restraint. "Saul said to his armor-bearer, 'Draw your sword and run me through with it' . . . but his armor-bearer was not willing [*lo' 'abah*] because he was so afraid" (1 Sam. 31:4). Power, as part of a *realpolitik*, is at issue from chapter 22 on, and it is dealt with in terms of its exercise—effective or ineffective, legitimate or illegitimate, restrained or unrestrained. I develop the latter two in the reading of chapters 24–27.

Inquiry of the Lord
David inquires of the Lord at least twice in the chapter; the first time is in the opening episode.

> (1) They told David, "The Philistines are right now fighting against Keilah and they are plundering the threshing floors." (2) David asked the Lord, "Should I go and attack these Philistines?" The Lord said to David, "Go, attack the Philistines and save Keilah." (3) David's men said to him, "Look, if we are afraid here in Judah, how much more if we go to Keilah against the Philistine armies?" (4) David again asked the Lord, and the Lord answered him, "Rise, go down to Keilah for I am giving the Philistines into your hand." (5) David and his men went to Keilah, fought the Philistines, and led away their cattle. He made a great slaughter among them, and David saved the people of Keilah. (6) When Abiathar the son of Ahimelech fled to David, he came down with an ephod in his hand.

V. 4 may report another inquiry or a continuation of the first; the placement of v. 6 leaves open whether or not David's inquiry employed the ephod. Inquiry of the Lord represents a limited insertion of the Lord into the narrative. Inquiries are restricted to a specific situation, usually a military encounter, and the responses are matter-of-fact, with little or no indication of divine motivation or purpose. For example, in Judges 20, there is no hint of the Lord's evaluation of the events and the parties involved that have led to the internecine war.

David's inquiries in chapter 23 and in 1 Sam. 30:6–8 have limited significance. The first inquiry concerns the attack on the Philistines at Keilah. The Lord's response does not show an approval of David that goes beyond the specific undertaking. Indeed, David's continuation of the inquiry immediately after his men's assertion of fear raises the possibility that David's inquiry has as much, if not more, to do with bolstering his men's courage as with obtaining divine approval.

> (8) Saul summoned the entire army to war, to go to Keilah to besiege David and his men. (9) David *knew* that Saul was plotting evil against him. He said to Abiathar the priest, "Bring the ephod." (10) David said [not, asked; is this an inquiry?], "O, Lord, God of Israel, your servant *has certainly heard* that Saul is seeking to come to Keilah to destroy the city on my account. (11) Will the leaders of Keilah surrender [*sagar*] me into his hand? Will Saul come down as your servant has heard? O Lord, God of Israel, please tell your servant." The Lord said, "He will come down" [*yered*]. (1 Sam. 23:8–11)

As usual, Saul is seeking someone or something. David knows what Saul is planning, and the fate of Nob leaves no doubt in his mind of the extent to which Saul will go to kill him. This "inquiry" is profuse compared to the straightforward question in v. 2, and David wants confirmation of what he already knows and has certainly heard. He asks two specific questions in v. 11. The Lord's abrupt one-word response to just the second question—*yered*—may indicate that he too thinks David should already have the answer. This would be akin to Samuel's response to Saul in 1 Sam. 28:15–19; Samuel tells Saul what Saul already knows. In v. 12, David re-asks his first question and again receives a one-word reply. "They will surrender" [*yasgiru*]. The Lord does not mention a direct object. "David and his men, who were about 600, rose and left Keilah; they went from place to place." The outcome is significant, since David and his men leave. The elaborate inquiry was intended for this purpose—to get his men to leave—and not to obtain divine confirmation of his knowledge. This David would share a characteristic with the Jonathan who could use "divine signs" to bolster another's courage.

Jonathan

Jonathan is on the scene in vv. 15–18.

> David saw [*ra'ah*] that Saul had come out to seek his life. David was in the Wilderness of Ziph at Horesh. Jonathan, Saul's son, rose and went to David at Horesh and strengthened his hand in God. He said to him, "Fear not for the hand of Saul my father will not find you; you will be king over Israel, and I will be next to you [or, your second-in-command]; Saul my father also knows this." The two of them made a covenant before the Lord. David remained at Horesh, and Jonathan went home.

Saul again seeks and does not find.

"He strengthened his hand in God." "Hand" (*yad*) can mean "power" or "position." The phrase is followed by Jonathan's assurance that "the hand of Saul my father will not find you." In the Amalekite episode in chapter 30, the army is thinking of stoning David; David is distressed, and "David strengthened himself in the Lord his God" (1 Sam. 30:6). This is immediately followed by an inquiry of the Lord that results in the assurance, " 'Pursue for you will certainly overtake and will certainly rescue.' David set out with the 600 men who were with him. . . ." All of the incidents in 1 Sam. 23:1–5, 8–13, 15–18, and 1 Sam. 30:6–9 emphasize the assurance of another or others and not just giving or obtaining knowledge; all are followed by the action of two or more, not just one. Intoning the Lord, as usual, carries little sure information on any divine activity.

"Fear not!" The only other time prior to this that the text speaks of David's fear is in 1 Sam. 21:13, when he is "much afraid of Achish the king of Gath." There is no other mention before or after 1 Sam. 23:15–18 of David's being afraid of Saul. The assurance "Fear not" is expressing the fact that David is afraid of Saul, although this is not stated elsewhere; at the same time, it is only expressing Jonathan's belief that David fears Saul; finally, and at the same time, it is an appropriate introduction to the rest of Jonathan's speech and expresses no facts or beliefs. The main point is not David's fears but the assurance. "The hand of Saul will not find you." This is analogous to his assurance, "Far from it! You will not die" (1 Sam. 20:2).

"You will be king over Israel." Is Jonathan stating knowledge, belief, or hope? Or is this persuasive flattery? "I shall be next to you" (*RSV*), or, "I shall be your second-in-command" (McCarter 1980b, p. 373). "[Jonathan] expects *nothing more* for himself than the position of second-in-command" (McCarter 1980b, p. 375; italics added), and "[Jonathan] himself *fades into the background,* like the 'friend of the bridegroom' when the hour comes" (Hertzberg 1964, p. 193; italics added). On the other hand, Jonathan is pushing himself into the foreground by demanding a position of high authority, if not a position equal to that of David. The word for "next to" or "second-in-command" is *mishneh,* which means "second-in-command" (2 Kings 23:4; Jer. 52:24), "second-born" (1 Sam. 8:2, 17:13), and "double" or "copy" (Gen. 43:12; Deut. 17:18). Jonathan is second to David in command or birth and, at the same time, his copy, his equal.

"Saul my father also knows this"—both David's future rule and Jonathan's being with him. Saul has said as much to him.

> Do I not know that you have chosen the son of Jesse to your own shame and to the shame of your mother's nakedness? For as long as the son of Jesse lives upon the earth, neither you nor your kingdom will be established. (1 Sam. 20:30–31)

Jonathan and David part company again after affirming their covenant. David stays, and Jonathan "goes home." Whatever Jonathan is about, however he views David and Saul, he does not break with his father. He goes home to him and from there to Mt. Gilboa, the next and last mention of Jonathan in 1 Samuel:

> The Philistines fought against Israel and . . . overtook Saul and his sons; the Philistines slew Jonathan and Abinadab and Malchishua, the sons of Saul. . . . On the morrow, the Philistines . . . found Saul and his three sons fallen on Mount Gilboa. (1 Sam. 31:1–8)

Escape

David asked about surrender (*sagar*) and Saul's coming down (*yarad*). In 1 Sam. 23:19–23, the Ziphites inform Saul of David's whereabouts and assert, "Now, according to all your heart's desire, O king, to come down, come down [*yarad*]; it will be up to us to surrender [*sagar*] him into the king's hand." Saul's reply in vv. 21–25, is more profuse than David's "inquiry" in vv. 10–11 and analogous, since the Ziphites have told him exactly where David is—"in the strongholds at Horesh, on the hill of Hachilah, which is south of Jeshimon." Saul does not at any time delay his pursuit because of a lack of precise knowledge of David's location. In 1 Sam. 26:1, the Ziphites give Saul less precise information on David's whereabouts, "and Saul rose and went down to the wilderness of Ziph." 1 Sam. 23:24–25 give no reason to think that Saul delayed his pursuit on this occasion. However, his elaborate response does stress the themes of assurance and clarity, even though there is little reason for Saul to seek them at this time. The themes continue in the following chapters.

Saul's pursuit is relentless and David is cornered:

> Saul went on one side of the hill, and David and his men on the other side of the hill. David was hard pressed to get away from Saul. Saul and his men were encircling David and his men to seize them when a messenger came to Saul, "come quickly for the Philistines have raided the land." Saul turned back from pursuit of David and went against the Philistines. (1 Sam. 23:26–28)

Ironically, the Philistines, not the Judahites, "save" David. Saul gives up his pursuit to act like a proper king; a national concern displaces his vendetta.

·7·

1 SAMUEL 24-26

At the close of chapter 23, Saul gives up his pursuit. He does not exercise his power when he has the opportunity to, because a larger issue and setting are involved—a Philistine attack on the land. This anticipates the theme of restraint, but it is David's restraint that is central to chapters 24–26; further, David restrains himself because of larger concerns—"the Lord's anointed" and his own future reputation. I treat chapters 24–26 as a quasi-unit analogous to chapters 13–15; there the issue was either restraint when there should have been action or action when there should have been restraint. Like chapters 13–15, chapters 24–26 comment on each other; the reading of one includes the reading of the others. All three chapters contain a great deal of dialogue, including some lengthy speeches that offer clarity and resolution but that either do not always produce it or produce an unexpected clarity. This is not to sever them from their context; they are enveloped by brutal exercises of power in chapter 22 and 1 Sam. 27:8–12. Chapter 23 and 1 Sam. 27:1–4 are paired by the "saving" role of the Philistines and by the theme of relentless and almost successful pursuit that is finally relinquished.

1 Samuel 24

Restraint

Saul does not yield his pursuit of David for long. Once he is told David's location in the wilderness of Engedi, he gathers 3,000 men to seek David. At this point of the story, we can say that Saul's career has been marked by seeking and not finding or by seeking one thing and finding another. Here Saul finally finds David, but the outcome of the encounter is not what he sought.

The encounter is by chance. "Saul went into [the cave] to relieve himself, and David and his men were sitting in the recesses of the cave." David's men present him with what could be a "word of the Lord."

> David's men said to him, "This is the time of which the Lord said to you, 'Look, I give your enemy into your *hand,* and you can do to him whatever is good in your eyes.' " David arose and secretly cut off the skirt of Saul's robe. After this David's heart struck him because he had cut off Saul's skirt. He said to his men, "The Lord forbid that I should do this to my lord, the Lord's anointed, to put forth my *hand* against my lord since he is the Lord's anointed." David persuaded his men with these words. (1 Sam. 24:5–8a; Eng., 1 Sam. 24:4–7a)

The play on *yad,* "hand" and "power," continues, now in a context of restraint. David rejects the "word" because of the larger context; Saul may be his enemy, but he is also the Lord's anointed.

David's express motive for his restraint may be sincere, but it is limited. "The Lord's anointed" recalls the difficult and tortuous terrain of chapters 8–16. What does it mean to be anointed at the Lord's command, whether Saul or David? What power, authority, and duties go with it, if any? What do Saul and David make of their anointing? David stresses that being anointed makes Saul's person sacrosanct, inviolable, but says nothing about any further significance of anointing.

> David rose afterwards and went out of the cave and called after Saul, "My lord the king!" When Saul looked behind him, David bowed with his face to the ground and paid homage. (1 Sam. 24:9)

Saul shows restraint. David is close to him, yet he takes no steps to capture or kill him.

David delivers a lengthy declaration, which I quote in full and then "unpack." It is marked by repetition, quotes, and emphasis on vindication.

> David said to Saul, "Why do you listen to the words of people who say, 'Look, David seeks to harm you'? This very day your eyes have seen that the Lord gave you today into my hand in the cave. One said to kill you, but I spared you. I said, 'I will not put forth my hand against my lord because he is the anointed of the Lord. My father, see, yes see the skirt of your robe in my hand for through the fact that I cut off the skirt of your robe and did not kill you, know and see that there is not in my hand evil or treason. I have not sinned against you, but you hunt my life to take it. May the Lord judge between me and you; may the Lord avenge me upon you, but my hand will not be against you. As the ancient proverb says: 'From the wicked comes

> wickedness,' but my hand will not be against you. After whom has the
> king of Israel come? After whom do you pursue? After a dead dog!
> After a flea! May the Lord be judge; may he judge between me and
> you; may he see and take up my cause so that he can save me from
> your hand." (1 Sam. 24:10–16)

David will not personally attack or kill Saul; whatever Saul may do,
however wicked he may be, "my hand will not be against you." But
David does not seek a reconciliation or even a cessation of Saul's
pursuit. He appeals to the Lord for vindication and protection; he
asks Saul only for the recognition that he means Saul no harm, is not
seeking evil for Saul.

David's speech includes far more than just his demand, since the
words and phrases are pregnant. "Hearing and seeing," which I focused on in 1 Samuel 1–3, are central here, but the order is reversed.
Eli mistook Hannah as a drunken woman because he saw and did not
hear; blind Eli knows that the Lord is speaking to Samuel. Hearing is
privileged over seeing; David switches the poles. "Don't listen, look
with your own eyes!" The seeing is to lead to knowledge and certitude, "know and see," which intones many previous passages, e.g.,
1 Sam. 12:17, if not the entirety of 1 Samuel and its undecidability.
What do we know after reading 1 Samuel? What can we know?

David appeals to retributive justice as he speaks of evil, sin, wickedness—"From the wicked comes wickedness"—and deciding or judging who is right. Canons of justice have been violated. "I have not
sinned against you, but you hunt my life to take it." David's demand is
not for punishment to redress Saul's unmotivated attack, but for
Saul's (public?) recognition that his pursuit of David is unjust. David's
sparing Saul is placed in a larger context; it functions as the "proof"
of David's innocence that underlies his demand for a clarification, a
statement of who is right and who is wrong. David's initial sincerity
and shock have possibly been taken as an opportunity for an effective
political statement.

Nebon Dabar
The statement is effective:

> When David finished speaking these words to Saul, Saul said, "Is
> this your voice, my son David?" And Saul lifted his voice and he
> wept. (1 Sam. 24:17)

There is no need to doubt the sincerity of Saul's emotion or the force
of his confession. Saul confirms that David is a "substitute son" but
will soon act to end David's status as royal son-in-law by giving Michal
to Palti (1 Sam. 25:44).

> He said to David, "You are more righteous than I for you have
> repaid me good and I have repaid you evil. You have told me today
> that you dealt well with me when the Lord surrendered [*sagar*] me
> into your hand; you did not kill me. If a man *finds* his enemy, will
> he dismiss him unhurt? May the Lord reward you with good for
> what you have done for me this day. And now [*we`atah*], I certainly
> know that you will surely be king and that the kingdom of Israel
> will be established in your hand. And now [*we`atah*], swear to me by
> the Lord that you will not cut off my descendants after me, and that
> you will not destroy my name from my father's house." David swore
> this to Saul. (1 Sam. 24:18–23a)

Saul provides the recognition or acknowledgment that David requests
and states it in terms of justice, notably in his opening sentences.

I focus on the closing statement and request, which are not so
subject to norms of justice. Saul's emphatic opening—"And now I
certainly know [*we`atah hinneh*]"—can mark a break and set off the
subsequent assertion. That is, Saul's knowledge may have its source
elsewhere and may not be the result of this incident. In 1 Sam. 18:8
and 1 Sam. 20:30–31, Saul expresses a similar knowledge or fear that
David is to be king, and Jonathan confirms it in 1 Sam. 23:17. Saul
finally speaks it himself and to David. What is left open is the larger
question of why David is to become king. Is he "more righteous" than
Saul in more than this one event? Is he better than (*tob min*) Saul
(1 Sam. 15:28)? If so, in what sense—morally, religiously, politically?
Saul does not mention the Lord in this affirmation of David's destiny.

Saul ends his pronouncement, as Jonathan did in chapter 20, by
requesting an oath from David not to cut off and destroy his descendants. An episode marked by restraint of power ends with a fear of
the exercise of power. David's hand may not be against Saul, but what
about the rest of Saul's family? "David swore this to Saul. Saul went to
his house, and David and his men went up to the stronghold." David
swears to both Jonathan and Saul. Given the disasters that befall the
house of Saul in 2 Samuel and 1 Kings (Shimei), is David's sparing of
Mephibosheth sincere maintenance of the oath or maintenance of the
oath only in letter? In accord with the chapter, the close is separation,
not reconciliation; David wanted clarification, not reconciliation or
even an end to the pursuit. But what is clarified? To answer the
question, let us return to a particular scene.

The Robe and the Kingdom

"See, yes see the skirt of your robe [*kenap me`il*] in my hand." Above I
discussed the certitude implied by "know and see" and previous passages alluded to, including those related to "hearing and seeing."
Samuel's denunciation of Saul is referred to.

> As Samuel turned to go, he seized the skirt of his robe [*kenap me`il*] and it tore. Samuel said to him, "The Lord has torn the kingdom [*mamlekuth*] of Israel from you this day." (1 Sam. 15:27–28)

The allusion, the symbolic power of the skirt in David's hand, is not lost on Saul, since he confesses that David will be king and that the kingdom (*mamlakah*) of Israel will be established (**qum*) in his hand. Saul, indeed, remembers Samuel's denunciation.

> You have done foolishly. You have not kept the commandment of the Lord your God . . . now the Lord would have established [**kun*] your kingdom [*mamlakah*] over Israel forever. But now your kingdom [*mamlakah*] will not be established [*lo' taqum*]." (1 Sam. 13:13–14)

What has been clarified? Because we have heard it, we know that Saul knows that David is to be king and will control the kingdom and also that Saul fears David's violent retaliation on his family. We are still left wondering, why David? In addition, after Saul's assertion, coupled with Jonathan's previous one (1 Sam. 23:15–18) and Samuel's earlier anointing, the question of David's reaction to and thoughts on these speeches and acts becomes critical; I will say more on it after discussing Abigail's analogous declaration of David's future in the next chapter.

We hear, but Saul sees the skirt of his robe in David's hand. The robe is a symbol of Samuel, of the kingdom, and of Saul's rejection. "She said, 'An old man is coming up and he is wrapped in a robe [*me`il*].' Saul *knew* that it was Samuel and he bowed with his face to the ground and paid homage" (1 Sam. 28:14). Saul is again told that "the Lord has torn the kingdom from your hand and given it to your neighbor, to David" (1 Sam. 28:17). For the first time, Samuel names Saul's successor. However, the cut or torn robe in chapter 24 is an ambiguous symbol of David's succession and success, since it points ahead to a future date when the Lord tears the kingdom from the hand of Solomon, David's son (1 Kings 11:11–13), and when another prophet from Shiloh, Ahijah, will tear his new "garment" as a symbol of the rending of the kingdom from the hand of Solomon (1 Kings 11:29–31). David is uttering far more than he is aware of when he tells Saul, "See the skirt of your robe in my hand." Now what has been clarified?

One thing has been clarified—David's restraint toward Saul—"My hand will not be against you." This holds true for the preceding and subsequent chapters; David does not personally attack Saul. In the encounter at Engedi, we can ascribe the restraint to laudable motives—personal respect and religious conviction (the Lord's anointed). There can be a hint of opportunism, since David realizes the advantages of his restraint. I will trace this aspect of restraint through the subsequent chapters, since they illuminate it and supply motives that are not so laudable, motives that are in accord with the "bad" David I have developed.

1 Samuel 25

Abigail and Nabal: Restraint and Power

1 Samuel 24 closes with David's oath to Saul not to eradicate Saul's house. "Saul went to his house, and David and his men went up to the stronghold." "And his men . . . to the stronghold"—the issue of power is still present. Samuel dies. "All Israel [including Saul and David?] assembled and mourned for him, and they buried him in his house at Ramah." Samuel departs the scene at a time when both Jonathan and Saul, regardless of their intentions, have explicitly asserted that David will be king (Gunn 1980, p. 95). The notice of Samuel's death at this point is a reminder of his absence, while he was still alive, from the narrative in chapters 20–24. The absence is notable in chapters 22 and 24. Doeg's massacre of the priests of Nob is a "perverse holy war," alluding to chapter 15; chapter 24 is concerned with the Lord's judging and vindication, with "setting things right."

David speaks of the Lord's anointed in chapter 24; the Lord and Samuel were the last to be associated with anointing and the anointed in 1 Sam. 16:1–13. David, in one limited sense, seeks a word of the Lord—judgment and vindication—akin to the words of Samuel and of the Lord in chapters 13 and 15. On the other hand, David does not address the Lord directly, by inquiry, or through his prophet Samuel; David speaks only to his men, to Saul, and perhaps to the assembled Israelite army. David's invocation of the Lord in 1 Sam. 24:10–16, as in 1 Sam. 17:45–47, may be more for its public effect than as an expression of his personal trust and belief in the Lord; indeed, this is a possible understanding of David's motives even when he formally inquires of the Lord.

Samuel's absence in view of this limited analogy draws attention to the contrast between the presentation of David and that of Saul. With David, there is no "word of the Lord" present in the sense of some command, directive, oath, or vow that he must obey or follow. In view of the earlier analysis of Saul, the word of the Lord, and interpretation in the reading of chapters 13–15, we can say that David is on his own. In a similar sense, we are on our own as we try to determine why

David is the Lord's anointed. Why will David be king? How do we even approach these questions when David is an undecidable character presented on a "character continuum"? The questions can be given a different focus. If Saul is condemned for violating a certain "word of the Lord," why not David? (Indeed, why not Saul in chapter 22?) Samuel denounces Saul's "restraint" at Gilgal in chapter 13; no explicit evaluation is made of David's "restraint" in the closing chapters of 1 Samuel when he is not with Saul at Mt. Gilboa. I trace the impact of these questions in the following readings.

A "Bad David"

To this point, I have stressed the ambiguity in the portrayal of David in the "continuum effect," stretching from the familiar pious, innocent David to the ambitious, brutal David who will stop at nothing to become king. The portrayal, however, has had a tilt toward the positive pole in the sense that it is "easy" to see a "good David" in chapters 16–24. In chapters 25–30, the portrayal has a tilt toward the negative pole, a "bad David," since it is "easy" to see a brutal, unscrupulous David in these stories, especially in chapters 25–27. However, it is a tilt, not a decision. We see in these chapters what David is capable of in the circumstances portrayed, which raises questions about his previous and subsequent actions and motivations.

A Vow Taken Back

In some respects, chapter 25 is a counter-point to chapter 24. Exercise of power or its restraint is at issue, and concern for the larger picture—David's future reputation—is the express motive for the restraint in regard to Nabal. "Good" and "evil" appear even more frequently in chapter 25 and are associated with principles of retributive justice. Play on *yad*, "hand" and "power," continues. In chapters 24 and 25, there is a concern with who is right and who is wrong and with how this should affect one's future actions. Finally, both are marked by verbose speeches.

David's roles in chapters 24 and 25 are in striking contrast. In chapter 24, David's men propose the violence against Saul, and David restrains himself for his own reasons. Saul is impressed with David's restraint and expressed motive. "You have repaid me good and I have repaid you evil." David has not followed a strict principle of justice, since Saul's evil leads to his good—David does not kill Saul—although David does ask the Lord to set things right. Indeed, Saul requests that the Lord "repay you with good" (1 Sam. 24:19).

In chapter 25, David sends ten young men—is ten an indication of force or of the size of the expected "gift" with which they are to return?—to speak of peace (*shalom*) to Nabal; the term *shalom* occurs four times in vv. 5–6. David has done only good for Nabal in protecting his herds and shepherds and now requests food:

> Ask your young men so that they may tell you and that my young men may find favor in your eyes for it is our feast day [*yom tob*]. Please give whatever you have at hand to your servants and to your son David. (1 Sam. 25:8)

Is this a request or a thinly veiled demand? That is, David and his men, and possibly Nabal's men too, are involved in a "protection racket" (Gunn 1980, pp. 97–98). Nabal will not honor the request or the demand but "returns evil for good" (1 Sam. 25:21). Nabal is the reverse of David in chapter 24, who returned good for evil, but Nabal is not dealing with that David, for now David does follow strict justice, since Nabal's evil is to be punished, repaid with evil. "David said to his men, 'Let each man gird on his sword!' Each man girded on his sword and David also girded on his sword." "Sword," a symbol of violence and power, occurs three times in rapid succession, offsetting the talk of peace in vv. 5–6.

Abigail is informed of the situation by one of the young men (vv. 14–17). The young man confirms the basis for David's request, or he confirms the existence of the "protection racket." Abigail is quite intelligent (*tobath śekel*) and beautiful (v. 3); both may be on display in her encounter with David. The narrative of the encounter is detailed, e.g., the "gift" in v. 18 and the lengthy speeches. Gunn and Levenson have both dealt with many of the rhetorical properties of Abigail's speech; I assume their analysis and go in a different direction of reading. I also have the parallel with chapter 14 as background, as a type of guide for the reading. Both stories are marked by vows or oaths involving death; in both someone is not told or does not hear— Jonathan does not tell Saul (1 Sam. 14:1); he does not hear Saul's oath (1 Sam. 14:27); Abigail does not tell Nabal (1 Sam. 25:19, 36)—and in narrative style both involve separate "scenes" that merge into climactic encounters between the two major characters.

Abigail implores David not to carry out his resolve to avenge himself. Her speech is tactful and persuasive; she, like David, is prudent in speech. She is also intelligent, since she comes not just with words but with a huge gift (*berakah*, vv. 18 and 27). David accepts the words and the gift. Abigail's argument is based on the larger picture of David's future, when the Lord will make for him "a sure house" (*bayith ne'eman*) and will appoint (*tsivvah*) him as *nagid* over Israel. Abigail, like Hannah, is a knowledgeable woman—in fact, her whole speech can be considered a pastiche of previous texts—and we are left wondering about the source of her knowledge and about its limits. She speaks of David becoming *nagid,* not *melek.* (The limitation is underscored by Nabal's feast, which is like that "of a king [*melek*]" [v. 36].)

Abigail proclaims that "the Lord has restrained you from going into blood and from saving yourself by your own hand" (1 Sam. 25:26). "Going into blood," i.e., bloodguilt, and taking matters into his own hands have not been problems for David before. Gunn may be correct to see in Abigail's speech not just a moral and practical argument but a specific offer of the gift and of her hand in marriage (Gunn 1980, pp. 100–01). "When the Lord has dealt well with my master, then remember your handmaid" (1 Sam. 25:31). Abigail is intelligent and beautiful after all.

Master and Servant/Slave

Abigail's speech and behavior are persuasive and obsequious. Twice she bows to the ground (vv. 23 and 41); she gives homage to David in her first meeting. In her speech in vv. 24–31, she refers to herself six times as handmaid—*'amah* five times and *shipchah* once—and fourteen times to David as lord or master (*'adon*). Indeed, the entire chapter teems with talk of masters—"lord," "husband," "king"—and servants—"servant" (*'ebed*), "young man," "handmaid," even "son." The height, or depth, of obsequiousness is reached in Abigail's response to David's messengers' marriage proposal: "She rose and bowed face down to the earth and said, 'Look, your handmaid [*'amah*] is a servant [*shipchah*] to wash the feet of my lord's servants' " (v. 41).

"Lord/master" and "servant/slave" are prominent in the chapter. *'Adon* occurs thirty-eight times in 1 Samuel; eighteen of these are in chapter 25, three in chapter 24, and six in chapter 26. Because of this prominence, I focus on "lord and servant" or "master and slave" as a major theme in chapter 25 and trace it in the succeeding chapters; it obviously involves issues of power and restraint. I use the term "servant" inclusive of all the above Hebrew terms and note that they, especially *'ebed,* can also carry the meaning "slave."

David introduces the theme in his initial request, which speaks of his and Nabal's young men and subordinates himself and his men to Nabal—"your servants . . . your son David" (vv. 6–8). He speaks as servant. Nabal continues the theme but in a denial; he speaks as master to David's servants. "Who is David? Who is the son of Jesse? Nowadays many *slaves* [*'abadim*] are running away from their *masters* [*'adonim*]" (v. 10). Nabal lives in Maon and has his herds in Carmel; should he give of his food to men "who come from I don't know where" (v. 11)? David's young men report to David; he responds to his men as master. He commands them to arm themselves. In his request, David spoke as servant but may already have been acting as lord.

Abigail is introduced in subservient status as "Abigail, Nabal's wife." However, she acts more as a lord by going to David with the gift, "but *her husband* Nabal she did not tell." I translate literally to show the stress given to "her husband" by being placed first. Vv. 21–22, in retrospect, inform us of David's oath, probably spoken at the time of his command to his men in v. 13. He now speaks in scorn of "this one" without name or title. The unusual oath formula and strong oath in v. 22—"God do so to the enemies of David and even more, if by morning I leave from all that is in his house a single male"—reflect the scorn and ironically forecast the conclusion of the story. David does leave all males who belong to Nabal, and God "does so" to David's enemy Nabal (vv. 29, 38). I have already commented on Abigail's obsequiousness in vv. 23–31 and now return to the reading of the close of chapter 25.

Unrestrained Power
In chapter 24, David appealed to the Lord for final vindication but without specifics as to how and when that vindication would come. In 1 Sam. 25:32–34, David replies to Abigail's entreaty with a pomposity befitting most of the speeches of the chapter. Three times he pronounces blessing (*baruk*) on "the Lord the God of Israel" and on Abigail, both of whom have prevented him from incurring bloodguilt and from saving himself by his own hand. Blessing, *baruk*, is a blatant pun on the gift, *berakah*, brought to him by Abigail. David acknowledges the Lord's and Abigail's activity but says little of his own wrongdoing or error. David comes close to saying that the Lord and Abigail are privileged because they were able to help him. David does not let pass an opportunity to remind Abigail of who is master, of who has the power of life and death.

> As surely as the Lord the God of Israel lives who *restrained me from harming you,* if you had not come quickly to meet me, then there would not have been left to Nabal at morning light [`ad 'or habboqer] as much as one male. (1 Sam. 25:34)

This is not all.

> David took from her hand that which she had brought for him and said to her, "Go up to your house; see, I have listened to you and have granted your request!"

The focus is on "I," not "you"; there is no doubt as to who is lord and master here.

Abigail may be servant to David but not to Nabal. She returns home to find Nabal drunk at a banquet "like the banquet of a king"; Nabal's pretensions to lordship are carried far. Abigail's equal or superior status is signaled by the text, which, in v. 36, speaks of Abigail and Nabal but does not cite their relation as husband and wife. Because of Nabal's drunkenness, Abigail says nothing until morning light (`ad 'or habboqer`). In the morning, "*his wife* told him all these things." The irony is heavy. The wife who would not tell when she probably should have now does when silence would be in her husband's best interest.

The Lord played no active role in chapter 24; now he intervenes directly. "Ten days passed and the Lord smote Nabal and he died." No motive or purpose is stated. His death was presaged by David in v. 22 and by Abigail. "Now may your enemies and those who seek evil for my lord be as Nabal" (v. 26). She clarifies this fate. "The lives of your enemies he will sling out as from the hollow of a sling" (v. 29). The image recalls David slaying Goliath with "a sling and a stone" (1 Sam. 17:50). When Abigail tells Nabal of her dealings with David, "his heart died within him and he became a stone" (1 Sam. 25:37).

David hears of Nabal's death and will not let a good opportunity pass. He apparently makes his pronouncement to anyone who wants to hear; no particular audience is indicated. He credits the Lord not only with restraining him from killing Nabal but with then killing Nabal to vindicate David.

> Blessed be the Lord who has taken up the cause of my disgrace from the hand of Nabal and has withheld his servant from evil and the evil of Nabal has been returned upon his head. (v. 39)

"Disgrace" (*cherpah*)—this is another allusion to the David and Goliath story, since the same root is employed for Goliath's "defiance" of the Israelite army (1 Sam. 17:10, 25–26, 45), and David speaks of killing Goliath and "removing reproach [*cherphah*] from Israel" (1 Sam. 17:26). Parallels there may be, but Nabal is no Goliath, and it is David's reputation, his reproach, that is at stake here, not defiance of the Lord of hosts, the God of the armies of Israel. The analogy can render the Abigail and David story a parody. Finally, David intones retributive justice, "evil," against Nabal but a justice that is defined by one's attitude and actions toward David; the Lord, for David, is his private judge and executioner. David asks for divine vindication, a setting of things right, vis-à-vis Saul, but God neither acts nor speaks. David threatens to kill vis-à-vis Nabal; he seeks no determination of right or wrong. God acts without speaking, and David declares vindication, pronounces that things have been set right. But to what effect? Nabal is neither a Goliath nor a Saul.

David ironically invokes the Song of Hannah.

> Talk no more so very proudly, let not arrogance come from your mouth for a God of knowledge is the Lord, and by him actions are weighed. (1 Sam. 2:3; *RSV* with *Qere*)

David, in chapter 25, is claiming the right to weigh actions. He "interprets" an act as an act of the Lord and then provides "the word" that led to it, i.e., "Thou shalt not disgrace David." David is master and has no Samuel to challenge either his right to interpret or his interpretation, but we the readers certainly can.

David restrains himself at Abigail's bidding for future considerations, possibly including her hand in marriage, and he blesses the Lord and her for restraining him and the Lord, in particular, for not restraining himself, for killing Nabal. David, the interpreter, the prophet, can be located in other statements. "God do so to the enemies of David and even more, if by morning I leave from all that is in his house *any that pisses against the wall*" (1 Sam. 25:22). He repeats the oath to Abigail, "If you had not hurried to meet me, there would not have been left to Nabal at morning light *any that pisses against the wall*" (1 Sam. 25:34). The oath does not necessarily include Nabal or even his men; the italicized phrase, previously translated "male," may refer only to Nabal's flocks. The graphic image is appropriate to many animals. The precise target of the oath is not clear. It is the messenger to Abigail—"evil is determined against our master and his whole house"—and then Abigail herself who speak of Nabal as the object of the oath and perhaps of murder (1 Sam. 25:17, 25, 31).

They, particularly Abigail, are certain that there is a threat from David but are not so certain of what the threat is; they speak of evil, shedding blood, and taking vengeance, but neither expressly speaks of David threatening to kill Nabal. Fear of David's violence is shared with Jonathan and Saul. David's oath may only have been a threat to kill flocks or even Nabal's men—"all that is his" and "there would not have been left to Nabal"—but given Nabal's death and Abigail's speech, David takes the opportunity to "reinterpret" the situation and to focus it all on Nabal and himself. David would have killed animals, but the Lord, the judge, kills Nabal because he has insulted David. David's rhetoric of morality, of restraint, is a self-centered rhetoric of a *realpolitik*.

He Sent and Took

The chapter that stresses restraint ends with the exercise of raw power. Abigail was correct to refer repeatedly to David as lord.

> When David heard that Nabal was dead, he said, "Blessed be the Lord . . . the evil of Nabal has been returned upon his head." David *sent* and told Abigail that he would *take* her as his wife. David's servants came to Abigail at Carmel and said, "David sent us to you to *take* you to him for a wife." (1 Sam. 25:39–40)

Gone are the verbosity and persuasiveness of the other speeches of the chapter; narration takes precedence over discourse. David sends and takes, as he does with another woman at a future time (2 Sam. 11:4; cf. Gunn 1978, pp. 94–111). David as master is like the king who is to take so much from the people (1 Sam. 8:11–17).

Abigail responds more as slave than as servant. "She rose and bowed face down to the earth and said, 'Behold, your handmaid is a servant to wash the feet of my lord's servants.' " Her response could not be further from that of Nabal in vv. 10–11. As before, in vv. 18–23, Abigail hurries to go to David and "became his wife."

Is Abigail eager to become David's wife because of love, like Michal, or has she, like the men of Keilah and Ziph, properly learned a lesson of power and violence, a lesson that Nabal did not learn? David may be arrogant in regarding Nabal's rejection of his demands as an evil to be punished, but this is all too often a fact of (royal) power. People who frustrate a king's desires frequently die as a result, e.g., the priests of Nob, Uriah the Hittite, and Naboth the Jezreelite (Miscall 1983, pp. 27–40). Chapter 25, in retrospect, is not so much about the restraint of power as about the exercise of power under the thin veil of a rhetoric of restraint.

> And Ahinoam David *took* from Jezreel, and the two of them became his wives. Saul had *given* Michal his daughter, the wife of David, to Palti the son of Laish, who was from Gallim. (1 Sam. 25:43–44)

There is no restraint here, and Saul's power is not yet at an end. Some equality between David and Saul is implied, since both can dispose of women. Saul, however, is still the master, since he takes David's wife and gives her to another.

Summary

This will bring together much of the preceding and lead into the reading of the rest of 1 Samuel. The exercise or restraint of power has been at issue from the opening pages of 1 Samuel; I have focused on it at this point in the reading because of its prominence, signaled by the frequency of *yad,* from chapter 23 on. With chapter 24, I narrowed the theme to David's restraint toward Saul and then Nabal, succinctly stated in the phrase, "My hand will not be against you." To this point, David will not harm Saul, because of respect for Saul as the Lord's anointed and possibly because David subsequently realizes that this will increase his reputation; after all, he is also the Lord's anointed. His restraint in chapter 24 has an immediate reward—Saul's confession. David will not harm Nabal, because he realizes that such violence will harm his reputation, or because he wants another reward—the gift and Abigail. David may not act, but why not is open—respect (including religious conviction), future reputation, or some other benefit that comes from the restraint. More possible motivations for David's restraint will be added from the subsequent chapters.

The possibility that David is concerned for his reputation must be qualified by the fact that most people already regard him with fear, specifically with fear of his violence—Jonathan, Ahimelech, Saul, and Abigail. Goliath does not and dies; Nabal does not and dies; Achish does not, and more on him shortly. David as the "man of blood" was introduced in the reading of chapter 18. Further, some—Jonathan, Saul, and Abigail—speak of David's future as king or *nagid* in very certain and precise terms, but David says nothing in response. This accords with the presentation of David from 1 Samuel 16 on; we have no explicit information on David's understanding of his future. Does he think he will be king? If so, does he believe that this is preordained by the Lord, that it is inevitable because of Saul's failures, that it is a good possibility, or that it is something for which he must strive, constantly and in every way possible? If kingship is on his mind, Abigail's talk of *nagid* could be an insult.

"Lord and servant" and "master and slave" were brought to center stage in chapter 25 and connected with power but not in a symmetrical fashion. One who is lord may or may not initiate action, i.e., restraint and exercise of power are the lord's options. Abigail demonstrates her authority by not telling and then by telling Nabal. A servant, on the other hand, responds to a command or previous act; Nabal is a good example. I have not used the terms, but much of my reading, mainly of the relations between Samuel and Saul and between Saul and David, could be recast in these terms. Who is lord, who is servant? This is significant when there is a clash, when both claim to be lord, e.g., Samuel and Saul in chapter 15, or when there is a hierarchy, e.g., Abigail is servant to David and master to Nabal. Finally, what of David and Saul? In chapter 24, David is in control. He does not act, and then he speaks; Saul responds. In some ways

both are masters—army commanders, kings, anointed of the Lord. At
the end of chapter 24, Saul is still king and returns to his house. In
chapter 25, David is dominant over Nabal and Abigail but is still not a
full equal of Saul.

1 Samuel 26

Replay of a Power Play

In chapter 26, even the thin veil of the rhetoric of restraint is de-
creased. The men of Keilah, the Ziphites and Abigail have all learned
lessons from the exercise of power and the value of allying oneself
with the one who has power. David, on the other hand, has learned
the strategic value of restraint, which can make him look good—"no
evil in you"—whether or not he is. The narrative in chapter 26 is a
"combination" of chapters 24 and 25 and now with an explicitly cold,
calculating David. The contrast with the David of chapter 24 is underscored by the contrast between the narratives of chapters 24 and 26,
which start similarly and then go their separate ways.

Chapter 24 was a study in David's restraint when given an opportunity to harm or kill Saul. Chapter 26 is a demonstration of David's
ability to put himself in the position to kill Saul; David is master and
demonstrates his position by not acting. This is no chance encounter
at Hachilah, as it was at Engedi. David "saw that Saul had come after
him into the wilderness; David sent spies, and he knew that Saul had
come." David's approach and view are described in the detail befitting
a careful plan.

> David rose and went to the place where Saul was camped. David
> saw the place where Saul lay; Abner the son of Ner, the commander
> of the army, and Saul were lying in the encampment, while the
> army was encamped around him. (v. 5)

Abishai and Abner

I deal briefly with these two characters, since treatment of them would
require reading extensive parts of 2 Samuel. The parallel between
them is interesting—both are generals in their respective armies, and
both drop suddenly from the narrative to reappear in 2 Samuel. Abishai volunteers to go with David to the camp. Why does David want an
accomplice and only one at that? David may want someone, especially a
man like Abishai, to go down to Saul's camp with him to serve as his
"straight man" by proposing to kill Saul on the spot.

God has now given [*sagar*] your enemy *into your hand;* now let me
pin him to the earth with one blow of the spear, and I won't strike
him twice. (v. 8)

Faced with Shimei, Abishai twice proposes to kill him on the spot (2
Sam. 16:9–10; 2 Sam. 19:21–23). Perhaps David wishes to impress
Abishai personally with his restraint and respect for Saul so that Abishai may have a similar regard for David in the future; only Abishai,
not David's men, hears David's speech in 1 Sam. 26:9–11. In any case,
Abishai introduces the theme of death; in 1 Sam. 24:5, David's men
speak only of doing whatever is good in David's eyes.

David picks up and elaborates the theme of death with four separate terms.

> David said to Abishai, "Do not *destroy* him for who can put forth his
> hand against the Lord's anointed and be innocent?" And David
> said, "As the Lord lives, the Lord will *smite* him, or his day will come
> and he will *die,* or he will go into battle and *perish.* The Lord forbid
> that I should put forth my hand against the Lord's anointed; now
> take the spear which is by his head and the jug of water, and let us
> go." (1 Sam. 26:9–11)

The statement is pregnant. The Lord smote Nabal and he died, and
Saul is to go into battle and perish. The spear is by Saul's head, "and
they cut off his head" (1 Sam. 31:9). "Cutting off" carries us back into
chapter 24.

"David took the spear and the jug of water from Saul's head, and
they went their way." The final phrase is the last mention of Abishai
in the story. "No one saw; no one knew; no one was awake for they
were all asleep since a deep trance of the Lord [*tardemath yahweh*] had
fallen upon them." Is this the intervention of the Lord; has he put
them to sleep? Or is this a use of "yahweh" akin to that of "elohim" in
1 Sam. 14:15 and possibly of "yahweh" in 1 Sam. 11:7 as a superlative
adjective—"an extremely deep sleep or trance"? If it is the Lord's
intervention, it would be in a class with the killing of Nabal and would
raise the question of whether it is on David's behalf or whether there
could be another purpose for the deep sleep. It does not appear to be
in the same class as the trance that came upon Adam (Gen. 2:21) and
Abraham (Gen. 15:12).

"David went over to the other side and stood on top of the hill at a
distance with a great space between them" (v. 13). Planning is evident.
Saul has no chance to capture David this time. David's first call is to
Abner, not to Saul, and the point is not David's restraint but Abner's
incompetence. "Why didn't you keep watch over your lord the king

since one of the army came to destroy the king your lord?" David
condemns Abner and the entire army. "What you [singular] have
done is not good. As the Lord lives, you [plural] deserve to die [liter-
ally, are sons of death] because you have not kept watch over your
lord, the Lord's anointed." The statement anticipates the defeat of the
army at Mt. Gilboa and Abner's absence or escape from Mt. Gilboa,
where he again fails to keep watch over his lord. Abner is not a
proper servant to his lord.

"You Will Certainly Do!"

Abishai and Abner drop from the story, which now concerns only
Saul and David. Saul's opening comment—"Is this your voice, my son
David?" (v. 17)—is exactly the same as in 1 Sam. 24:17; this time he
does not weep. Saul has been through this before. David's speech in
vv. 18–20 begins and ends with reminiscences of his statement in
chapter 24, but there the resemblance ends; David here has little
interest in revenge or vindication. He speaks only of his own death,
not Saul's. Although the "lord" and "servant" contrast continues in
David's mouth, he is the one in control in this situation.

> Why does *my lord* pursue *his servant?* For what have I done [*meh
> `asithi*]? What evil is there in my hand? [cf. 1 Sam. 24:12, 16] But
> now let *my lord* listen to the words of *his servant.* If it is the Lord who
> incited [*swt*] you against me, may he be appeased by an offering,
> but if it is men, cursed be they before the Lord because they have
> driven me out this day so that I have no share in the heritage of the
> Lord. They say, "Go, serve other gods." Now, do not let my blood
> fall to the earth away from the presence of the Lord for *the king of
> Israel* has come out to seek *one flea* like one who pursues a partridge
> in the hills. (1 Sam. 26:18–20)

David's concern with being driven from the Lord's presence and heritage does not mesh with his cavalier assumption that the Lord can be
appeased (*ravach*) with an offering; is he thinking of his own appease-
ment or refreshment (*ravach*) of Saul with his lyre (1 Sam. 16:23)?
The Lord, as inciter (*swt*), is not so easily appeased elsewhere (cf. 2
Samuel 24). This is the David who quickly fled the Lord's heritage to
go to the Philistines and the Moabites (1 Sam. 21:11–6; 1 Sam. 22:3–
4) and who returns to the Philistines to take up a lengthy residence
(1 Sam. 27:1–28:2). Does David already have the latter move in mind
and now is attempting to blame it on Saul and to cast it in theological
rather than political-military terms?

Saul's reply is a "confession" like 1 Sam. 24:18–22, but now Saul
says nothing about David becoming king, and he does not invoke the
Lord.

> I have done wrong [or, I have sinned]. Return, my son David, for I will do no more evil to you because my life was precious in your eyes today. Yes, I have acted foolishly [*hiskalti*, cf. 1 Sam. 13:13] and have erred very greatly. (v. 21)

The statement is terse and ambiguous. This could be a sincere admission by Saul of serious sin against both the Lord and David, or it could be a weaker admission that Saul has done a few things wrong, including letting himself get caught in his present predicament. "To do wrong/sin," "to act foolishly," and "to err" do not necessarily carry a heavy theological or religious denotation. "Return!" can then have a sinister aspect; we encountered a similar ambiguity in 1 Sam. 19:1–7.

David's answer is much wordier.

> David answered, "Here is the spear, O king! Let one of the young men cross over and get it. The Lord rewards everyone for their righteousness and faithfulness. The Lord is he who gave you into a hand today, but I was not willing to put forth my hand against the Lord's anointed. Look, as your life was valued this day in my eyes, so may my life be valued in the eyes of the Lord so that he will save me from all harm." (vv. 22–24)

David drops the "master-servant" rhetoric and speaks plainly, even scornfully: "O king!" Only the spear is to be returned; keeping the water jug, a symbol of life, could be a sign of David's control. Although David invokes the Lord, it is more as guarantor of his future prosperity than as vindicator. There is no affirmation that David will not take future action against Saul. Saul's rejoinder is more terse than his first, and in view of his declaration in 1 Sam. 24:20–22, it verges on mockery.

> Blessed are you, my son David! Indeed, you will certainly do! Indeed, you will certainly succeed!

(*RSV:* "You will do many things and will succeed in them." My translation stresses the balance and brevity of the statement.)

The narrator matches Saul's brevity and balance. "David went on his way; Saul returned to his place." This contrasts with the geographical details at the opening of the story and anticipates the continuing narrative of David's "way" to kingship and Saul's "place" on Mt. Gilboa. Or, with a different evaluation, it refers to David's wandering on his way and to Saul's stability, his place. Finally, there is even more balance between Saul and David than at the end of chapters 24 and 25; there is no contrast in power here.

Summary
Chapters 24–26 have, from one perspective, charted a rise in David's
fortunes as he acts more and more like lord and master, more and
more independently, and a corresponding slippage in Saul's fortunes.
He recognizes David's destiny, and although he can take away David's
wife, Saul's authority in southern Judah is apparently limited. Neither
Abigail nor Nabal mentions the possibility of appealing to Saul or of
reporting David to Saul, as the Ziphites do. Finally, in chapters 24 and
26, Saul is actually at David's mercy in at least two incidents. To some
extent, the three chapters are analogous to chapters 16–18, which
chart another rise for David, a slippage for Saul, including his recognition of David's prowess and success, and David's marriage to Michal.
But there is no mention by the narrator in chapters 24–26 that the
Lord is with David, despite claims by David and others to that effect.

David acts with authority and independence, but why? Is David the
leader of a powerful outlaw band who is flexing his muscles, who is
showing that he controls a considerable expanse in southern Judah?
Does David believe himself to be a child of destiny who is separated
from the throne only by time? "As the Lord lives, the Lord will smite
him, or his day will come and he will die, or he will go into battle and
perish." He would be supported in this belief and others in varying
ways by Jonathan, Saul, and Abigail and by the memory of his anointing by Samuel. The questions arise because of the explicit references
to David's future and because of the absence of any explicit reaction
on David's part to the various pronouncements.

A final motive for David's restraint toward Saul can be added to
personal respect and concern for his reputation. In chapter 26, David
restrains himself, he does not act, to demonstrate the opposite—his
power and ability to act. To show in an impressive manner that he can
kill, David does not kill.

·8·

1 SAMUEL 27-31

"Thus David Has Done"

David, who shortly before was publicly perturbed with being driven from the Lord's heritage, now proposes "in his heart":

> One day soon I may perish by the *hand* of Saul; there is nothing better for me than that I immediately escape to the land of the Philistines so that Saul will quit seeking me any longer within the territory of Israel, and then I will escape from his *hand.* (1 Sam. 27:1)

The motif of *yad,* "hand" and "power," is maintained. David's statement is matter-of-fact; is it best characterized as fear or as a realistic appraisal? In either case, we have another possible motive for David's restraint vis-à-vis Saul, i.e., he recognizes Saul's power and will avoid Saul at almost all times. At Hachilah, David was willing to gamble, as he did with Goliath, because of the great gains he could make. David may have more in mind than just the escape from Saul when he goes to the Philistines, but we are told nothing explicit about that. Finally, David speaks of the Lord to others; "in his heart" he does not mention the Lord. David, in fact, does not mention God or the Lord while with Achish, even though Achish refers to both God (1 Sam. 29:9) and the Lord (1 Sam. 29:6).

David's escape is no small undertaking, since he is accompanied by "the six hundred men who were with him . . . every man with his household, and David and his two wives, Ahinoam the Jezreelite and Abigail the Carmelite, wife of Nabal" (v. 3). Nor is it a brief stay; "David dwelled in Philistine territory for a year and four months" (Driver 1890, p. 163). The strategy works. "When Saul was told that David had fled to Gath, he sought for him no more" (v. 4). But why does Saul give up the chase? Does he consider David to be out of reach in Philistia, or does he think that David has deserted and gone over to the Philistines for good? Does David know that Saul has given up?

David and Achish

> David said to Achish, "If I have found favor in your eyes, let a place be given me in one of the country towns that I may dwell there; why should *your servant* dwell in the royal city with you?" (1 Sam. 27:5)

"Saul sent to Jesse, 'Let David stay in my service for he has found favor in my eyes' " (1 Sam. 16:23). The story of David, servant to King Achish, forms a counterpoint to the story of David, servant to King Saul. Is David master or servant? Over whom or to whom?

David's request of Achish is granted. "That very day Achish gave him Ziklag; therefore Ziklag has belonged to the kings of Judah to this day" (1 Sam. 27:6). One can wonder when "this day" is in light of this passage and similar ones throughout Genesis-Kings. The statement is intriguing, since it presumes the existence of "kings of Judah to this day"—is this the same "day" when a *ro'eh* is called *nabi'*?—and does not say "house of David" or "Davidic" kings in a context dominated by David. There is an explicit anticipation of David as king, and here he is depicted as master of his own city. Is there a hierarchy here? David is lord of Ziklag and of his men but servant to Achish. Or is David servant only in name to Achish?

David's "Mishpat" (Holy War?)

David and his men do not idle away their time but raid (*pashat*) the Geshurites, the Girzites, and the Amalekites. "David smote [*hikkah*] the land and left alive neither man nor woman [*lo' yechayyeh*], but took sheep, oxen, asses, camels, and garments" (1 Sam. 27:8–9). This story, and that in 1 Samuel 30, are reminiscent of the holy war legislation in Deut. 20:10–18. The latter makes a distinction between "cities which are very far from you" and "the cities of those peoples whom the Lord your God is giving to you as an inheritance . . . the Hittites, the Amorites, the Canaanites, the Perizzites, the Hivites, and the Jebusites." With the first, all the males are to be killed (*hikkah*, Deut. 20:13) and the women, children, and cattle to be taken as booty; in the second group, nothing that breathes, human or animal, is to be left alive (*lo' techayyeh*, Deut. 20:16).

David does not make the distinction. In distant cities, he kills all humans, men and women, and takes the cattle "and the garments" as booty. This is not surprising, since David is not "fighting the battles of the Lord"; he is securing his own position. He "took sheep, oxen . . . and returned and came to Achish." The text is evasive; it does not tell us what David did with the booty. Did he give it to or share it with Achish? His motive for leaving none alive is personal, not theological.

> David left alive neither man nor woman to bring to Gath, thinking, "Lest they might say, 'Thus David has done.' " This was his custom [*mishpat*] all the time he dwelt in the territory of the Philistines." (1 Sam. 27:11)

David's inner motive is expressed matter-of-factly, as in v. 1. Why is he concerned with someone, particularly Achish, finding out what he has done? Does he fear retaliation? The people are not Judeans, and there is no reason to think of them as Philistine allies. Or, with an eye to David, is he just trying to make the best of a bad situation; is he looking to the future and attempting to establish some further basis for his power? This can still mean that he will avoid a direct battle with Saul at all costs.

David took skirt, spear, and water jug as "witnesses" to his restrained action—"See the skirt of your robe in my hand . . . and know and see that there is not in my hand evil"—now he leaves no witnesses to his unrestrained brutality. The narrative comments obliquely through terseness and punning. "This was his custom." David's custom, *mishpat*, is raiding, *pashat*. In chapter 27, we are twice afforded a glimpse of David's "true" motives, of what he says in his heart. In neither is there a reference to the Lord. In vv. 1–3 and 8–11, David acts to avoid danger from a king. The man who knows well the strategic value of restraint and flight also knows well the strategic value of battle and wholesale massacre. David, indeed, does and, indeed, succeeds. He succeeds in part because no one comes to say, "Thus David has done." Saul relinquishes the search, "and Achish trusted [*ya'amen*] David, thinking, 'He has made himself odious to his people Israel, and he will be *my servant forever* ['*ebed olam*]' " (v. 12).

Reprise: Master and Servant

Is Achish stupid and gullible; is David an extremely capable confidence man? What of the booty from the raids? If Achish is receiving large amounts of booty from David, is he then blinded, perhaps knowingly, by it? Achish may share with Nabal's men a self-interested involvement with David. On the other hand, like Nabal, Achish seriously underestimates David by regarding him as a servant or slave. David serves Achish for his own present interests or future plans, not because he is Achish's servant, let along "a servant forever." This is analogous to a major thread of my reading of the relationship between Saul and David. Saul may be obsessed with his pursuit of David and may gravely overstep his authority, as in the massacre of the priests of Nob, but whom is he pursuing? Is this one of the king's "faithful servants" (`ebed ne'eman, 1 Sam. 22:14) and loyal general of his army? Or is this a cunning and unscrupulous rival whose hand will not be against the king, but neither will it be with the king in his hour of need? Achish errs when he considers David a permanent servant; does Saul err when he considers David a permanent enemy (cf. 1 Sam. 18:29)?

Again we can consider questions of David's motives and long-range plans revolving around his future kingship. Is he convinced that he will be king? If so, is he waiting for things to work out his way, or is he doing all in his power to bring them about? Is he capable and cunning? Is he a man caught in the middle between Saul and Achish and then between Achish and the Philistine generals? At this pole of the spectrum, David is in great distress, and violence and brutality are all that occur to him as a way out, i.e., his fear of Achish and the Philistines in chapter 21 is still present. And, regardless of the moral evaluation, David is certainly a "man of blood." He does not want to attack Judeans directly, but he lies to Achish lest Achish send him back to Saul.

---

1 Samuel 28–31

The Final Battle

The concluding chapters are composed of four major episodes—1 Sam. 28:3–25 and 1 Samuel 29, 30, and 31—which are connected by the background of battle, building to the climactic defeat of Israel on Mt. Gilboa. 1 Sam. 28:1–2 continues the story of David and Achish from chapter 27 and introduces the battle. "In those days the Philistines gathered their forces for war to fight Israel" (1 Sam. 28:1). Similar statements are found in 1 Sam. 28:4, 1 Sam. 29:1; and 1 Sam. 31:1.

Against the background of the muster, Achish makes David an ambiguous proposal. "Know certainly that with me you will go into the camp, you and your men" (1 Sam. 28:1). "Into the camp" (*bammachaneh*) is frequently translated "in the army" (*RSV*) or "into battle" (McCarter), but elsewhere in 1 Samuel *machaneh* means "camp," not "army" or "battle," with the possible exception of 1 Sam. 29:6. Thus it is not explicit that Achish wants David to join in the actual battle; David and his men may only be Achish's personal bodyguards. "Know certainly!"—is this a proposal, an assurance, or a command? David's response is no less ambiguous. "Very well, you will know what *your servant* can do." David echoes Achish's stress on knowledge and Saul's pronouncement, "Indeed, you will certainly do." David implicates his fears that survivors might tell Achish, "Thus David has done." David's fears—past, present, and future—become themes; depending on the circumstances David will do almost anything. "What have I done?" could more accurately be, "What haven't I done?" 1 Sam. 28:1–2, however, leaves open whether this might include battle against Saul and Israel; the question is resumed in chapter 29.

"Achish said to David, 'Very well, I make you bodyguard [literally, watcher of my head] for life'" (1 Sam. 28:2). In accord with one of the above readings, Achish now confirms and extends the term of David's duty. Achish's trust and misjudgment of David continue. So does the play on "head" (*ro'sh*). David is the man who once cut off the head of another Philistine from Gath and whom the Philistine generals fear will reconcile himself to Saul "with the heads of the men here" (1 Sam. 29:4). David once bound himself to Saul as son-in-law by killing and then cutting off the foreskins of 200 Philistines. We certainly know what David can do.

1 Samuel 28:3–25

A Night in Endor

My reading of the story is indebted to the studies of Beuken and Gunn (1980), includes other texts and themes, and goes in other directions than they do. 1 Sam. 28:3 provides two pieces of information about the past. The report of Samuel's death is not new, since it was noted in 1 Sam. 25:1 before the Abigail and David story; Saul's dealings with a knowledgeable woman are to have a radically different outcome from David's. We were not informed that "Saul had removed the mediums and the wizards from the land," which is in accord with the Mosaic legislation in Deut. 18:9–14 and in Lev. 19:31 and Lev. 20:6, 27. "Do not turn to mediums and wizards; do not *seek* them" (Lev. 19:31).

But Saul does not follow another piece of Mosaic legislation. "Saul saw the Philistine camp, and he feared and his heart trembled greatly." The Israelites are not to fear even if they "see horses and chariots and an army larger" than theirs (Deut. 20:1). At an earlier time, Saul was in fear because of a Philistine challenge (1 Sam. 17:11); David came on the scene to answer the challenge and kill the Philistine. Saul may be in fear at Mt. Gilboa, because neither Samuel nor David is there with him to tell him what to do or to do it for him. Saul inquires of the Lord, "and the Lord did not answer him either by dreams, or by Urim, or by prophets" (1 Sam. 28:6). We are not told what Saul is inquiring about. Battle with the Philistines seems a foregone conclusion; does he want a guarantee of victory? Or do we take Saul's explanation to Samuel at face value (v. 15)? Saul is in great distress and does not know what to do. In this instance he is similar to David in distress but different in the response. David does and succeeds; Saul does and fails.

Saul does not respond to the Lord's lack of an answer by assuming sin, as he did before (1 Sam. 14:37), but responds as one of his servants did when Saul was terrified by an evil spirit—by seeking out someone to help in his distress (1 Sam. 16:14–16). David served in the first case, the "witch of Endor" in the second. Neither provides the aid or relief that Saul seeks.

"Saul disguised himself and dressed in other ['*acherim*] garments" (v. 8). This is the man who was given another ['*acher*] heart and turned into another ['*acher*] man by God (1 Sam. 10:6–9). Saul's first nocturnal meeting with Samuel is "repeated," but with the message of 1 Samuel 15, not that of 1 Samuel 9–10. This is a tale of ends, not beginnings. Saul wants the witch to divine for him; chapter 15 is included once more. "The sin of divination is rebellion" (1 Sam. 15:23). The woman is fearful for her life since "Saul . . . has cut off the mediums and wizards." Ironically, Saul swears to her by the Lord—"as the Lord lives"—however, the story is about death, not life. This is the last time that Saul will speak the name of the Lord.

Samuel is to be brought up. "The woman saw Samuel and cried out in a great voice and the woman said to Saul, 'Why have you deceived me? You are Saul!' " (v. 12). The divining powers of the woman are not employed; Samuel simply appears. This is another "knowledgeable woman" like Hannah and Abigail. The source of her knowledge is not indicated, since she sees Samuel and immediately realizes that she has been deceived by Saul. The woman tells Saul that she sees "gods ['*elohim*] coming out from the earth." What does he look like? "An old man is coming up and he is dressed in a robe [*me`il*]." This is enough for Saul. "Saul *knew* that he was Samuel and bowed with his face to the ground and did homage."

> Samuel said to Saul, "Why have you disturbed me by bringing me up?" Saul said, "I am in great distress. The Philistines are fighting against me, and *God* has turned from me and will not answer me again either by the hand of prophets or by dreams. Therefore, I have summoned you to make known to me what I should do" (v. 15)

This is a Saul of old—he cannot act on his own but needs Samuel's guidance, needs a "word of the Lord." This is not the Saul of chapters 22–23 who acts on his own, even though in murderous fashion, and this Saul stands in sharp contrast to the David of chapters 25–27. This is the Saul presented in the analysis of chapters 13–15, a Saul who has to have a certain guide in order to act, whether Samuel's command or his own oath. His statement fits this portrayal. Saul speaks first of his distress and of the Philistines before mentioning God's turning away and God's refusal to answer him. Saul's response reads as though it were directly addressed to Samuel's earlier directive in 1 Sam. 10:7–8.

> When these signs come to pass, do whatever your hand finds for God is with you. Go down before me to Gilgal . . . and I will make known to you what you should do.

God has turned from Saul, Saul's hand finds nothing to do, and he turns to Samuel for direction.

> (16) Samuel said, "Why ask me? *The Lord* has turned from you and become your enemy. (17) *The Lord* has done to you as he spoke by *my hand,* and *the Lord* has torn the kingdom [*mamlakah*] from *your hand* and has given it to your neighbor, to David. (18) Because you did not obey the voice of *the Lord,* and you did not carry out [`aśah, do] his fierce wrath against Amalek, *the Lord* has done this to you this day. (19) *The Lord* has also given Israel with you into *the hand* of the Philistines; tomorrow you and your sons will be with me; also *the Lord* has given the camp of Israel into *the hand* of the Philistines.

Saul said "God" once; Samuel says "the Lord" seven times. The denunciation is balanced, especially in vv. 17 and 19, and plays upon the terms "hand" and "do." Retributive justice is invoked: "Because you did not do, the Lord has done." Yet more is involved, since Israel also is to be given into the hand of the Philistines; what has she done to have this done to her?

"Why ask me?" Samuel is not the issue or the source of a word of the Lord, since he is dead. "The Lord has turned from you." This is Samuel's first point, not his third, and it is the Lord, not God, who has turned. Previous texts are summoned. "Saul feared David because the Lord was with him, but had turned from Saul" (1 Sam. 18:12; cf. 1 Sam. 16:14). Samuel tells Saul no more than he should already know, i.e., why ask me, since you already have the word of the Lord? Or, with a slight twist, why ask me, since I am dead and can only tell you what you already know? Samuel condenses the entire narrative of 1 Samuel 16–27 and even chapter 28 into the fulfillment of his denunciation in 1 Sam. 13:13–14 and 1 Sam. 15:22-29. Samuel says nothing of Saul's sin of divination and consulting a medium. He speaks not of a vague and distant future but of "this day" and "tomorrow." And he names Saul's neighbor this time, David, confirming Saul's declaration in 1 Sam. 24:21.

"The Lord has also given Israel with you into the hand of the Philistines." Saul and his sons, like Eli and his sons, die on the same day, a day on which the Philistines defeat Israel. The elders of Israel, like Samuel, declare that the defeat is the work of the Lord; in neither instance does the Lord himself or the narrator confirm the declaration. Even if the declaration is accurate, we are given no hint in either case of the Lord's motivation. The deaths of the families of Eli and Saul may make sense as punishment for sin, but why is Israel included in the debacles?

A Meal
Saul begins and ends the episode in fear.

> Saul immediately fell full length on the ground; he was in great fear because of the words of Samuel. Moreover, there was no strength in him since he had not eaten any food all day and all night. (v. 20)

The closing scene can be read on different tracks; in any reading, some attention must be given to the previous texts that are recalled. As seeking and eating, particularly at night, marked Saul's beginning, they mark his end.

Possible readings—Saul is weak because he has not eaten; Saul is weak because he has been fasting. Hannah lingers in the background. Beuken argues that the knowledgeable woman of Endor is now ignorant, for she thinks that Saul's dismay or terror can be remedied by a good meal; she does not understand that Saul's terror stems from the death sentence that he has just heard and that is to be carried out the next day (Beuken 1978, pp. 11–13). Gunn reads differently. Saul is weak from fasting, and his eating marks his acceptance of life "even when he knows that this time life holds only death in store for him" (Gunn 1980, p. 109).

I propose a third possibility based on Samuel's pronouncement, an interpretation that can complement either of the above. Saul is weak from not eating or from fasting and at first refuses food because of his consternation. The climactic moment of Samuel's return from the dead has produced only the return of the past for Saul. He remembers the denunciations; he realizes David's destiny; he knows that this battle may well result in his death and Israel's defeat. The dead have nothing new to say.

The woman's statement to Saul plays upon "listening to" (*shama*`), recalling Samuel's accusation, "You did not listen to the Lord." Saul eats because the woman tells him to; she makes known to him what he is to do.

> Now listen to the voice of your handmaid so that I may place a morsel of bread [*path lechem*] before you; eat that you may have strength when you go [*halak*] on your way [*derek*]. (v. 22)

The latter phrase could be translated "when you go to your fate." *Derek* has the sense of purpose, goal, journey, and mission in 1 Sam. 9:6, 8, and in 1 Sam. 15:18, 20. Texts return, and some are ominous. "The Lord sent you on a mission . . . I went [*halak*] on the mission" (1 Sam. 15:18–20). In addition, the judgment speech against the house of Eli is attached to the house of Saul.

> Anyone who is left in your house will come to implore him . . . and say, "Please attach me to a priestly position to eat a morsel of bread [*path lechem*]." (1 Sam. 2:36)

And once more the parallel between the defeats at Ebenezer and Mt. Gilboa asserts itself, accompanied by the question of the Lord's possible intervention and motivation.

"And they ate and they rose and they went that night." What effect has the encounter at Endor had on Saul, if any? Has it produced a death sentence, a certitude that he did not have before? Or has it only confirmed what he already knows? Is Saul to be considered brave or tragic? Does he accept death with resignation and calm, or is he so afraid that he does not know what else to do? Is he accepting death at all? He has heard Samuel's recriminations and fulminations before and has still lived through battles with the Philistines.

Conjurings

What effect has the encounter at Endor had on the reader? Are we enlightened on Saul's character, especially as he goes to Mt. Gilboa? I could add questions but turn instead to a positive effect that takes into account Samuel's "coming up from the underworld." This is presented as an actual event, not a dream or a vision, even though dreams are explicitly mentioned by Saul. This tale of the conjuring of the dead itself conjures previous texts. The allusiveness forces rereadings, reinterpretations, that deepen all the texts, even if the deepening means increased complexity and undecidability, even if it is an unending reading and rereading. For example, 1 Samuel 4—the defeat at Ebenezer—is parallel to 1 Samuel 31—the defeat at Mt. Gilboa—but the focus of the two is different. Israel is defeated at Ebenezer, and Hophni, Phinehas, and Eli also die on that day; Saul and his sons die on Mt. Gilboa, and Israel also is defeated on that day. Israel's defeat is in the foreground in the former, in the background in the latter.

On the other hand, Samuel's denunciation of Saul does offer a clarification by way of a reduced and narrowed focus—Saul is to lose the kingdom and to die because he violated the word of the Lord in the attack on the Amalekites. Samuel's denunciations in chapters 13 and 15 are combined and ascribed to one sin. This certainly simplifies the situation we encounter in reading chapters 13 and 15, where Samuel's condemnations occur amid a cloud of enigma and possible readings. Neither incident at Gilgal could be read simply according to a norm of retributive justice—Saul has sinned and is punished. Samuel could not be regarded simply as a faithful and stern prophet of the Lord announcing a definitive word of the Lord.

Yet this is how 1 Samuel 28 portrays him. He returns from the dead to cut through all the events that have occurred since 1 Samuel 15, including the present conjuring, and to get to the core—Saul sinned once and must die. This is attractive and could nullify my readings. The undecidable has been decided—Saul has sinned and must die. Possible power plays, jealousy, realistic fear of a brutal rival and perhaps of a scheming son, etc., can be put aside; we now have the answer, the decision, from the Lord's own prophet. This "allusion," this conjuring of past texts, calls for an end to reading and rereading; the enigma has been solved, the analysis can be terminated—Saul has sinned and must die. Yet nothing is nullified, since nothing is decided; this is a word from the dead that repeats the past by simplifying it. Samuel adds nothing to his assertions in chapters 13 and 15; he only narrows them. He names David but says nothing more about why David. The only point that Samuel adds and clarifies is a time of death. "Tomorrow you and your sons will be with me." Faced with the Philistine army, Saul may already suspect, if not know, this.

The night at Endor cuts two ways. It depicts the futility of conjuring the dead, since this results in an announcement of death; to speak with the dead is to join the dead. It also depicts the emptiness of seeking the certitude and simplicity that Samuel offers; only the dead and death have such certitude and simplicity. The only certitude and simplicity we can have are that such a certain and simple explanation as Samuel's is meaningless and dead.

1 Samuel 29

What Will David Do?

The chapter can be read as a contrast to the story of Saul in chapter 28, which is framed by the story of David among the Philistines (1 Sam. 27:1–28:3; 1 Sam. 29). Unlike David, Saul is paralyzed; he does not know what to do. In his final hour of distress, he returns to his beginning, to Samuel, and has that "beginning" repeated to him. David, in his troubles, knows well what to do, even if it means leaving "the heritage of the Lord" and going to the Philistines in Gath; David, in a distorted way, goes back to his beginnings, since he slew Goliath of Gath and later fled to Achish of Gath. David shows no concern for the Lord's or God's role in events; he says neither "Lord" nor "God" in the narrative of his stay with Achish. Why is open to debate. The omission may be intentional on the part of a deliberate and self-centered David, or it may be due to his distress and haste. He does and says what he thinks will best serve the present crisis.

1 Sam. 28:1–2 left open the question of whether David would go into battle against Saul and Israel; chapter 29 continues the question and still leaves it unanswered. We are far from Endor and now do not receive even an offer of clarity and decision. Several readings are possible that are based on David's possible responses to Achish's regarding him as a perpetual servant and lifelong bodyguard. First, David will not fight Saul and Israel under any circumstances, but he faces just this probability because of Achish's actions. Chapter 29 explains why David never had to face the situation, whether by chance or by divine intervention. Second, David will fight Saul and Israel, analogous to his subsequent battles against Absalom and Sheba; chapter 29 explains why he did not actually have to, whether by chance or by divine intervention. Third, an "in-between reading"— David does not want to fight Saul and Israel but would in these circumstances; he does not have to because of chance or God. David's character dissolves into a spectrum, since we are presented with a wide range of possible readings of his actions and motivations, including his reaction to Achish's opinion of him and his promotion of him.

Achish
Achish is presented in a complex portrayal that picks up the master-servant theme and does not resolve the ambiguity surrounding David's status as lord or as servant. The Philistine generals question Achish about the presence of "these Hebrews"; Achish replies by speaking about David.

> Is this not David, *servant of Saul* the king of Israel, who has been
> with me these days and years; I have found nothing [*me'umah*] in
> him from the day *he deserted* until this day. (1 Sam. 29:3)

To the Philistines, Achish says "servant of Saul"; to himself and
David, he had said "my servant forever" and "my bodyguard." In
both chapters 27 and 29, David's relationship is with Achish alone and
not with the other Philistines.

Achish mentions nothing of David's raids and says that David "deserted." The generals reply angrily that Achish must send David back
to his place; they fear for their heads, since they remember the couplet sung to David when he returned from slaying the Philistine Goliath (1 Sam. 18:6–7). Do they also know of David's first visit to Achish
(1 Sam. 21:11–16)? They, like so many others, fear David's violence.

Achish accepts the generals' demand, dismisses David, and speaks,
surprisingly, of the Lord. His speech brings back into play themes of
good and evil, "in the eyes of" (seeing), and finding and doing.

> As the Lord lives, you have been honest [*yashar*]. It is *good* [*tob*] in
> my eyes that you go out and in with me in the camp since *I have not
> found* in you any *evil* [*ra'ah*] from the day that you came to me until
> this day. But in the eyes of the Philistine generals you are *not good*
> [*lo' tob*]. Now return and go in peace; do nothing *evil* [*ra'*] in the eyes
> of the Philistine generals. (vv. 6–7)

The statement has some points of contrast with the one to the Philistine
generals, which was shorter and did not employ "good" and "evil." Like
David, Achish is a man prudent in speech (*nebon dabar*). His statement
to David is flattering and persuasive, while his statement to the generals
was matter-of-fact. With them, he played down the relation between
himself and David. David's desertion is now, "You came to me." Achish
speaks of "the Lord," probably to show David that he respects David's
god. With the generals, he uses the neutral term *me'umah*, "something,"
once; with David, he uses the evaluative terms "honest," "good," and
"evil" a total of five times. Retributive justice is alluded to for the
purposes of flattery and persuasion.

Achish's final assertion to David could be paraphrased, "The generals don't trust you; go, before you do something that will confirm
their distrust." That is, Achish may be worried not so much about the
present battle and David's participation in it as about the lucrative
booty he is receiving from David. He readily accepts the generals'
demand, because he does not want to jeopardize the relationship he
has with David.

Achish can join a lengthy list of people who might be involved with

David because of self-interest, because of what they gain or could gain from alliance with him. These are possible, not definitive, interpretations. The list includes Jonathan, Abiathar, David's men, Nabal's men, and Abigail. David demonstrates an awareness of the value of giving booty to others when he distributes the Amalekite spoil to several cities, including Hebron (1 Sam. 30:26–31), the city where he is anointed king of Judah (2 Sam. 2:1–4). To reiterate an earlier point, Achish does not appear here as someone so stupid and gullible that he does not have some idea of what David is about; Achish is not so much gulled as bought.

David answers Achish with a familiar question, the meaning of which is again undecided. "What have I done?" (*meh `asithi*). He has "asked" this of Eliab (1 Sam. 17:29), of Jonathan (1 Sam. 20:1), and of Saul (1 Sam. 26:18). In all cases, it can be taken either as an assertion that David has done nothing to deserve his present treatment or as a sincere question and answered with a statement of what he has in fact done to merit his present treatment.

> What have I done? *What have you found in your servant* from the day that I have been with you until this day that I cannot go and fight against the enemies of *my lord the king*? (v. 8)

The questions are superfluous, since Achish has already answered them. Is David breathing a secret sigh of relief that he will not have to go and fight Saul while proclaiming to Achish that he feels insulted? "My lord the king"—is this Achish or Saul? Is David being ironic? Is he breathing a sigh of relief that he has not been forced to turn against Achish? The issue will not be decided; we will not finally know whether David would or would not desert the Philistines and fight with Saul and Israel. Is David servant to Achish or Saul, to both, to neither?

> Achish answered David, "I know that you are as good in my eyes as an angel of God. Nevertheless, the Philistine generals have said, 'He will not go up with us to the battle.' Now, rise early in the morning; *the servants of your lord who came with you,* all of you rise early in the morning and as soon as you have light, go!" David and his men rose early in the morning to go, to return to the land of the Philistines, and the Philistines went up to Jezreel. (vv. 9–11)

Achish's response is eloquent and very insistent that David is not to go to the battle. The wise woman of Tekoa, in a speech that is both deceptive and persuasive, also speaks of David, who is "like an angel of God in discerning good and evil" and who has "wisdom like the wisdom of an angel of God to know all that there is on earth" (2 Sam.

14:17–20). Mephibosheth attempts to persuade David by saying that he is like an angel of God (2 Sam. 19:27). The phrase "like an angel of God" does not readily connote sincerity or accuracy. In 2 Samuel, Shimei is probably the sincere and accurate man: "Go away, Man of Blood!" (2 Sam. 16:7).

There is one final reminder in Achish's speech of David's undecidable status—"you and the servants of your lord." "Your lord"—is this Achish, who is thereby emphasizing his right to command David? Is this Saul? Achish recognizes David's true allegiance but has still profited from his alliance with this bandit leader.

Emphasis is on departure at morning's first light. Does David's departure coincide with Saul's departure from Endor? In any case, Saul and the Philistines are on their way to Jezreel, while David and his men are returning to "the land of the Philistines." David leaves both Achish and Saul; he is now on his own; he is lord. While Saul and the army of Israel are being crushed in the far north by the hand of the Philistines, David is in the far south in the land of the Philistines. He does not fight with the Philistines. "As the Lord lives, the Lord will smite him, or his day will come and he will die, or he will go into battle and perish" (1 Sam. 26:10). David knows both the Israelite and the Philistine armies. Does he feel certain that Saul is to perish in this battle? David later uses battle to destroy Uriah.

When David returns to the land of the Philistines, does he do so willingly, begrudgingly, fearfully, with a sense of relief? Would he or would he not fight against Saul? Or would he have deserted Achish and fought with Saul, "his lord the king"? He is too close to Achish, and the Philistine generals' distrust is too sharp for him to desert; they would destroy him and his men if he tried. This departure from Achish and from Saul could lead to a thorough rereading of previous chapters, particularly chapter 24 on, with focus on the various motives for David's restraint vis-à-vis Saul. The rereading would revolve around a different question—why isn't David at Mt. Gilboa? Is he a coward, a realist, a man trapped by circumstances? He went to Achish to flee Saul, and now Achish ironically prevents him from being with Saul at Mt. Gilboa. Indeed, a good deal of 1 Samuel could be reread around twin questions,—why is Saul at Mt. Gilboa, and why isn't David?

Chapter 29 is a "typical chapter" in view of this forcing of a rereading and in view of its detail, repetition, and ambiguity. What of Achish and his perception of David? What of David and his perception of Achish, Saul, his own future, and the coming battle at Mt. Gilboa? What of the whole chapter? Why this lengthy presentation of David with the Philistines at this point? From one perspective, the ambiguity and equivocations of the living characters, especially Achish and David, underscore the failed certitude of the dead in chapter 28. Saul will die and David will be king, but why is not certain, particularly in regard to the word and the doings of the Lord. Does Saul die because of divine judgment, because of his own failures and weaknesses as leader and general, or because the Philistines fight courageously and valiantly? Retributive justice is invoked by dead Samuel as an ultimate explanatory principle. It is, in one sense, mocked by Achish, who employs its terms to persuade and flatter David; Abigail had done so once before, and David himself had spoken to Saul of good and evil to demonstrate his power. The proffered clarity of chapter 28 is opposed by the undecidability of chapters 29 and 30, which interpose themselves between Samuel's pronouncement and its "fulfillment."

1 Samuel 30

David and the Amalekites

1 Samuel 30 is similar to chapter 29 in its detail and explicit statements and in its lack of definitive resolutions. The analysis of the story focuses on its narrative techniques, its portrayal of David, and its place in a complicated network of analogies. The latter is traced by noting terms and themes shared with other texts; the tracing is not exhaustive and is more of a pointing into the maze. The narrative techniques are familiar—detailed and explicit statements and descriptions, repetition of some of them, gaps that block a definitive and exhaustive reading.

David now moves front and center as lord and independent leader. He is separate from Achish, Saul, and the Philistines. The terminology "lord" ('*adon*) and "servant" (`*ebed*) occurs in vv. 13–15, although it is not applied to David. David acts as and is regarded as the leader. He is not yet fully in control, since his actions in the chapter, however decisive they may be, are in reaction to the acts of others—the Amalekites and his own men. David's independence and power contrast with his absence from Mt. Gilboa. He is weak from distress and weeping, not from military setback.

Holy War(?)

1 Samuel 13–15 are implicated because of the Amalekites and the "holy war" theme, but there is a major shift. We now see the effects of holy war from the victims' perspective. I note the analogy with the Ark Narrative in chapters 4–7 but do not develop the issue of viewpoint.

> The Amalekites had made a raid upon the Negeb and upon Ziklag; they had taken [*hikkah*] Ziklag and burned it with fire. They had taken captive the women who were in it from small to great. They had killed no man. They carried off the women and went their way. (1 Sam. 30:1–2)

The description is a flashback to three days before David's return to Ziklag. The Amalekite raid is in accord with the holy war legislation in Deut. 20:10–15, i.e., what is to be done to distant cities. "You will put [*hikkah*] all its males to the sword, but the women and the little ones, the cattle, and everything else in the city, all its spoil, you can take as booty." It turns out that they had done the latter. The Amalekites killed no man, because there were none there; they were off with David. The Amalekites perform bloodless holy war.

Surprisingly and in the same categorical fashion,

> David rescued all that the Amalekites had taken; David rescued his two wives. *Nothing was missing*, whether small or great, sons or daughters, spoil or anything that had been taken; *David brought everything back.* (1 Sam. 30:18–19)

David is clearly the leader; only he acts, and he is named three times. However, the remarkable recovery is not what happens with David's raids in 1 Sam. 27:8–11—there David killed all; none was left alive. David does not now annihilate the Amalekites, since "400 young men mounted camels and fled" (v. 17). Is this an insignificant number, *only 400,* or is it a large number? The group is equal in size to David's army at the time. Unlike chapter 15, nothing is made of this. Holy war is implicated in allusive fashion, not as an explicit theme or as a direct command to David; he is reacting to a raid, not conducting a divine mission.

Another holy war theme is the concern with spoil (*shalal*) and its proper division, vv. 21–25. Indeed, chapter 30 reads like a gloss on the destruction of the Midianites in Numbers 31; the Israelites kill all the males, take captive the little ones, and burn the cities with fire (*śarap be'esh;* vv. 7–9). The booty that is taken is divided into two parts—"between the warriors who went out to battle and the entire congregation" (v. 27). David's "statute and ordinance" (1 Sam. 30:25) is a specification of the warriors' part, which is to be divided equally among those who guard the baggage and those who actually go into battle. David, in good holy war fashion, ascribes the booty to the Lord (1 Sam. 30:23, 26), but his men may better describe the situation in v. 20: "This is David's booty."

David in Distress

Vv. 1–2, quoted above, present the reality of the Amalekite raid. V. 3 presents the perception of David and his men—the city—"Look! it has been burned with fire [*śarap ba'esh*] and their wives, sons, and daughters have been taken captive"—they do not know who did it. Their ignorance is a theme in the first section of the story. "David and the army raised their voices and wept until they had no more strength to weep." Weakness is an important theme in the chapter and is attached to David.

We are explicitly informed that David's two wives were taken captive—Ahinoam the Jezreelite and Abigail, wife of Nabal, the Carmelite.

> David was greatly distressed for the army spoke of stoning him since they were all bitter about their sons and daughters, and David strengthened himself in the Lord his God. (v. 6)

Alter has noted the ambiguity of David's weeping and distress; how much, if any, concerns his wives, and how much stems from the army's threat to stone him (Alter 1981, pp. 121–22)? When David strengthens himself, is this because of his weeping and distress, or is it a ploy to lessen the army's bitterness? Further, is anyone worried about his own wife? The army is bitter because of "sons and daughters," not wives. The young Egyptian talks of a raid and burning of Ziklag, and David asks him nothing about the fate of women or children.

This is only the second time that we have been informed that David is afraid or distressed (1 Sam. 21:13), and the narrative in chapter 30 provides an "anchor" for a fearful and distressed David who is not so cunning and confident of his actions. It is easy to read the chapter as portraying a troubled David—faced with possible mutiny and not sure what to do. He inquires of the Lord about pursuing "this band." He apparently has no idea who or where they are. He may not even know that they are Amalekites. The pursuit begins with no set destination, since David does it to placate the army; chasing an unknown band is better than getting stoned.

He leaves in such haste that 200 of his men are too tired to continue the chase; these are not similar to the 200 he had, on another occasion, left with the baggage (1 Sam. 25:13). The theme of weakness appears again here and in vv. 11–15; the Egyptian lad is weak because he has not eaten or drunk for three days. The detail of the food and drink emphasizes David's straits; the lad, who must first be well fed, is his only hope of ever locating "this band." The lad replies to David's demand in familiar terms—swear, kill, deliver. At first encounter, even a young Egyptian lad fears David and enters into an explicit relation of mutual self-interest with David. "Swear to me by God that you will not kill me or hand me over [*sagar*] to my master, and I will bring you down to this band" (v. 15). There is poignancy to his speech, since it intones both Saul's earlier request for an oath from David not to kill him (1 Sam. 24:22) and Saul's death on Mt. Gilboa. Previously Saul had been hungry and weak from not eating.

When the army returns to the 200 exhausted men, a group of "wicked and horrid men" (*'ish ra`ubeliyya`al*) wants to give them nothing but their wives and children. David once more faces dissension in the ranks and again "strengthens himself in the Lord."

> (23) "You cannot do this, my brothers, with what the Lord has given us; he protected us and gave into our hand this band which came up against us. (24) Who would listen to you in this matter? As his share who goes down into the battle, so his share who stays with the baggage; they will share alike." (25) From that day forward he made it a statute and an ordinance for Israel to this day.

This may be a sincere statement based on solid principle, or it may be David's way of keeping the army intact through the use of booty. He has too few men at this point to lose any, for whatever reason, and he understands the value of booty, since he soon distributes booty to cities to gain or buy their allegiance. In any case, his decision is somewhat off the point, since the 200 men in question stayed behind because they were exhausted, not because they were with the baggage. David, who is *nebon dabar,* speaks effectively if not accurately.

Whether David is acting with initiative and foresight or under the pressure of the circumstances, whether his decision is to or off the point, the decision is stated formally as a law, is a serious matter, and is effective. It is not just standard practice that David refines but the word of the Lord; it is not an interpretation of Moses. The law in Num. 31:26–30, describing the division of booty, is introduced, "The Lord said to Moses." David's independence and authority increase and are confirmed by the narrative; this is not just a custom (*mishpat*) but "a statute and an ordinance" (*choq umishpat*). Again we can ask the question if David, why not Saul? This is particularly pertinent, since David has apparently kept a large amount of booty for himself, which he then distributes to Judean cities; perhaps "this is David's booty" (v. 20) makes a distinction between what is his and what is the army's. It is only the latter that is divided between the warriors and the baggage guards.

We can portray David on a continuum. At one end is the shrewd and calculating David who has regained much spoil "from the land of the Philistines and from the land of Judah" (v. 16) and is putting it to the most effective use he knows to buy the allegiance of others. Loyalty to David is profitable. Or we can see a troubled and distressed David who buys the allegiance of his army and others, because he does not know what else to do under the circumstances. Finally, he may perceive a need to offset the reaction to his absence from Mt. Gilboa.

Chapters 29–30 in all their detail and ambiguity, in all their possible readings of David's character and motivations, come to a close with the brief list of cities in 1 Sam. 30:16–31. The first city mentioned is Ziklag, where David is independent leader; the last is Hebron, where David is soon to be anointed king of Judah and Israel. The obfuscation, the clouds, surrounding David can be put aside in favor of a statement by Saul—David has certainly done, David has certainly succeeded. But if we ask why, then the obfuscation, the clouds, return. Looking to the next chapter, we can put aside the ambiguities and uncertainties surrounding Saul and say—Saul has certainly done, Saul has certainly failed. But the ambiguities and uncertainties return if we ask why, which I do, twice. If Saul, why not David? If David, why not Saul?

1 Samuel 31

The Final Chapter

Chapter 30 and 31 gain in poignancy and power if we regard their events as simultaneous. In the far south, David is anxious about his own and about spoil, while in the far north Saul and the Israelite army perish. The contrast is increased by the length of the chapters— thirty-one verses in chapter 30 to thirteen verses in chapter 31. The defeat of Israel is so devastating that the Philistines are able to seize and inhabit Transjordanian cities. Did David foresee this and avoid being engulfed by it? If so, is this a cowardly or a realistic response?

David pursues (*radap*) a band that has raided (*pashat*) the land; he does not go to save Saul from a Philistine invasion. Saul had pursued (*radap*) David and had had him cornered but let him go to face a Philistine raid (*pashat*, 1 Sam. 23:24–28). David, faced with the sack of Ziklag three days afterward, inquires of the Lord and immediately pursues the raiding band. Informed of Saul's death and the defeat of the Israelite army three days afterward, David kills the messenger, recites a lamentation—and has it published!—and inquires of the Lord about returning to Judah; David's actions stand in contrast to

those of the inhabitants of Jabesh-gilead. There is no mention in 2
Sam. 1:1–2:4 of any pursuit or rescue.

While David smites (*hikkah*) the Amalekites, and they flee (*nus*), the
Philistines smite (*hikkah*) Saul and his sons, and Israel flees (*nus*).
While David is dividing up his spoil, the Philistines

> cut off his head and stripped off [*pashat*] his armor. They sent
> messengers to announce the good news [*lebaśśer*] in the house of
> their idols and to the people. (1 Sam. 31:9)

Is their announcement the same as that brought by a Benjaminite
messenger (*mebaśśer*)? "Israel has fled [*nus*] before the Philistines, and
there has been a great slaughter [*maggepah*] of the army" (1 Sam.
4:17). Israel has been defeated, and fathers and sons have died on the
same day.

The narrative spends little time on the actual battle; it concentrates
on Saul's death and the treatment of his body. The encounter with
Samuel at Endor lingers in the background; we now have certitude—
Saul is dead and his bones are buried at Jabesh-gilead. But where is
his head? The battle and the Israelite defeat are reported in v. 1. The
narrative centers on Saul and his sons; the latter are killed, and Saul is
alone with his armor-bearer. Saul asks the armor-bearer to kill him
"lest these uncircumcised come, thrust me through, and ridicule me."
The armor-bearer refuses, and Saul falls on his own sword. Saul, in
his last moment, is not supported by his armor-bearer—this one or his
earlier armor-bearer. "David came to Saul . . . and became his armor-
bearer" (1 Sam. 16:21–22). Again we are subtly reminded that David
is not there at Mt. Gilboa; David is not one to commit suicide, even
though he knows well how to ridicule "these uncircumcised," at least
200 of them.

V. 7 reports the cataclysmic effects of the defeat and is a division in
the chapter between live Saul and his dead body. The latter receives
better treatment than the former. The Philistines come to strip the
dead. Saul is there. They cut off his head and strip off his armor. We
are returned to previous wars and texts that end in beheading and
stripping; we enter a network of analogies from another point.

The Philistines put Saul's "armor in the temple of Ashtaroth, and
they hung his corpse on the wall of Beth-shan." Saul's end is ignominious, yet the book of 1 Samuel closes by putting aside allusions to
Saul's dark and clouded days. It closes with an act that is not a power
play, a calculated show of restraint, a deception, or an attempt to buy
someone's loyalty; it closes with pathos, with a memory of Saul's finest
hour.

The inhabitants of Jabesh-gilead heard what the Philistines had done to Saul. All the warriors rose and traveled all night and took the corpse of Saul and the corpses of his sons from the wall of Beth-shan; they came to Jabesh and burnt them there. They took their bones and buried them beneath the tamarisk tree in Jabesh, and they fasted seven days.

POSTSCRIPT

The postscript is brief and highlights two major aspects of the work—networks of analogies and undecidability. Chapter 31 is typical of 1 Samuel, but then all the book is typical of itself and of OT narrative. The story of Saul's death and the fate of his corpse is told in a detailed manner, but several important issues are not explicitly raised or dealt with amidst the detail. Why is Saul at Mt. Gilboa? Why isn't David? Why is Israel defeated? The questions are raised by the specific texts and by the allusions to Israel's defeat at Ebenezer, to Saul's former armor-bearer, to Samuel's return from the dead, and to a myriad of other texts. Jabesh-gilead, for example, is a double-edged allusion to Saul's finest moment in chapter 11 and to one of Israel's most sordid moments in Judges 20–21.

To read chapter 31 is to reread previous texts, indeed all of 1 Samuel and beyond, with new information and from new perspectives. Such a constant rereading, retraversing of already trodden ground, has been a hallmark of my reading of 1 Samuel. To read OT narrative is to enter its labyrinth. A chapter or section marks an advance in the narrative and, at the same time, calls for another look at what precedes and what follows. "Already trodden ground"—the phrase describes chapter 31 by the time we reach it in the sequential ordering of this book. It has been alluded to frequently in the course of the reading. The labyrinth of OT narrative has no set entrance, and once in it, there is no set direction; we trace and create the labyrinth, the maze, as we read and do not simply follow a preordained route with a limited number of entrances. Chapter 31 itself refers ahead to the opening chapters of 2 Samuel, to the return of Saul's and Jonathan's bones to Gibeah in 2 Samuel 21, and to the death of Saul's neighbor and rival in 1 Kings 1.

"Undecidability"—the term retraces 1 Samuel and this book. It returns us to the introduction. Throughout 1 Samuel, various issues, problems, questions, etc., have been raised and frequently treated extensively, e.g., retributive justice, the Lord's intervention, violence, and the characters Saul and David. But the issues are not defined or resolved in a final, conclusive fashion. For example, we cannot finally decide why Saul dies at Mt. Gilboa. It may be his fault, the Lord's punishment, the result of superior Philistine strength, or some combination of these or other causes. But "undecidable" and "unanswerable" do not mean "unaskable." The analysis may be interminable, but it does begin. We do ask who Saul is and why he is at Mt. Gilboa; we do ask who David is and why he is to be king; we do ask what the Lord is doing, if anything. We ask these questions and pursue them, although there are no final answers that can preclude the necessity of asking them again.

I employ a biblical metaphor. To read OT narrative is to follow the way of the Lord, but the way is a labyrinth, a network, without a beginning, a center, or an end. To follow means movement, not stasis; to follow is to traverse a path, not to arrive at a destination—the meaning, the explanation, the word of the Lord. Samuel offered this to Saul at Endor, but such certitude and clarity belong only to the dead. "The embrace of meaning turns out to be but the embrace of death; the grasp of the signified turns out to be the grasp but of a corpse" (Felman 1977, p. 174). Saul's destination, his *derek,* is Mt. Gilboa, not Endor.

Interminable and undecidable—analysis and reading cannot stop because the final answer, interpretation, or signified meaning has been found. Reading is unending, incessant, because we must read 1 Samuel again if someone were to ask, what is 1 Samuel about? There is no essential, definable "what" that 1 Samuel is "about." Reading does not stop because the goal has been reached, but practically it can be halted quickly and simply.

BIBLIOGRAPHY

Ackroyd, Peter. 1971. *1 Samuel (The Cambridge Bible Commentary)*. Cambridge: University Press.

Alter, Robert. 1981. *The Art of Biblical Narrative*. New York: Basic Books.

Barthes, Roland. 1968. "L'effet de reel." *Communications* 11:84–89.

———. 1971. "L'analyse structural du récit. A propos d'Actes 10–11." In *Exégèse et hermeneutique*, pp. 181-204. Paris: Seuil.

———. 1974a. "The Struggle with the Angel: Textual Analysis of Genesis 32:23–33." In *Structural Analysis and Biblical Exegesis* (Pittsburgh Theological Monograph Series, 3), pp. 21–33. Pittsburgh: Pickwick.

———. 1974b. *S/Z*. New York: Hill and Wang.

———. 1975. "An Introduction to the Structural Analysis of Narrative." *New Literary History* 6:237–72.

Berlin, Adele. 1982. "Characterization in Biblical Narrative: David's Wives." *JSOT* 23:69–85.

Beuken, W.A.M. 1978. "1 Samuel 28: The Prophet as 'Hammer of Witches.'" *JSOT* 6:3–17.

Burke, Kenneth. 1970. *The Rhetoric of Religion*. Los Angeles: University of California.

Culler, Jonathan. 1975. *Structuralist Poetics*. Ithaca: Cornell.

———. 1981a. "Convention and Meaning: Derrida and Austin." *New Literary History* 13:15–30.

———. 1981b. *The Pursuit of Signs: Semiotics, Literature, Deconstruction*. Ithaca: Cornell.

———. 1982. *On Deconstruction*. Ithaca: Cornell.

Curtis, John Briggs. 1979. "A Folk Etymology of NABI'." *VT* 29:491–93.

de Man, Paul. 1971. *Blindness & Insight*. New York: Oxford.

———. 1979. *Allegories of Reading*. New Haven: Yale.

Derrida, Jacques. 1974. "White Mythology: Metaphor in the Text of Philosophy." *New Literary History* 6:5–74.

———. 1976. *Of Grammatology*. Baltimore: Johns Hopkins.

———. 1977a. "Signature Event Context." *Glyph* 1:172–97.

———. 1977b. "Limited Inc." *Glyph* 2:162–254.

———. 1978. *Writing and Difference*. Chicago: Chicago.

———. 1981. *Dissemination*. Chicago: Chicago.

Dillard, Annie. 1982. *Living by Fiction*. New York: Harper and Row.

Driver, S. R. 1890. *Notes on the Hebrew Text of the Books of Samuel*. Oxford: Clarendon.

Erdmann, C.F.D. 1960. *The Books of Samuel*. Vol. V of the Old Testament in *Lange's Commentary on the Holy Scriptures*. Grand Rapids: Zondervan.

Eslinger, Lyle. 1983. "Viewpoints and Points of View in 1 Samuel 8–12." *JSOT* 26:61–76.

Felman, Shoshana. 1977. "Turning the Screw of Interpretation." *Yale French Studies* 55/56:94–207.

Fish, Stanley. 1980. *Is There a Text in This Class?* Cambridge: Harvard.

———. 1981. "Why No One's Afraid of Wolfgang Iser." *Diacritics* 11, no. 1:2–13.

Frei, Hans. 1974. *The Eclipse of Biblical Narrative.* New Haven: Yale.

Gasché, Rodolphe. 1979. "Deconstruction as Criticism." *Glyph* 6:177–215.

Gros Louis, K.R.R. 1977. "The Difficulty of Ruling Well: King David of Israel." *Semeia* 8:15–33.

Gunn, David M. 1978. *The Story of King David: Genre and Interpretation* (JSOT Supplement #6). Sheffield: JSOT.

———. 1980. *The Fate of King Saul* (JSOT Supplement #14). Sheffield: JSOT.

Hartman, Geoffrey. 1980. *Criticism in the Wilderness.* New Haven: Yale.

———. 1981. *Saving the Text: Literature/Derrida/Philosophy.* Baltimore: Johns Hopkins.

Hertzberg, H. W. 1964. *I & II Samuel.* Philadelphia: Westminster.

Humphreys, W. Lee. 1978. "The Tragedy of King Saul: A Study of the Structure of 1 Samuel 9–31." *JSOT* 6:18–27.

———. 1980. "The Rise and Fall of King Saul: A Study of an Ancient Narrative Stratum in 1 Samuel." *JSOT* 18:74–90.

———. 1982. "From Tragic Hero to Villain: A Study of the Figure of Saul and the Development of 1 Samuel." *JSOT* 22:95–117.

Iser, Wolfgang. 1974. *The Implied Reader.* Baltimore: Johns Hopkins.

———. 1981. "Talk like Whales: A Reply to Stanley Fish." *Diacritics* 11, no. 3:82–87.

Janzen, J. Gerald. 1983. " 'Samuel opened the doors of the house of Yahweh' (1 Samuel 3:15)." *JSOT* 26:89–96.

Jobling, David. 1978. *The Sense of Biblical Narrative* (JSOT Supplement #7). Sheffield: JSOT.

Johnson, Barbara. 1980. *The Critical Difference.* Baltimore: Johns Hopkins.

Keil, C. F., and Delitzsch, F. 1971. *Commentary on the Old Testament in Ten Volumes.* Part Two of Vol. II: Samuel. Grand Rapids: Eerdmans.

Knierem, Rolf P. 1968. "The Messianic Concept in the First Book of Samuel." In *Jesus and the Historian,* ed. F. T. Trotter, pp. 20–51. Philadelphia: Westminster.

Kugel, James L. 1981. *The Idea of Biblical Poetry.* New Haven: Yale.

Leach, Edmund R. 1970. "The Legitimacy of Solomon." In *Introduction to Structuralism,* ed. M. Lane, pp. 248–92. New York: Basic Books.

Leitch, Vincent B. 1983. *Deconstructive Criticism.* New York: Columbia.

Levenson, Jon D. 1978. "1 Samuel 25 as Literature and as History." *CBQ* 40:11–28.

McCarter, P. Kyle, Jr. 1980a. "The Apology of David." *JBL* 99:489–504.

———. 1980b. *1 Samuel (The Anchor Bible,* 8). Garden City, N.Y.: Doubleday.

Miller, J. Hillis. 1978. "Ariadne's Thread: Repetition and the Narrative Line." In *Interpretation of Narrative,* eds. M. J. Valdes and O. J. Miller, pp. 148–66. Toronto: Toronto.

———. 1979. "The Critic as Host." In *Deconstruction and Criticism,* eds. H. Bloom, *et al.,* pp. 217–53. New York: Seabury.

Miscall, Peter D. 1979. "Literary Unity in Old Testament Narrative." *Semeia* 15:27–44.

————. 1983. *The Workings of Old Testament Narrative.* Philadelphia: Fortress.

Perdue, Leo G. 1984. " 'Is There Anyone Left of the House of Saul . . . ?' Ambiguity and the Characterization of David in the Succession Narrative." *JSOT* 30:67–84.

Polzin, Robert. 1980. *Moses and the Deuteronomist.* New York: Seabury.

Preston, Thomas R. 1982. "The Heroism of Saul: Patterns of Meaning in the Narrative of Early Kingship." *JSOT* 24:27–46.

Radday, Yehuda T. 1974. "Chiasm in Samuel." *Linguistica Biblica* 9/10:21–31.

Ritterspach, A. D. 1974. "Rhetorical Criticism and the Song of Hannah." In *Rhetorical Criticism,* eds. J. J. Jackson and M. Kessler, pp. 68–74. Pittsburgh: Pickwick.

Rorty, Richard. 1979. *Philosophy and the Mirror of Nature.* Princeton: Princeton.

Rose, Ashley S. 1974. "The 'Principles' of Divine Election. Wisdom in 1 Samuel 16." In *Rhetorical Criticism,* eds. J. J. Jackson and M. Kessler, pp. 43–67. Pittsburgh: Pickwick.

Sanders, James A. 1979. "Text and Canon: Concepts and Methods." *JBL* 98:5–29.

Scholes, Robert. 1974. *Structuralism in Literature.* New Haven: Yale.

Scholes, Robert, and Kellogg, James. 1966. *The Nature of Narrative.* New York: Oxford.

Shaviv, Shemuel. 1984. "NABI' and NAGID in 1 Samuel 9:1–10:16." *VT* 34:108–13.

Simon, Uriel. 1981. "Samuel's Call to Prophecy: Form Criticism with Close Reading." *Prooftexts* 1:119–32.

Smith, Henry P. 1899. *The Books of Samuel (The International Critical Commentary).* Edinburgh: T. and T. Clark.

Speiser, E. A. 1964. *Genesis (The Anchor Bible,* 1). Garden City, N.Y.: Doubleday.

Spivak, Gayatri C. 1976. "Translator's Preface." In *Of Grammatology* by J. Derrida, pp. ix-lxxxvii. Baltimore: Johns Hopkins.

————. 1980. "Revolutions That as Yet Have No Model: Derrida's *Limited Inc.*" *Diacritics* 10, no. 4:29–49.

Stoebe, H.-J. 1973. *Das erste Buch Samuelis (KZAT).* Gütersloh: Gerd Mohn.

Todorov, Tzvetan. 1977. *The Poetics of Prose.* Ithaca: Cornell.

Veijola, Timo. 1984. "David in Keila." *Revue Biblique* 91:51–87.

White, Hayden. 1978. *Tropics of Discourse.* Baltimore: Johns Hopkins.

————. 1979. "The Discourse of History." *Humanities in Society* 2:1–15.

————. 1980. "The Value of Narrativity in the Representation of Reality." *Critical Inquiry* 7:5–27.

Whitelam, Keith W. 1984. "The Defense of David." *JSOT* 29:61–87.

Weiss, Meir. 1965. "Weiteres über die Bauformen des Erzählens in der Bibel." *Biblica* 46:181–206.

Willis, John T. 1973. "The Function of Comprehensive Anticipatory Redactional Joints in 1 Samuel 16–18." *ZAW* 85:294–314.

INDEX

Biblical Passages Cited
(Page numbers in boldface indicate major treatment.)

Genesis–Kings, vii–xvi, 54, 117, 164
Genesis, x–xi, 1, 35

2:21	159
6:6–7	102
10:10	63
10:13–14	35
15:12	159
15:19–21	35
16	1
18:20–21	31–32
20:9	63
21:22–34	36
24	55
26:26–33	36
29	1, 55, 121
31	127
32	121
34	121
35:16–20	29, 127
37:2	x
39	119
41:46	x
43:12	142
49	xi
49:10	5

Exodus–Deuteronomy, 4, 40, 79
Exodus, 60, 121

2:1–10	1, 55
2:23–24	32
3	45
3–4	58, 116
10:2	32
15	xi
17:8–16	99
19–24	74
19:4–6	63, 74
23:23,31	35
24:13	17
25:7	17

Exodus (*cont.*)

25:10–16, 22	10
28:1–43	17
32:11–14	102
33:2	35
33:11	17
39:1–29	17
40:16–21	10

Leviticus

8:7	17
19–20	167

Numbers

1:50	17
6:3–5	12–13
7:89	10
11:16–30	61
13:29	35
16–17	108
20:26–28	111
23–24	xi
23:19	111
25:10–13	9
27:12–23	2
31	178, 180
32:33	63

Deuteronomy, xv, 54, 114, 129

2:16–23	35
5,9,10	74
5:22–31	45
7:1	35
10:1–8	10
10:8	17
13	99
13:1–5	53–54, 60, 86
16–17	40, 73
16–18	108
16:18–20	42–43
17:8–13	4, 42–43, 45, 77–78
17:12–20	47–48
17:15–20	63, 65, 142
18:1–8	17, 109

Deuteronomy (*cont.*)
18:9–14	108, 167
18:15–22	xii, 3, 44–46, 50–51, 53–54, 70–71, 86, 109
19:15–21	4
20	xv, 86
20:1–8	4, 167
20:10–18	35, 99, 164, 178
21:5	17
25:17–19	99
28:25	63
31	78–79
31:19	49
31:24–29	108
31:26	10, 49
32	49
32:36	102
33	xi
34:9	2, 78
34:10–12	2–3, 44, 70–71

Joshua, viii, 4, 8, 79, 129
1–11	xv, 86
1	11, 35
1:1	T1746
1:7	100
2:12–14	100–101
3:10	35
6–8	83, 99
6:1–5	96
7–8	4–5
7	64, 94–96, 102
7:6	4
8:23–29	101, 112
9:1,7,17	35
10:2, 11:10	63
13:1–6	2, 35
14:1,6	4
17:4	4
18:1	4, 10
18:8–10	4
19:51	4–5, 10
21:1	4
22:13,30–32	4
24	5, 74

Judges, viii, x, xiv–xv, 4, 7–8, 16, 20, 34, 39, 42, 70, 74, 78–79, 121
1:1	5
2	11
2:18	102
3:1–5	2, 35
3:5–6	7
3:9	57
3:30	7

Judges (*cont.*)
5	xi–xii
5:31	7
6:2	84
6:8–10	64
6:15	58
6:17,36	60
8:27	18
8:28	7
10:6–8	3
10:10–16	74
10:10	37
11	66, 93
11:35	94
13–16	3, 13, 117
13	1–2, 8
13:1	3, 7, 76–77, 105
13:4–5	1–2, 13
14:4	3
14:5–9	94
15:7	93
15:11	3
16:20–30	2, 30, 93
17–21	3, 5, 8, 14, 28, 79
17:5	18
17:6	4, 7
17:13	27
18:1	7
18:5–6	6, 27
18:14–20	18
18:30–31	5
19–21	3, **5–8,** 29, 50–52, 65, 89, 184
19:22	17, 66
20	140
20:13	17
20:27–28	9, 11
21	9–10, 94
21:1–7	27
21:2–4	12
21:8–15	67
21:25	4, 8, 46

Samuel–Kings, xiii, 47, 54
1–2 Samuel, xii, xvii, xxiii–xxiv, 97
1 Samuel
1–16	xii, 113, 119
1–12	xiii
1–3	3, 146
1:1–2:6	10
1	**10–15**
1:1	8, 51
1:3	10, 27
1:7	39
1:9	9
1:10,12	19
1:11,22	20

1 Samuel (*cont.*)

1:16	17
1:19	xiii
1:23	102
1:28	1
2:1–10	xi–xii, **15–16**
2:3	155
2:10	46, 56, 59
2:11–36	**16–24,** 110–11
2:12–17	28
2:20	14
2:21	16
2:22	9–10
2:25	xiii, 28, 77, 107
2:27–36	xiii, 9, 29, 87, 122–23
2:30	98
2:34	28
2:35	14
2:36	16, 171
3	xiii, 19, **24–25,** 45, 54, 56, 70, 79, 87, 116
3:3	9
3:11–14	22–23
3:12	14
3:13–14	19
3:19–4:1	xiii, 14–15, 23, 26, 44–46, 53, 70, 97
4–6	x, 52, 122, 177
4	xvi, 3, 10, **26–30,** 39, 79, 172
4:3–4	9, 93
4:4–10	37
4:17	182
4:18	79
4:20	112
4:21–22	90
5:1–7:1	**30–35**
5:6–11	37
5:6	xiii
6:2–3	109
6:14–18	39, 88
7–8	79
7:2–12	**36–39**
7:2ff	x–xi
7:3–8	36
7:3	77
7:5–11	19
7:6–9	42
7:9–10	61
7:10–12	41–42
7:13–17	10, 37, **41–43**
7:13–14	35–36, 82, 87, 98
7:15–8:20	42
8–16	145
8–12	40–41, 47, 78, 81
8–11	71–72

1 Samuel (*cont.*)

8	xii–xiii, **43–51,** 57, 64–65
8:2	142
8:5,6,18,22	57
8:7–9	64, 76, 102–103, 109
8:11–17	156
8:19–22	69–70, 72, 75, 87
9–31	xvii
9–11	41, 51, 57, 67–70, 81
9–10	63–64, 71, 85, 111, 168
9:1–26	**51–58,** 118
9:1–2	64, 116
9:6–11	xi, 171
9:9	62, 70, 164
9:11–27	105
9:11–14	64
9:16	60, 87, 115
9:17	132
9:27–10:16	**58–62**
10:1–8	58, 86, 124, 169
10:2	55, 127
10:5–13	70
10:5	82, 89
10:6–10	117, 168
10:7	68, 87
10:8	84–87, 103
10:11	97
10:12	9, 128
10:16	63
10:17–27	53, **63–69,** 74, 83, 90
10:25	49, 63, 108
10:26	89, 98, 138
11	xv, **66–72,** 73–75, 81– 83, 85, 97, 100, 113, 118, 124, 184
11:4	89
11:7	159
11:12–13	127
11:14	63
11:15	51, 97
12	xii, xxv, 51, 71, **72– 78,** 85, 109
12:2	44
12:6–15	23
12:10	37
12:11	79
12:12–20	102
12:13	98
12:17	105, 146
12:25	36
13–31	xii
13–16	79–80
13–15	67, 71, 81, 85, 102, 113–14, 135, 144, 149, 169, 177

1 Samuel (*cont.*)

13–14	97–101
13	xv, 61, 80, **81–89,** 90, 93, 99–100, 103, 107, 122, 149–50, 172
13:6–7	93
13:9	112
13:11	96
13:13–14	102, 105, 111, 148, 161, 169
13:14	52, 63
14	**89–98,** 122, 136, 151
14:3	20–21
14:6–12	120, 141
14:15	159
14:23	xiii
14:24	103
14:32	105
14:37	168
14:38–44	64
14:45	127
14:47	63
14:48	99
14:50	16, 62
14:52	138
15	xiii, xv, 53, 80, 97, 116, 122–24, 136, 149, 157, 172, 178
15:1–9	**98–101,** 102–106, 136
15:1–3	102
15:10–11	**101–103,** 104
15:11–13	14
15:12–23a	**103–109**
15:18–20	171
15:22	18
15:23b–35	**109–14,** 169
15:23	168
15:27–28	63, 147–48
15:35	102
16–27	169
16–24	150
16–18	121, 162
16–17	xvii, 131
16	**115–20,** 124
16:1–13	59, 121, 149
16:1–5	61, 65, 113, 131
16:6–7	102
16:14–16	104, 113, 168–69
16:18	121
16:20	11
16:21–22	182
16:23	160, 164
17–18	**120–25,** 129
17	131, 154
17:11	167

1 Samuel (*cont.*)

17:12	16
17:13	142
17:17–18	11
17:29	175
17:42	119
17:45–47	149
17:50–51	xxv, 154
18:4	111
18:5–16	23
18:6–7	133, 174
18:8	63, 147
18:10–11	62, 118–19, 126
18:12–15	119
18:12	113, 169
18:14	xiii
18:25–27	166, 182
18:29	166
18:30	126
19–22	137–38
19	**126–29**
19:1–7	161
19:9–10	119
19:19–24	62, 111, 137–38
20	126, **129–31,** 147
20:1	175
20:2	142
20:30–31	142, 147
20:31	63
21:2–10	**131–33**
21:2–8	21, 134–35
21:11–16	**133,** 160, 166, 174
21:13	142, 179
22	xv, 113, 131, **133–39,** 144, 149–50, 169
22:3–4	160
22:3	16
22:6–20	21
22:14	23, 132, 166
22:17	xiv, 139
22:22	133
23	xiii, **139–43,** 144, 157, 169
23:6–24	136
23:6–12	18
23:10–12	xiv
23:15–18	147–48
23:26–28	138, 181
24–26	126, 161–62
24	110–11, 122, 139, **144–49,** 150–54, 157–62, 165, 176
24:5	xiii
24:12–22	160–61, 170, 180
25–27	169
25	94, 122, **149–58,** 161
25:1	167

1 Samuel (*cont.*)
25:13	179
25:28	23
25:39	xiii
25:44	146
26	152, **158–62,** 165
26:1	143
26:10	176
26:18	175
27	xv, 144, 160, **163–66,** 173–74
27:1–4	53, 127, 133
27:5	63
27:8–11	178
27:12	23
28:1–2	**166–67,** 173
28:3–25	96, 108–10, 166, 167–72, 177
28:14–19	xiv, 113, 141, 148
28:20–25	16, 53
29	93, 133, 166–67, **173–77**
29:4–6	167
29:6,9	163, 166
30–31	xviii, 166
30	xv, 113, 164, **177–82**
30:6–8	xiv, 140–41
30:12	16
30:26–31	175
31	22, 111, 113, 142, 172, **181–83,** 184– 85
31:4	139
31:9	159
31:11–13	67

2 Samuel, x–xii, xviii, 41, 119, 121–22, 147, 158, 184
1:1–2:4	181–82
1:17–27	xi–xii
2:1–4	175
3:28	63
5:4	x
6	xi
6:23	xxiv
7:8–15	121
7:13,16	23, 63
8:1	35
8:17	21
9	22, 147
11:4	156
12:9–10	121
12:12	126

2 Samuel (*cont.*)
12:26	63
13:23,38	x
14:17–20	175–76
16:5–8	22, 63, 121, 176
16:9–10	159
19:21–23	159
19:27	176
21	184
21:2	35
21:1–9	22
21:8,19	xxiv
22	xi–xii
24	138, 60
24:16	102

1–2 Kings, x–xiii, 21, 122

1 Kings, 41, 79
1	184
1:46	63
2	147
2:15,22	63
2:27	21–23, 75
5:1	35, 63
6:1	x
9:5	63
11–14	10
11	148
11:35	63
12:21,26	63
21:7	63

2 Kings
9:1–3	59
10:31	59
11:1	63
14:5	63
15:19	63
19	xi
23:4	142
25:25	63
25:27–30	22

Isaiah, viii, xi–xii
55:8	117

Jeremiah, 54
52:24	142

Psalms, viii

1 Chronicles
10:10	30

Hebrew Words and Roots

'acher (other), 168
'adon (lord), 152, 177
'akar (to trouble), 94
'am (army; people), 67, 79, 110
'amah (maidservant), 152
'amar (to say), 49
'arur (cursed), 94
'asah (to do), 97, 100, 109, 169
'atsar (to restrain; rule), 56–57, 132
'azar (to help), 39

beliyya'al (worthless), 17, 65, 180
bachar (to choose), 56, 65
berakah (gift), 151, 153
baruk (blessed), 153
biqqesh (to seek), 52
bo' (to go; happen), 53–54, 60

chamal (to spare), 99, 101, 136
chapets (to delight in), 107, 126
chereb (sword), 121
cherem (to annihilate), 83, 99, 106
cherpah (disgrace), 154
chesed (love; loyalty), 100, 121
chiddesh (to renew), 69

dabar (word), 14, 18, 25, 43, 46, 62
derek (way), 53, 171, 185

'ebed (slave), 23, 50, 152, 165–66, 177
'eben (stone), 39
'ed (witness), 49
'elohim (God), x, xiv, 15, 92, 159, 168

halak (to go), 53, 171
hikkah (to kill), 164, 178, 182
hinneh (here!), 108, 147
hith'allel (to make sport of), 32
hithpallel (to intercede), 18–19, 37, 77
hodi'a (to make known), 109
hoshi'a/moshi'a (to save; savior), 56–58, 60, 67

kabed/kabod (to honor; glory), 20, 29–32
kiy (indeed; for), 108
kun (to establish), 23, 148

lechem (bread), 16, 171
lo' 'abu (to be unwilling), 136, 139
lo' yechayyeh (not to let live), 164

machaneh (camp), 166
maggepah (slaughter), 182
malak/himlik (to be king/to make king), 48, 56–57, 63, 67, 69, 72
mashach (to anoint), 56

matsa' (to find), 52
mebasser (messenger), 182
meh 'asithi or 'asitha (what have I done?), 85, 96, 130, 160, 167, 175
me'il (robe), 17, 110–11, 147–48, 168
melek (king), 46, 63–65, 68–69, 72, 79, 97, 152
   malkuth, 63
   mamlakah, 63, 86, 148, 169
   mamlakuth, 63, 168
   melukah, 62–63, 69, 97, 111
me'adannoth (fearfully; hopefully), 112
me'umah (something), 174
mishneh (second), 142
mishpat (justice; custom; cf. shapat), 17, 42–43, 49, 65, 164–65, 180
   mishpat hammelek, 42, 48–50, 65
   mishpat hammelukah, 49, 65
mitsvah (commandment), 102
mo'ed (appointed time), 84–85, 87
muth (to die), 28, 112

nabi' (prophet), 46, 53–54, 56, 62, 70–71, 164
   hithnabbe', 61
nacham (to repent), 102
natan (to give), 46–47, 56, 139
natsib (prefect; garrison), 82
*nbt (to see), 118
neéman and ye'amen (to be sure; to trust), 22–23, 151, 165–66
nebon dabar (prudent in speech), 104, 119–20, 146, 174, 180
netsach yisra'el (Glory of Israel), 111
*ngd
   higgid (to tell), 42–43, 49, 53–54, 57, 62, 105
   nagid, 53–59, 68, 79, 85–87, 98, 111, 116, 151–52, 157
niskalta (to do foolishly), 86, 160
nus (to flee), 182

'olam (forever), 9, 20, 23, 165
'or (light), 94, 153–54

pak (vial), 59
pashat (to raid), 111, 164–65, 181–82

qalal (to treat lightly), 20, 32
qara' (to call), 24, 109
qeren (horn), 59
qum (to rise up; establish), 14, 86, 104, 148

ra'ah (to see), 115, 118, 134, 141
   roéh, 54, 62, 70, 118, 164

ra` (evil), 174, 180
radap (to pursue), 181
ravach (to refresh), 160
ro´sh (head), 106, 167

sagar (to surrender), 139–41, 143, 147, 159, 180
sapah (to be swept away), 78
śarap be´esh (to burn in fire), 178–79
sha´al (to ask), 1, 5, 14
shalal (booty), 94, 105, 178
shalom (peace), 151
shama` (to hear), 18, 50, 58, 85, 171
shapat (to judge), 42, 46–47
sha´ul (Saul), 1, 14
shemu´el (Samuel), 14
shipchah (maidservant), 152
śim (to set up), 46–47, 56

sur (to remove), 113, 121
**swt* (to incite), 160

tob (good), 106, 111, 118, 147, 151, 174
tohu (nothingness; vanity), 77
tsivvah (to command; appoint), 86–87, 151

we`atah (and Now!), 20, 98, 110, 147

yad (hand), 139–41, 145, 150, 157, 163
yahweh, x, xiv, 15, 159
yarad (to go down), 140–41, 143
yarah (to teach), 43, 77
yasap (to continue to; add to), 77–78
yashar (to be honest), 174
za`aq (to cry out), 56–57

General Index

Abiathar, 21, 75, 132, 137–40, 175
Abigail, 23, 129, 148–58, 162, 167–68, 175, 177, 179
Achan, 64, 83, 94–96, 99, 102–103
Achish, king of Gath, 23, 127, 129, 131, 133, 138, 142, 157, 163–67, 173–77
Ackroyd, P., xvi, 132
Agag, 101–104, 106, 112, 136–37
Ahab and Jezebel, 36, 59, 156 (Naboth)
Ahijah of Shiloh, xii, 10, 148
Ahijah, son of Ahitub, 20–21, 90, 93, 95
Ahimelech, 21, 113, 131–37, 140, 157
Ahinoam, 156, 163, 179
Ai, 4, 83, 99–102, 112
Alter, R., xii, xvii, 10, 55, 58, 98, 118–19, 124, 127, 131–32, 134, 179
Amalek(ites), 99–114, 123, 136–37, 141, 164, 169, 172, 175, 177–79, 182
Ambiguity/Undecidability, ix, xiii–xiv, xvi, xviii–xx, xxiii–xxiv, 6, 8, 11–12, 14–15, 25–26, 29–30, 33–35, 37–40, 46, 49–50, 56, 60–65, 69–72, 78, 88–89, 91, 95–96, 112–15, 120–25, 127–29, 131–32, 146, 150, 161–62, 166–67, 169–77, 179, 181, 184–85
Ammonites, 3, 15, 35, 66–67, 82, 84–86, 93, 100, 117, 124
Anoint, xvii (messianic), 15, 22–23, 56–59, 73, 87, 98–99, 102, 105, 115–18, 122–25, 128–29, 131, 139, 144–45, 148–50, 157–62, 175, 181
Ark, 1, 4–6, 9–10, 17, 26–35, 37–39, 49, 83, 88, 92, 108–109

Baals and Ashtaroth, 8, 36–38, 59, 74, 77, 182
Barthes, R., xviii
Bathsheba, 119, 121, 126
Benjamin (tribe and ancestor), 4–7, 10–11, 17, 29, 52, 55–58, 64, 88–89, 94, 105, 127, 135–36, 182
Bethel, 4–7, 9–12, 42, 59
Beuken, W.A.M., 167, 170
Blood, 94–96, 121, 126, 132–33, 152–53, 155–56, 160, 166, 176
Burke, K., xviii

Canaan(ites), 2, 7, 32, 94, 164
Characterization, xiii–xiv, xviii, 40, 46–47, 53, 58, 70–73, 81–82, 84–86, 90–92, 103, 109–11, 120–21, 128, 130–31, 150, 165–66, 173–74, 180–81
Culler, J., xix, xxi
Cultic order, 1, 4–5, 8–12, 16–21, 37–38, 79, 97, 107, 110, 112, 132, 134–35
Curtis, J.B., 53–54

Dan(ites), 5–7, 24, 44–45
David, x–xi, xiii–xiv, xviii–xix, xxiv–xxv, 15–16, 21–23, 35, 52–53, 59, 70–71, 80, 82, 94, 98, 111, 113–185 *passim*
Deconstruction, xx–xxv, 39–40, 74–75
de Man, P., xxiv
Deuteronomistic History, xv, 100
Derrida, J., xx–xxv, 75

Dichotomies, xx–xxv, 38–39, 74–75, 78, 117, 128–29

Dillard, A., xxiv–xxv, 128, 131

"Disappearance from the narrative," xvi, 3, 5, 10, 21, 23, 30, 158–60

Disobedience and not hearing, 18, 24, 43, 50, 64, 75–77, 104, 106–14, 171

Dissemination/dispersion/displacement, 13–15, 20–24, 53, 81, 87–88, 113–14, 122–23, 171–72, 177, 182, 184–85

Divine intervention and motivation, xiii–xiv, 16, 18–20, 25, 27–28, 30–34, 38–39, 41–42, 90–93, 96, 101–104, 111, 115–25, 128–29, 138, 140–41, 147, 153–56, 159, 161, 169–73, 177, 181, 184–85

Doeg, 21, 131–36, 149

Driver, S.R., 163

Eating and drinking, 11–13, 16, 22, 55, 57–58, 93–96, 132, 151, 170–71, 179–80

Ebenezer, 3, 20, 26–28, 30–31, 34, 37, 39, 79, 124, 171–72, 184

Egypt(ians), x, 2, 9, 11, 16, 20, 27, 32, 35, 47–48, 63, 76, 99–101, 119, 179–80

Eli, xvi, 1, 4, 9–30, 34, 40, 43, 45, 75, 77–79, 87, 89–90, 107, 110, 122–24, 134, 139, 146, 170–72

Eliab, 102, 116–17, 175

Elkanah, 1, 10–11, 14–17, 102

Endor, 16, 58, 96, 108–109, 167–73, 176, 182, 185

Engedi, 144, 148, 158

Ephod, 5, 17–18, 20, 90, 92, 132, 136, 139–40

Erdmann, C.F.D., xvi

"Evil in the Eyes of the Lord," xii, 7–8, 12, 17, 24, 34–35, 77–78, 93–95, 105, 108–109

"Eyes of Samuel," 46–47, 51

"Eyes of the Philistines," 174

Feldman, B., xxiv

Felman, S., xx, 185

Fish, S., xix

Frei, H., xix

Fulfillment, "literal," 21–24, 74–75, 122–23

Gasché, R., xx

Gath, 2, 31, 36, 127, 131, 133, 138, 163, 165, 167, 173

Gibeah (Geba), 5, 9, 17, 21, 52, 65, 82,

88–90, 97, 113, 133, 135, 137–38, 184

Gideon (Jerubbaal), xiv, 18, 58, 60, 64, 74, 79, 84, 94

Gilboa, Mt., 22, 111, 142, 150, 160–61, 166, 168, 171–72, 176–77, 180–85

Gilgal, 4–5, 10, 42, 60, 69, 83–88, 96, 103, 106, 112–13, 123, 169, 172

Goliath, xix, xxiv–xxv, 113, 119–20, 124–27, 131–34, 154–55, 157, 163, 167, 173–74

Gros Louis, K.R.R., xvii, 124

Gunn, D.M., xvii, 139, 149, 151–52, 156, 167, 170

Hachilah, 143, 158, 163

Hannah, 1, 10–19, 24, 39, 146, 151, 168, 170

Song of, xi–xii, 15–16, 20, 46, 56, 59, 155

Hartman, G., xxiii

Hertzberg, H.W., 117, 142

Holy War, xv–xvi, 4, 83, 86, 94–96, 98–114, 133–34, 136, 149, 164–65, 177–78

Hophni and Phinehas, 1, 9, 16–20, 27–28, 40, 43–44, 107, 112, 172

Humphreys, W.L., xviii

Ichabod, 20, 29–30, 90

Inquiry of the Lord, xiii–xiv, xviii, 1, 4–7, 10–14, 17, 23, 26–27, 31–32, 53–54, 64, 90, 92–93, 95–97, 134–35, 139–43, 149, 168, 179, 181

Inquiry and ritual, 4–7, 12, 39

Intercession and prayer, 10–13, 18–19, 24, 37–39, 46, 70, 77, 103, 107, 110

Interpretation (of God's word), xv, xxiv, 2, 50–51, 70, 74–75, 85–88, 95, 98–114, 122–23, 128–29, 136–37, 149, 154–55, 180

Iser, W., xix

Jabesh-gilead, 7, 28, 39, 52, 55, 67, 182–84

Jacob, xi (Blessing: Gen 49), 5, 29, 55, 121, 127

Jephthah, 3, 66, 74, 93–94

Jericho, 4, 83, 94, 99

Jesse, 11, 58, 115–18, 164

son of Jesse, 134, 142, 152

Jobling, D., 111

Johnson, B., xx, xxiv

Jonathan, xii, 15, 64, 71, 82–83, 89–97, 111, 113, 120–21, 125–31, 134, 137–39, 141–42, 147–48, 151, 155–57, 162, 175, 184

Joseph, x, 119
Joshua (Book and Leader), xv, 2–5, 17, 35, 40, 49, 61, 74, 78–79, 83, 99–101, 112
Judah, xv, 22, 66, 133, 138–40, 143, 162, 164–66, 175, 180–81
(To) Judge, 8–9, 37, 40, 42–47, 51, 53, 66–67, 70, 73, 77–79
Justice and/or mercy, viii, xiv–xv, 1, 7–8, 16–20, 24, 28, 34–35, 38–39, 76–78, 87–88, 99–100, 102, 107, 109, 112, 114, 122–23, 129, 145–47, 150–51, 154, 161, 169–70, 172, 174, 177, 184

Keil and Delitzsch, xvi
Keilah, 136, 139–41, 156, 158
King and kingship, xii–xiii, 4, 7–8, 12, 15, 25, 40–42, 46–53, 57–59, 62–80, 83, 85–88, 97–98, 101–103, 105, 109–11, 113–16, 123–26, 128–29, 133, 136, 141–42, 147–48, 150–52, 156–58, 161, 164, 166, 169, 174–77, 181
    The Lord as king, 48–49, 72–73, 75
Kiriath-jearim, x, 35–36
Knierem, R., xvii, 124
Knowledge and/or ignorance, 2, 6–8, 13, 15–16, 24, 27, 30–35, 46, 70, 79, 89–90, 115, 121–22, 140–41, 142, 145–47, 151–52, 155, 166–70, 172, 175–76, 179, 182
Kugel, J., xi–xii

Laish (city), 28, 39
Leach, E.R., xvii
Levenson, J.D., 151
"The Lord is with him", 24, 45, 119–20, 125, 128, 162, 169
The Lord, Yahweh, as distinct from God, Elohim, xiv, 15, 27–28, 58–59, 92–93, 134–35, 163, 168–69, 173–74
Lot selection, 4–5, 64, 83, 95–97
Lure (literary device), 9–10, 15–16, 21, 41

McCarter, P.K., viii, xvi–xvii, 13, 29, 58, 68, 131, 137–38, 142, 166
Mephibosheth, 22, 147, 176
Micah, 5–6, 18, 27–28, 35
Michal, xxiv, 71, 120–21, 126–27, 137–38, 146, 156, 162
Michmash, 83, 89, 96, 106, 124, 136
Miller, J.H., xxv
Miscall, P.D., vii, xvi, 120, 129, 156
Mizpah, 5–6, 10, 37–39, 41–42, 64–65, 69, 74

Moses, xi (blessing), xv, 1–3, 10–11, 42–50, 52–53, 58, 61–62, 65, 71, 74, 78–79, 99, 108–109, 111, 116, 167, 180

Nabal, 129, 149–59, 162, 165, 175
Nathan, xii, 71, 121
The nations, xvi, 2, 7, 35–36, 42, 46–47, 50, 109, 164
Nob, 21, 131–38, 141, 149, 156, 166
Oath/vow, 3, 6–7, 10–11, 66, 92–97, 101, 106, 127, 130, 147, 149–55, 168
Obedience and hearing, 18, 24, 43–51, 54, 56–57, 60–61, 69–70, 72, 75–76, 78–79, 86–87, 98, 104–14, 122, 169, 171

Palti, son of Laish, 146, 156
Paradigmatic Story, 67, 82, 100
Peninnah, 1, 10
Perdue, L.G., xviii
Philistines, xviii, xxv, 1–3, 15, 26–42, 52, 56, 60, 66, 82–98, 109, 111, 117, 120, 124–25, 129, 131, 133, 138–39, 160, 163–77, 181–85
Phinehas, son of Eleazar, 4–5, 9
Polzin, R., xii, xiv–xvii, 2, 30, 49, 83, 100
Power politics/realpolitik, 100–101, 107–109, 112, 114, 122, 128–29, 139, 155–56, 172, 182
Priest(s), 1, 4–10, 12, 14, 16–21, 27, 32, 35, 40, 42–43, 47, 50, 59, 75, 79, 83, 86, 109, 131–32, 134–36, 139, 149, 156, 166, 171
Preston, T.R., xviii
Prophet and prophecy, xii–xiii, xvi, 2–3, 10, 12, 19, 22–25, 37, 40, 44–54, 56–62, 64, 70–73, 77, 79, 103, 109–11, 116, 121–23, 128–29, 149, 155, 168–69, 172
    True Prophet, 44–46, 53, 60–62, 85–87

Rachel, 1, 29, 55, 121, 127
Radday, Y., xii
Ramah, 1, 10, 16, 42, 46, 50, 62, 65, 69, 75, 88, 113, 127–28, 137, 149
Reading, Mode of, vii–xxv, 7–8, 14–15, 18–19, 23–24, 33–34, 41–42, 51, 57–58, 68–71, 73, 78, 81, 85–89, 99–110, 114, 121–23, 129, 137, 144, 150–51, 156–58, 162, 171–72, 176–77, 181, 184–85
Rejection, 48–49, 64, 66, 72–73, 75–77, 79–81, 86–87, 98, 101–103, 108–17, 123–25, 128–29, 148, 169–70, 172

Repetition, xvi, xviii–xix, xxiv–xxv, 8,
    13, 37–39, 75, 101, 103–106, 131,
    145, 159–61, 168, 177
Retrospect, "literal," xiii, 23, 74–75,
    122–23.
Rose, A.S., 119

Sacrifice, 4, 6, 11–12, 17–20, 24–25, 33,
    37–38, 55, 60–61, 69, 84–87, 95, 97,
    101, 104–108, 112, 116, 131, 160
Samson, xiv, 1–3, 8, 12–13, 30, 52, 93–
    94, 117
Samuel, x–xiii, xviii, 1–125 *passim;* 127–
    28, 131, 137–38, 141, 146, 148–50,
    155, 157, 162, 167–73, 177, 182,
    184–85
Saul, x–xiv, xviii, 1, 12–16, 21–23, 35,
    41, 51–185 *passim*
Scholes, R., xx
Seeing and hearing, 13, 18, 24–25, 54,
    82, 146, 148
Seeking and finding, 23, 52–54, 57, 59–
    60, 62, 64, 75, 87–89, 114, 118, 130,
    141–42, 144–45, 147, 163–64, 167–
    69, 174–75
Shaviv, S., 54
Shechem, 4–5, 121 (Gen 34)
Shiloh, xi, xvi, 1–31, 45, 52, 75, 90
Shimei, 22, 121, 147, 159, 176
Sign, 2, 28, 33–34, 59–61, 76–77, 86–
    87, 91–92, 110–11, 117, 120, 130,
    141, 169
Sin and wickedness, xiv–xv, 15–20, 24,
    34, 39, 73, 75–78, 87, 94–97, 101–14,
    126–27, 130, 145–47, 154–55, 160–
    61, 168, 170, 172
Smith, H.P., 131

Solomon, x, xviii, 21–22, 35–36, 75, 148
Speiser, E.A., 29
Spirit of the Lord, 61, 66, 78, 104, 111,
    113, 117–18, 128, 168
Spivak, G.C., xxi, xxv
Succession and successors, xvii, 2, 5, 46,
    49, 70, 72–73, 77–80, 123–25, 148
Sword, xxv, 67, 89, 121, 132–37, 151,
    182

Tent of meeting, 4–5, 9–10, 16–17
Text criticism, viii, 13, 34, 68, 76, 82
Todorov, T., xx
Truncated story (literary device), 30–34,
    36–37, 39, 88–89, 128

Uriah the Hittite, 121, 156, 176

Veijola, T., xviii
Violence, xviii, 3–4, 7, 22, 67, 113, 116,
    119, 121–22, 126–28, 130–31, 133,
    135–36, 144, 147–48, 151, 153–56,
    158–59, 162, 164–67, 169, 173–74,
    178–80, 184

White, H., xx
Word of the Lord, xiii, xv–xvi, xxiv, 1–
    3, 10, 14–15, 17–18, 21, 23–27, 32–
    35, 37, 45–46, 49–51, 53–54, 56–60,
    70, 75–79, 85–88, 90, 92–95, 98–114,
    121–23, 128–29, 134–36, 145, 149,
    154–55, 168–70, 172, 176–77, 180,
    185

Ziklag, 164, 178–79, 181
Ziph(ites), 136, 141, 143, 156, 158, 162